# The Autobiography
# *of*
# Alexander Luria

*A Dialogue with*
*The Making of Mind*

# The Autobiography
## *of*
# Alexander Luria

*A Dialogue with*
*The Making of Mind*

Michael Cole
Karl Levitin
*and*
Alexander Luria

 LAWRENCE ERLBAUM ASSOCIATES, PUBLISHERS
Mahwah, New Jersey                    London

Originally published 1979 as *The Making of Mind*.

Lawrence Erlbaum Associates, Inc., Publishers
10 Industrial Avenue
Mahwah, New Jersey 07430
www.erlbaum.com

Cover design by Kathryn Houghtaling Lacey

**Library of Congress Cataloging-in-Publication Data**

Cole, Michael, 1938–
    The autobiography of Alexander Luria : a dialogue with the
    making of mind / Michael Cole, Karl Levitin, Alexander Luria.
            p.  cm.
    Includes bibliographical references and index.
ISBN 0-8058-5499-1 (pbk. : alk. paper)
1. Lurïëiïa, A. R. (Aleksandr Romanovich), 1902–1977. 2. Psychologist
    —Soviet Union—Biography.  3. Psychology—Soviet Union.   I.
    Levitin, Karl, 1936–  II. Lurïëiïa, A. R. (Aleksandr Romanovich),
    1902– Making of mind.  III. Title.
BF109.L87C65   2005
150'.92—dc22                                                    2004061929
                                                                      CIP

Books published by Lawrence Erlbaum Associates are printed on acid-
free paper, and their bindings are chosen for strength and durability.

Printed in the United States of America

# Contents

# Preface

## PUTTING A SCIENTIFIC AUTOBIOGRAPHY INTO ITS SOCIAL AND PERSONAL CONTEXTS

So far as we are aware, the origins and contents of this book have no analogues, either in historical writings on science, or in the genres of biography and autobiography. Consequently, we feel we owe the reader some explanation for the texts that follow.

Alexander Romanovich Luria was born in Kazan, Russia, in 1902 and died 75 years later in Moscow, USSR. He was one of the leading psychologists of the 20th century. Among his accomplishments, which are described at length in this book, he

1. Founded the discipline of neuropsychology on the basis of a theory of brain functioning in relation to the environment that remains the cornerstone of basic research on the brain and behavior to this day.
2. Conducted the first, and still one of the most influential, studies of changes in human thinking associated with rapid cultural/historical change. This work is considered a classic of cross-cultural psychology.
3. Conducted the first large scale study comparing identical and fraternal twins designed to tease apart the role of nature and nurture in development.
4. Invented a psycho-diagnostic procedure that allows valid inferences about other people's mental states which he

called "the combined motor method." This method is widely used in such fields as the study of infant cognition and forensic psychology, where it serves as the basis for polygraph tests.
5. Invented an overarching approach to psychology that enables reconciliation of laws based on studies of large groups and the idiosyncracies of individual human natures.

His earliest article in English appeared in 1928 and over the following 50 years he published more than two dozen books and hundreds of articles in many of the world's languages as well as his native Russian—A prodigious outpouring of scientific work which remains influential to this day.

In the quarter century that has passed since Alexander Luria's death, the Soviet Union, which came into being when he was a schoolboy, has passed into history. The scientific discipline of psychology to which he made so many contributions has also undergone enormous changes owing in part to changing technologies unavailable to Luria and unimagined by his contemporaries. Nevertheless, several of his books are still in print, and his publications are still widely cited by scientists from all over the world.

Perhaps most remarkable is evidence that the theoretical framework that he and his colleagues began to formulate late in the 1920s, when Russia was undergoing cataclysmic changes, are finding (sometimes unwitting) resonance in contemporary sciences. Central to their theorizing was the idea that human psychological process are unique in that the biological functioning of the human brain depends crucially upon immersion in human culture—the circuits of the human brain develop through their interaction with a culturally organized environment, without which the brain can neither develop nor function normally. In recent years this idea has been taken up by a variety of scholars in many fields. In anthropology, Clifford Geertz declared that if it were biologically possible, a human being growing apart from culture would not be a potentially talented ape, but a monstrosity (Geertz, 1973). Gerald Edelman (1992), Nobel Prize winning neuroscientist, has pointed to "re-entrant" brain processes, that is, circuits completed through the culturally organized environment, as the key to human consciousness. Computational neurobiologists Stephen Quartz and Terrence Sejnowksi (2002) argue that development of the prefrontal cortex depends crucially on inhabiting a cultural environment. All of these scholars discovered independently what Luria and his colleagues had asserted many decades earlier, a discovery neatly described in the title of a recent book by Matt Ridley (2003), *Nature via Nurture*. Clearly, Luria is a scientist worth remembering.

## AUTOBIOGRAPHIES AND BIOGRAPHIES OF A. R. LURIA

For a variety of reasons which we explore in detail in the later sections of this book, Luria's life and work have never been adequately described, although there have been several attempts, for some of which we have ourselves have been responsible.

The earliest attempt at eliciting an autobiographical account of Alexander Romanovich's life that we know of occurred in the early 1960's when he received a letter from Edwin. G. Boring, a professor of psychology at Harvard University. Boring, who had written the then-canonical history of psychology, had also been editing a series of autobiographical essays by prominent psychologists since 1930. As Alexander Romanovich later described matters:

> In 1963 Professor E. Boring proposed that I participate in the preparation of the volume, *A History of Psychology in Autobiography* ... and submit written material to be held until 1970.

> If you live to 1970, wrote Professor Boring, the material you have written will go in the next volume of *A History of Psychology in Autobiography*. If you die before then, it will be published as an autonecrology.

Professor Boring's invitation seemed more than a superfluous
diversion. In fact, retrospective analysis of the road one has traveled is always useful. Therefore, I have responded to the proposition with complete seriousness and I have prepared the present
material in order that it might be useful in one or the other forms
proposed by Professor Boring. (Luria, 1974, p. 253)

This essay, which was written some time during the 1960s,
was translated by Michael Cole and published in the 6th volume
of the series in 1974 (Luria, 1974). Oddly, at the time Michael
Cole edited the 1979 autobiography, the earlier publication had
completely slipped his mind, which was a shame because a comparison of the two accounts is interesting in several respects. In
that essay, Luria denied the relevance of personal information in
this early biographical essay with even more determination than
in the current volume. Autobiographical sketches, he asserted,
"would not be likely to result in a true picture of the history of
science" (p. 253). He drove home the point by writing a 10-para-
graph account of various facts about his career, which were presented in small type and indented, to mark them off from the
main text. He then moved resolutely into the history of psychology in Russia, with only two additional sentences devoted to
social context.

Alexander Romanovich returned to matters autobiographical
in the 1970s when an academic film maker sought to make a film
about his life and work, but this project never really got off the
ground; when the film makers arrived in Moscow, Alexander
Romanovich was suffering from heart insufficiency, an illness
which would kill him a few years later. In 1979 his autobiography was published in English. It was edited by Michael Cole in
collaboration with his wife, Sheila. They had succeeded in editing the early chapters of the book while in constant communication with Alexander Romanovich. When he died, they
completed the editing in the pattern already established. The
Russian title, *Looking Backwards: A Scientific Autobiography*
was changed at the request of the English language publisher to

*The Making of Mind.* Michael Cole wrote an introduction and an epilogue. A year later, the Russian version of the autobiography was published in the USSR.

Nor have Russian biographers and non-Russian historians of psychology ignored Luria. As a science journalist, Karl Levitin spent a good deal of time with Luria while completing a monograph on the psychological ideas of Lev Vygotsky and his followers of whom Luria is the best known outside of Russia (*One is Not Born a Personality*, 1975/1982). He subsequently wrote the first biography of Luria, *Mimoletny Uzor* (*A Dissolving Pattern*), 1978/1990. Evgenia Khomsakaya, a close colleague of Luria's, wrote a biography that appeared in English in 2001 (Homskaya, 2001) and his daughter, Elena contributed a biography, which appeared in Russian (E. Luria, 1994). In addition, aspects of his ideas and life have appeared in books devoted to the history of Soviet/Russian psychology (Joravsky, 1989; van de Veer & Valsiner, 1991).

With all of this recent attention, the reader is justified in wondering—why take the trouble to publish yet another book about Luria? The answer is complex, because its subject was a complex man living at a complex time.

First, and most obviously, the 1979 English language autobiography which provides the most complete information on the complex interconnectedness of social events and Luria's scientific ideas has gone out of print, and is not readily available. But this is only part of the answer. After all, there are other biographies to draw upon.

Second, and more importantly, the 1979 autobiography was written in the Soviet Union by a man who considered himself a Soviet scientist. All of the biographies of Luria were written by authors (including Michael Cole) whose publications had to be acceptable to Soviet literary bureaucrats, and most were themselves writing as Soviet citizens, or as people who had lived almost all of their lives under Soviet rule. Other accounts of Luria were written by non-Soviets, some of whom had met him, many of whom were writing from secondary sources.

It is almost impossible to overstate the sometimes subtle, sometimes terrifyingly evident, problems of all kinds that faced Soviet citizens during Luria's lifetime. It must be remembered that in the 1970s, when Luria wrote his autobiography and Levitin his biography, in the Union of Soviet Socialist Republics, the Communist Party governed the USSR. The Party controlled the lives of its citizens with a heavy ideological, and often, physical hand. There were still gulags (concentration camps) for anyone deemed an enemy of the state, places which many people entered, but many fewer lived to walk away from. All publications within the country were subject to censorship, and publications that appeared in translation were even more heavily censored to ensure their ideological appropriateness, as determined by the organs of the Party.

As a consequence of these historical circumstances as well as more personal circumstances surrounding Luria's life (about which we have more to say in the course of this book) Luria emphasized that he was writing a biography focused on **science**—a history of ideas in which the concrete history of the individual and his times are rarely visible beyond the first chapter, which recounts the events that initially propelled his scientific inquiries. Evgenia Homskaya's biography is also explicitly a "scientific biography" which, although written after the end of the USSR, shares with Luria's autobiography an almost uncanny absence of information about the circumstances of Luria's life and how he dealt personally and scientifically with the rapidly shifting, often dangerous social context in which he worked. Only a biography about her father, written by Elena Luria (1994), gives the reader some idea about her father's personality, much of it gleaned through diaries he kept as a youth. But Elena Luria was a microbiologist, not a psychologist, so she depended upon her father's autobiography for the scientific part of her text and her account remains oddly devoid of the kind of integration of the personal, the social, and the scientific that one finds, for example, in such well known autobiographical books as Francis

Crick's *Double Helix* or the writing of Jean Paul Sartre, Peter Brook, Jerome Bruner, and many others.

The absence of such personal and socio-historical information would be missed in any autobiography, but it is particularly damaging in the case of Alexander Romanovich. The narrative he presents portrays his life as a combination of lucky events and a more or less logical sequence of somewhat disparate projects in different fields of ideas, most of them derived from Vygotsky, as if he had little part in their development. From the material presented, a reader unfamiliar with what was occurring simultaneously in the USSR can easily come away with the impression that he voluntarily shifted from one topic to another in order to take advantage of circumstances that would insure that the entire, vast, landscape of Vygotsky's theoretical ideas received empirical confirmation.

We were made acutely aware of the inadequacy of previously published accounts of Luria's life and work at a series of memorial meetings held in 2002 in a number of European countries to which a few of Luria's close Russian colleagues were invited in addition to non-Russians. Despite the potential for an integrated portrait of Luria's work, by and large, these meetings paid tribute to Luria as the "father of neuropsychology," the study of the brain bases of behavior. When Luria, the person, or Luria, the Soviet citizen struggling to lead a decent life in indecent circumstances were discussed, as they were on at least one occasion, these personal memories were simply not linked to Luria's scientific career.

Whether we looked to our own past biographical efforts or the efforts of others, the result was distinctly unsatisfactory. The shortcomings were certainly not the result of indifference or lack of effort. Rather, the difficulties of the subject are not easily overcome in any orthodox manner. Once he reached adulthood, Alexander Romanovich was extremely reticent; both as a matter of personal preference and political caution, about his personal life, and few people are left alive who could speak authoritatively about it. Some of the information, presented here for the first time, comes from interviews we have conducted with this re-issue of the autobiography in mind. We have also drawn upon from Luria's extensive correspondence. We present some of these voices in the new epilogue written for this re-issue of his autobiography and in the accompanying DVD.

The social context of Luria's work presents far fewer difficulties. There is a voluminous literature on the history of the USSR that is more than sufficient to provide non-specialist readers with adequate information about the interplay between Luria's scientific preoccupations and the conditions under which they arose, only to go underground for years or decades before reappearing, often dressed in new language that obscures their origins and history.

Michael Cole, as we mentioned, wrote an introduction and epilogue to the published version of Alexander Romanovich's autobiography. This introduction, we believe, stands the test of time. It was written in a style that Alexander Romanovich himself would approve. Drawing upon a variety of lectures that Luria had delivered on the history of psychology over many years, it provided the scientific context at the beginning of the century that set the stage of Alexander Romanovich's career.

In contrast with the introduction, written as he thought Luria would have liked it, his epilogue to the English edition of the autobiography sought to fill in some of the personal and political context of Luria's work, which, he acknowledged, Alexander Romanovich would never have approved of. The effort was only partially successful. Although written with what he thought was reasonable caution, the Soviet agency (VAAP), which negotiated translations for all Soviet authors refused to permit publication of the book unless the epilogue was censored to make it ideologically acceptable. The facts were not disputed, only the possibility of them appearing in print. Luria's family sought to have the book translated with the epilogue as Cole wrote it, but in the end, State power prevailed. One of Luria's students, and a close friend of Cole's and the Luria family, the well-known Russian psychologist, Vladimir Zinchenko, "edited" the epilogue with great care and artistry. When he was done, the epilogue, although it included many episodes the authorities would just as soon have forgotten, was accepted. Zinchenko had artfully deleted just those phrases and incidents that had to be omitted from a Soviet point of view. At the same time, the absence of just these materials made it impossible for English language readers, unfamiliar with Soviet reality, to understand the real circumstances of Luria's life and work, and hence his special qualities as a scientist.

Consequently, the epilogue was not even adequate to its own times, let alone our times, when the USSR is no more, and the memory of Alexander Luria, based as it is on egregiously inadequate foundations, is being eroded.

We became acutely aware of this situation over the past two years during which we have been deeply involved in various centennial celebrations of Luria's life and work—occasions that, by their nature, were designed to restore memory and strengthen links to valued treasures from the past. But these events left us deeply concerned. The sharp contradiction between what we know to be the realities of Luria's life and work, combined with the impoverished impressions transmitted by Luria's autobiography and the biographies written about him by his colleagues and daughter, became impossible to ignore. The issue for us became to find a way to help preserve the memory of this extraordinary man and his work because of its **contemporary relevance** while at the same time allowing Luria to speak as he himself had spoken.

This book represents our effort to deal with the difficult problem of respecting Luria's account of his scientific career while providing the world with a fuller account of the connections between his life and work and the social conditions of that life in the historical context of his country. To achieve this goal we have put his autobiography and various existing biographical accounts into dialogue with his own past and the future in a manner that would make his ideas and his remarkable life more accessible to future generations. Consequently, the current manuscript is constructed in a polyphonic manner that retains the original and clearly distinguishes it from the many voices that we put it into dialogue with, including our own. To accomplish this, we have sought to construct a framework in which the whole of *The Making of the Mind*, including its introduction and epilogue, are flanked by new materials. The first of those new materials is this preface. Following presentation of the text of his 1979 autobiography and the two essays written at the time by Cole, we present a summary of the extraordinary social context that accompanied and often shaped the lines of work they describe. We then present information contributed by Luria's former colleagues that convey something of his unique character as well as material drawn from a number of recent publications in Russia and the West that cast light upon the complexities of this very complex man. We hope that in this manner, we may simultaneously provide the reader with a fuller appreciation of Luria's life and work and restore to human memory events that he himself would have wished never to have had to remember. We have also added a supplemental bibliography, and have added a DVD containing not only photographs from Luria's archive, but interviews with several leading scholars who knew him, again following our main goal to make the book as personal as it is in our power to do so. The reader is also invited to consult the website constructed to accompany this book, which may be found at http://luria.ucsd.edu.

Michael Cole and Karl Levitin,
September 2004
San Diego-Moscow

# The Making of Mind

*A Personal Account
of Soviet Psychology*

# A. R. Luria

Michael Cole and Sheila Cole, eds.

*Introduction and Epilogue
by Michael Cole*

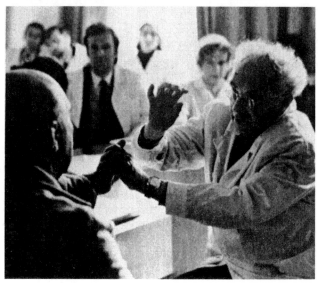

Luria with his father (above)
and performing a neuropsychological analysis

# Introduction:
# The Historical Context

JUST AFTER the turn of this century the German psycholgist Hermann Ebbinghaus reflected that psychology "has a long past, but a short history." Ebbinghaus was commenting on the fact that whereas psychological theorizing has existed as long as recorded thought, only a quarter of a century had passed since the founding of the first scientific groups that were self-consciously known as "psychology laboratories." Until the period around 1880 to which Ebbinghaus was referring, psychology was nowhere considered an independent scholarly discipline; rather it was a facet of the "humane" or "moral" sciences which was the official province of philosophy and the amateur pastime of any learned person.

Although three additional quarter-centuries have passed since Ebbinghaus' remark, the history of psychology is still short enough to make it possible for the career of one individual to span all, or almost all, of its brief history as a science. Such an individual was Alexander Romanovich Luria (1902–1977), born into the second generation of scientific psychologists but raised in circumstances that immersed him in the basic issues which had motivated the founders of the discipline.

Scientific psychology was born almost simultaneously in America, England, Germany, and Russia. Although textbooks credit Wilhelm Wundt with founding the first experimental laboratory in Leipzig in 1879, the new approach to the study of the mind was not really the province of any one person or country.

At almost the same time William James was encouraging his students to conduct experiments at Harvard; Francis Galton in England was initiating the first applications of intelligence tests; and Vladimir Bekhterev opened a laboratory in Kazan that explored most of the problems which would later come to dominate the new science. Learning mechanisms, alcoholism, and psychopathology were all under investigation in Bekhterev's laboratory while Luria was growing up in Kazan.

Although historical hindsight makes it possible to divide eras in psychology according to the ideas that dominated its practitioners, the changes in the early years of the twentieth century that were to render the "new psychology" of the 1880s and 1890s an obsolete psychology by 1920 were by no means clear. Dissatisfaction with the dominant psychologies had not yet resulted in a coherent opposition with a positive program of its own. If matters were unclear in western Europe and America, they were even murkier in Russia, where science labored under the burden of heavy government censorship, guided by conservative religious principles and autocratic political policies. Not until 1911 was the first officially recognized Institute of Psychology founded at Moscow University. But even this progressive step was blunted by the choice of a director whose research was based squarely on German psychological theory of the 1880s.

Under such conditions, a young Russian who became interested in psychology found himself in a curious intellectual time warp. If he restricted himself to reading Russian, his ideas about the subject matter and methods of psychology would be old-fashioned. Translations of important western European work became available slowly and only in a quantity and range of subject that suited the tsar's censor. Because of the sketchy evidence available in Russian, psychology in Kazan in 1910 was at the same point as psychology in Leipzig or Wurzburg a generation earlier.

But if a young Russian read German, more recent work was available, especially if his family moved in intellectual circles whose members went off to Germany to study. Such was the case with the Luria family. So at a very young age, young Luria began to read more widely in contemporary experimental psychology than work in translation would permit. Perhaps because his father was a physician interested in psychosomatic medicine, the new work in psychiatry spearheaded by Jung and Freud also fell into Luria's hands. To this he added the humanistic, philosophical ideas of the German romantic tradition, especially those works which criticized the limitations of laboratory psychology of the sort propounded by Wundt and his followers.

Thus, although Luria was by virtue of his birth, a member of psychology's second generation, he began his career immersed in the basic issues of those who had founded psychology a quarter-century earlier. Throughout his sixty years of active research and theorizing, Luria never ceased to be concerned with these fundamental problems. He constantly sought their resolution in the light of new knowledge accumulated as succeeding generations of psychologists worked their transformations on the fundamental material inherited from their progenitors.

The general amnesia that afflicts the ahistorical discipline of psychology makes it difficult to recover the dilemmas which Luria confronted as a young man. Perhaps there is comfort to be derived from the notion that psychological ideas at the turn of the century are as obsolete today as the automobiles which were then being manufactured. But the course of material technology has proved a poor analogy for progress in scientific psychology. A better analogy, which has an honorable history in Russian thought of the late nineteenth century and in Marxist writings of both the nineteenth and twentieth centuries, was provided by Lenin, who remarked of progress in science that it is "a development that repeats, as it were, the stages already passed, but repeats them in a different way, on a higher plane . . . a development, so to speak, in spirals, not in a straight line" (Lenin, 1934, p. 14).

The state of psychology's spiral as Luria surveyed the intellectual landscape at the start of his career was contentious. The major disagreement dividing scholars found expression in several seemingly independent arguments. Primary among these was whether psychology could be an objective, experimental science.

The "new" element in the "new psychology" of the 1880s was experimentation. There was little innovation in the psychological categories and theories offered by Wundt, whose main concepts could be traced back through empirical philosophers like Locke all the way to Aristotle. For Wundt, as for the psychologically inclined philosophers before him, the basic mechanism of mind was the association of ideas, which arise from the environment in the form of elementary sensations. Wundt's innovation was his claim that he could verify such theories on the basis of controlled observations carried out in carefully designed laboratory experiments. Introspection remained an essential part of his method, but now it was "scientific" introspection that could yield the general laws of the mind, not armchair speculation.

Wundt's specific, theoretical claims did not go unchallenged. He was opposed from within the new psychology by a variety of scholars whose data led them to construct alternative theories of mental events. The disagreements that ensued often centered on the validity of introspective reports, and a great deal of controversy was generated about basic matters of fact. Eventually, the failure to resolve these arguments, as well as the suspicion that they might be irresolvable in principle because the events to which they referred were internal reports of individuals rather than events observable by any unbiased observer, brought an end to the first era of scientific psychology.

In many standard discussions of this period (e.g. Boring, 1925, 1950) it goes unnoticed that the arguments between Wundt and his critics within psychology were part of a larger discussion about the appropriateness of experimentation altogether. While Wundt and his successors were gathering facts and prestige for their burgeoning new science, skeptics mourned the loss of the phenomena that had originally made the human mind an important topic of study. This criticism was captured nicely by Henri Bergson in quoting Shakespeare's phrase, "We murder to dissect." Or as G. S. Brett later put the choices "One way will lead to a psychology which is scientific but artificial; the other will lead to a psychology which is natural but cannot be scientific, remaining in the end an art" (Brett, 1930, p. 54).

The objection to experimentation from critics was that restricting psychology to the laboratory automatically restricted the mental phenomena it could investigate. There is more to mental life than elementary sensations and their associations; there is more to thinking than can be discerned in reaction time experiments. But it seemed that only these elementary phenomena could be investigated in the laboratory.

Wundt was not indifferent to these criticisms. He acknowledged that the experimental method has limitations, but he chose to confront them by making a distinction between elementary and higher psychological functions. Whereas experimental psychology was the appropriate way to study elementary psychological phenomena, the higher functions could not be studied experimentally. In fact, the actual processes of higher psychological functioning could probably not be ascertained at all. The best that could be done was to study the products of the higher functions by cataloguing cultural artifacts and folklore. In effect, Wundt ceded the study of higher psychological functions to the discipline of anthropology as he knew it. He devoted many years to this enterprise, which he termed *volkerpsychologie*.

The basic choice between experimental and nonexperimental methods was of central concern to Luria as he began his career, but he did not like any of the ready-made choices with which he was confronted. On all sides he saw compromise formulations, none of which satisfied him. Like Wundt, Bekhterev, and others, he believed firmly in the necessity for experimentation. But he also sympathized with Wundt's critics, especially Wilhelm Dilthey, who had searched ways to reconcile the simplifications entailed by Wundt's experimental approach with humanistic analyses of complex human emotions and actions. Dilthey eventually despaired, rejecting experimentation as an altogether inappropriate way to study human psychological processes. Luria, never given to despair, chose a different route. He sought a new, synthetic method that would reconcile art and science, description and explanation. He would remove artificiality from the laboratory, while retaining the laboratory's analytic rigor. Having made this choice, he then faced a new series of choices concerning method and theory that would make possible his attempt at scientific synthesis.

Like countless psychologists before him, Luria believed that a full understanding of the mind had to include accounts of both the knowledge that people have about the world and the motives that energize them as they put such knowledge to use. It was important to know the origin of the basic processes through which knowledge is acquired and the rules that describe psychological change. Change, for Luria referred to the new kinds of systems into which the basic processes can be organized. His very large task, still unrealized by any psychological theory today, was to try to provide both a general framework and a set of specific mechanisms to describe and explain all the systems of behavior that emerge from the workings of the many subsystems that comprise the living individual.

Using this global characterization of the human mind as a starting point, Luria had to survey the existing experimental methods that could render his own approach more than empty phrase-mongering. Within the arena of knowledge, all major techniques were elaborations of the notion that the structure of ideas can be found in the structure of the associations into which they enter. German laboratories had begun to use mechanical timing devices which they hoped would yield a precise chronometry of mental associations. This technology had advanced to the point where many investigators believed that it would be possible to record the time required for different kinds of mental events. Arguments focused on defining the units of mental activity and on determining whether it was the association of elements or of mental acts that was being "measured."

During this same period associative responses were being used for a quite different purpose by medically oriented scholars such as Jung and Freud. While recognizing that associations among words provided information about relations among ideas, they were less interested in mapping their patients' conscious knowledge systems or in timing associative responses than in using associations to discover knowledge that the person was not aware of. Even more important was the possibility that word associations could yield information about the motives, hidden from consciousness, that were energizing otherwise unexplainable behavior.

Luria saw in these two disparate approaches to the method of word associations—one experimental, the other clinical—the possibility of enriching the study of knowledge and motivation, both of which he believed to be intricately combined in any psychological process. His efforts to create a unified psychology of mind from these beginnings represented the central theme of his life's work. His willingness to work with motivational concepts put forth within the psychoanalytic school might have placed him outside of academic psychology altogether, but this did not happen for a number of reasons. First, Luria was committed to the experimental method. Just as important was his commitment to the use of objective data as the basis for theorizing. When many psychologists began to insist not just that observable behavior had to represent the basic data for psychologists but also that psychological theories could not appeal to unobservable events, Luria demurred, anticipating a position similar to that defended by Edward Tolman years later. He treated consciousness and the unconscious as intervening variables, that is, as concepts that organized the patterns of behavioral data obtained.

Another issue confronting psychologists at the turn of the century was their attitude toward the "more basic" knowledge then accruing in physiology, neurology, and anatomy, an area now termed the "neurosciences." The major achievements of nineteenth-century biology and physiology had made it virtually impossible to ignore important links between the central nervous system and the "mental" phenomena that were the psychologist's focus. But the question was whether psychology need restrict itself to the phenomena that had been discovered in the physiological laboratory. Here opinion was divided along two important lines.

As a matter of principle, many psychologists rejected the notion that mind could be reduced to "matter in motion" and that such matter could be studied in the physiologists' laboratory. Mind, according to their view, had rather to be studied introspectively, using itself as a basic investigative tool. At the opposite extreme were scientists who claimed that psychology was no more than a branch of physiology, which would provide a unified theory of behavior. This position was taken by the Russian physiologist I. M. Sechenov, whose *Reflexes of the Brain* contained an explicit program for explaining mental phenomena as the central link in the reflex arc.

Between these extreme positions, were many psychologists, including Luria, who believed that psychology should develop in a manner that was consistent with, but not entirely dependent on, the neurosciences. They accepted the notion that psychological phenomena were part of the natural world, subject to the laws of nature. But they did not necessarily agree that any existing model of how the brain was linked to psychological processes, especially complex processes, was correct. So psychology had to proceed on its own, keeping an eye on physiology as it progressed. Luria was among a very few psychologists who sought to extend the areas of consistency, deliberately confronting both psychology and the neurosciences with each other's facts and theories. Forty years after he had begun such activities, a new, hybrid branch of psychology, called "neuropsychology," won recognition as a scientific enterprise.

Another basic distinction within psychology formed around the basic "building blocks" of mind that the psychologist assumed. One group, associated variously with the names of Wundt, E. B. Titchener, John Watson, and Clark Hull, attempted to identify the basic elements of behavior as sensations that combined according to the laws of association to form elementary ideas, or habits. Another group, among whom can be counted Franz Brentano, William James, and the Gestalt psychologists, resisted this "elementarism." Their analyses suggested that basic psychological processes always reflected organizational properties that could not be discovered in isolated elements. This idea was expressed variously in terms like the "stream of consciousness," "unconscious inference," and "properties of the whole." The essence of this position was that the reduction of mind into elements obliterated properties of the intact, functioning organism that could not be retrieved once the reduction had taken place.

In this controversy Luria clearly sided against the elementarists, but his insistence that basic units of analysis must retain their emergent properties did not reduce to the arguments and phenomena then being explored by the Gestalt psychologists. Luria very early insisted that the basic units of psychological analysis were functions, each of which represented systems of elementary acts that controlled organism-environment relations.

Because of the cross-cutting choices and competing claims to scientific legitimacy in psychology which constituted Luria's early intellectual milieu, it is not possible to assign him to any one school. On each of the systematic issues confronting psychology he made clear-cut choices from the same set of possibilities as his contemporaries, but his combination of choices was unique, making him both a part of and separate from the major schools of psychology of the early 1920s.

The new mixture that Luria developed in collaboration with Lev Vygotsky, retained its distinctiveness up to 1960. Luria's interest in the way that motives organize behavior, coupled with his willingness to talk about "hidden complexes," his use of free association techniques (albeit in conjunction with tried-and-true reaction time methods), and his promotion of psychoanalytic ideas make it tempting to view him as an early, experimental Freudian. But even in his early writings on the subject, this designation would not have fit. Luria was not interested primarily in revealing the nature of the unconscious, and he attributed far too great a role to man's social environment as a prime shaper of individual behavior to be comfortable with Freud's biologizing of the mind.

From the outset, Luria carefully defended a methodology which relied upon objective data, whether in the form of spoken responses, movements, or physiological indicators, as the only acceptable data in psychology. This position might have placed him among the behaviorists, had it not been for his willingness to talk about unobservable states of mind and his insistence on the possibility of using objective indicators to yield information about them. Luria would also have been difficult to classify as a behaviorist because of the strong link between early behaviorism and stimulus-response, or reflex, theories. For Luria, word associations were a useful tool with which to ferret out the workings of a complicated psychological system, but he never accepted the idea that associations among ideas, or between stimuli and responses, represented a theory of how the mind works.

He unfavorably identified stimulus-response theories with the "telephone station" theory of how the central nervous system organized behavior, which likened the central nervous system to a giant switchboard. He remarked wryly that "it would be an interesting work to follow the complete history of the twentieth-century natural science of analogy . . . of those models which are accepted as a basis for the construction of ideas concerning forms and mechanisms of human vital activity. This history should reveal many naive sources of human thought . . . This tendency to introduce naive concepts to explain the nervous system on the basis of analogies with artificial things is more common in the study of behavior than anywhere else" (Luria, 1932, p. 4). In place of a telephone station, Luria suggested the idea of a dynamically organized system, composed of subsystems, each of which contributed to the organization of the whole. In the 1920s this might have sounded like a version of Gestalt psychology, but it could come as no surprise to cognitive psychologists when more than thirty years later Luria seized upon Miller, Galanter, and Pribram's *Plans and the Structure of Behavior,* a pioneering effort to apply computer systems analysis to psychology, as a kindred expression of concern for the limitations of stimulus response theory and as a mechanical analogy which, despite its limitations, began to approach his idea of what human systems might be like.

It might also have been possible to consider Luria a physiological psychologist because of his lifelong interest in the brain bases of behavior, except that for him the study of the isolated brain could not reveal how behavior was organized. Rather, he kept firmly in mind the fact that properties of the entire system could not be reliably obtained from a study of its parts operating in isolation. The brain was part of both a larger biological system and a surrounding environmental system in which social organization was a powerful force. Consequently, a psychological theory of the intact organism that preserved its history of interactions with the environment and its task at the time of study was a necessary complement to purely physiological or neuroanatomic investigation.

All of these ideas, which are to be found in Luria's writings as early as the 1920s, render him a prematurely modern psychologist who happened to begin life before his ideas could find confirmation in existing technologies or data. But it is not possible or appropriate to locate Luria's ideas only in terms of world psychology and neurophysiology. The fact that he was a Russian intellectual actively involved in the building of Soviet science and psychology shaped his career from its earliest days.

For approximately a decade following the Revolution there was a great deal of experimentation and improvization in the conduct of Soviet science, education, and economic policy. Less well known than the political struggles after Lenin's death are the experiments with new forms of schooling, free market agriculture, modern means of expression in the arts, and new branches of science. During the 1920s, virtually every psychological movement existing in western Europe and the United States found adherents in the Soviet Union. Perhaps because psychology as an academic discipline was embryonic at the end of the tsarist era, with only a single institute devoted to what was then recognized as psychology proper, an unusual variety of viewpoints and activities competed actively for the right to determine what the new Soviet psychology should be like. Educators, doctors, psychiatrists, psychoanalysts, neurologists, and physiologists often contributed to national meetings devoted to discussions of research and theory.

As the decade progressed, three issues came to dominate these discussions. First, there was increasing concern that Soviet psychology should be self-consciously Marxist. No one was certain what this meant, but everyone joined in the discussion with their own proposals. Second, psychology must be a materialist discipline; all psychologists were obliged to search for the material basis of mind. And third, psychology should have relevance to the building of a socialist society. Lenin's exhortation that theory be tested in practice was a matter of both economic and social urgency.

Toward the end of the 1920s this discussion had progressed to a point where there was agreement on some general principles, but the major conclusions did not single out any existing approach as a model for others. At the same time, the country experienced new economic and social upheavals with the advent of the rapid collectivization of agriculture and a greatly accelerated pace of heavy industrial development. Existing psychological schools were found to be wanting in their practical contributions to these new social demands as well.

A major result of these ideological and performance deficiencies was a deliberate reorganization of psychological research in the mid-1930s. While the specific events associated with this reorganization grew out of dissatisfaction with the use of psychological tests in education and industry, the result was a general decline in the authority and prestige of psychology as a whole.

During World War II many psychologists, like Luria, devoted

their efforts to rehabilitation of the wounded. Educational and medical psychology mixed freely in the face of the devastation wrought by modern warfare. Following the war, these two aspects of psychology continued to dominate Soviet psychology as the country rebuilt itself. Psychology as a separate discipline remained dormant, while psychological research was treated simply as a special feature of some other scientific enterprise.

Then in the late 1940s, interest in the field of psychology revived, with a focus on the work of Ivan Pavlov, Russia's renowned physiologist. Although many Americans think of Pavlov as a psychologist, perhaps because his methods for studying conditioned reflexes were adopted as both a key method and a theoretical model in American psychology between 1920 and 1960, Pavlov resisted association with psychology for most of his life. Soviet psychologists returned the compliment. They were willing to grant Pavlov pre-eminence in the field of the material basis of mind; but they reserved the province of psychological phenomena, particularly such "higher psychological processes" as deliberate remembering, voluntary attention, and logical problem solving, to themselves.

As in this country, many Soviet physiologists concerned with relations between the brain and behavior did not like this division of scientific labor. In fact, they considered psychology altogether unscientific. Given the opportunity, such people, many of whom were students of Pavlov, were delighted with the chance to make the study of "higher nervous activity" a model for psychology to follow. As the result of an extraordinary set of meetings under the auspices of the Academy of Medical sciences in 1950, psychologists began devoting major energy and attention to the application of Pavlovian concepts and techniques in their work. Special prominence was given to Pavlov's ideas concerning language, which appeared a likely area for psychologists to exploit.

In the past quarter-century, Soviet psychology has grown enormously in size and prestige. Important scientific advances in western European science, particularly in the study of brain functioning and computer technology, have been adopted and become a part of indigenous Soviet science. Psychology has not only gained recognition as an independent discipline but also been included among the disciplines that make up the prestigious National Academy of Sciences.

Throughout the first six decades of Soviet psychology Alexander Luria labored to make it a science that would fit the dreams of its originators, a Marxist study of man which would be of service to people in a democratic, socialist society. In pursuing this goal, Luria brought to bear firsthand experience with all of the problems and insights accumulated throughout the world in psychology since its inception one hundred years ago. His work is a monument to the intellectual and humanistic traditions that represent the best of the human culture he labored to understand and improve.

# The Making of Mind

# 1 . . .

# Apprenticeship

I BEGAN my career in the first years of the great Russian Revolution. This single, momentous event decisively influenced my life and that of everyone I knew.

In comparing my experiences with those of Western and American psychologists, there is one important difference. Many European and American psychologists possess outstanding personal gifts. Like good scientists anywhere, they have made their share of important discoveries. But most of them have spent their lives in a comparatively quiet, slow-moving environment. Their histories reflect the course of their work as well as the people and events that have shaped them: their parents, teachers, colleagues, and the intellectual issues in which they have participated. Their work as scholars consists of doing research and sometimes moving from university to university.

The difference between us lies in the social and historical factors that influenced us. From the outset it was apparent that I would have little opportunity to pursue the kind of well-ordered, systematic education that serves as the cornerstone for most scientific careers. In its place life offered me the fantastically stimulating atmosphere of an active, rapidly changing society. My entire generation was infused with the energy of revolutionary change—the liberating energy people feel when they are part of a society that is able to make tremendous progress in a very short time.

I was only a youngster of fifteen when the 1917 Revolution

broke out. Our family resided in Kazan, an old university town of about 140,000 people on the Volga River, 600 miles east of Moscow. My father was a doctor, specializing in stomach and intestinal diseases, who taught at the Kazan Medical School. Following the Revolution, he became an influential contributor to Soviet medicine. He established an independent institute for advanced medical studies in Kazan and after several years moved to Moscow where he was vice-director of the Central Institute for Advanced Medical Studies. My family was typical of what in Russia is called "the intelligentsia." We considered ourselves progressive and had no religious traditions. Although we were sympathetic to the revolutionary movement, we were not directly involved in it.

The stifling restrictions of the tsarist period are difficult for modern people to understand. Prerevolutionary Russian society was comprised of strictly divided classes: workers and peasants, intellectuals (physicians, teachers, and engineers), merchants and businessman, and the gentry (aristocrats and high government officials). The repressive nature of the regime was reflected in the educational system, which was designed to see to it that everyone stayed in his or her "natural" station in life and nothing changed. To make sure that this was the case, the Ministry of Education ruled that the gymnasium and the schools which prepared students for the gymnasium "shall be freed from the attendance of children of drivers, footmen, cooks, laundrywomen, small traders, and other persons similarly situated, whose children, with the exception perhaps of the exceptionally gifted, should not be encouraged to abandon the social environment to which they belong."

Of course the revoltuion changed all this. It broke down the barriers between classes and gave all of us, no matter what our social class, new perspectives and new opportunities. For the first time in Russia people were able to choose their own careers without regard to their social origins.

The Revolution freed us, especially the younger generation, to discuss new ideas, new philosophies and social systems. Neither

I nor any of my friends were familiar with Marxism or scientific socialist theory. Our discussions had not gotten beyond the utopian socialist schemes that were in the air in those days. I had no idea of the real causes of the Revolution. But my friends and I immediately threw our whole beings into the new movement because we recognized the opportunities that it offered. My enthusiasm came more from a strong emotional, romantic feeling toward the events of the time than from any deep intellectual appreciation of their social roots.

The content and the style of our lives changed almost immediately. Instead of cautiously groping for a foothold in life, we were suddenly faced with many opportunities for action—action that went far beyond the confines of our own tiny circle of family and friends. The limits of our restricted, private world were broken down by the Revolution, and new vistas opened before us. We were swept up in a great historical movement. Our private interests were consumed by the wider social goals of a new, collective society.

This atmosphere immediately following the Revolution provided the energy for many ambitious ventures. An entire society was liberated to turn its creative powers to constructing a new kind of life for everyone. The general excitement, which stimulated incredible levels of activity, was not at all conducive, however, to systematic, highly organized scientific inquiry.

These new conditions immediately changed the course of my education. By 1917 I had completed only six years of an eight-year gymnasium curriculm. About all I can remember now from those years of formal, classical education was the five hours a week of Latin lessons at which we learned to write extemporaneously on various subjects. This Latin training later proved useful in helping me learn English, French, and German. I did not complete the regular gymnasium course of training. Instead, like many of my classmates, I earned my diploma in 1918 by taking shortened courses.

I then entered Kazan University, where the situation was especially chaotic. The doors of the universities had been thrown open to all secondary school graduates, no matter how poorly prepared the graduates were. Thousands of students entered, but the universities were hardly in a position to educate them. There were shortages of all kinds in those days. Perhaps most important was the scarcity of professors prepared to teach under the new conditions. Some of the old, conservative professors were opposed to the Revolution. Others who were disposed to accept it had no clear idea of its import for what and how they taught.

The traditional curriculum had included such courses as the History of Roman Law and the Theory of Jurisprudence for prerevolutionary society, which now, of course, were inappropriate. But no one had yet decided what the new programs should be, and our professors were confused. I remember the pathetic efforts of one professor who had taught the History of Roman Law for many years to adapt to the new situation. He changed the name of his course to "The Social Foundations of Law," but his attempts to modernize his lectures were hopeless. While this kind of confusion was minimal in the medical school and in physics, mathematics, and chemistry, it was rampant in the social sciences, where I was a student.

Under these conditions student discussion and student-initiated projects soon came to dominate the professors' lectures. There were countless meetings of student groups and scientific associations which spent their time discussing general topics, especially politics and the shape of the future society. I took part in many of these activities and under their influence became interested in utopian socialism, thinking it would help me understand future developments.

These discussions about contemporary history also led me to become absorbed in certain basic questions concerning man's role in shaping society: Where do social ideas come from? How are they developed? How do they spread? And how do they become a force leading to social conflict and change?

I searched for books that would deal with these questions. I remember a book by Petrazhiskis about the psychological roots of law and emotion. I also remember reading the economist L.

Brentano's *Theory of Human Drives*. I even translated it into Russian and published it through the student's Association for Social Sciences. Both these volumes led me to want to develop a concrete psychological approach to the events of social life. I even developed a naive plan to write a book on these issues. Such projects were typical of the time, and although there wasn't the slightest chance that I could really write such a book, this kind of ambition shaped my intellectual development.

I found little of value in the dry, prerevolutionary academic psychology that then dominated the universities, which was strongly influenced by German philosophy and psychology. Most psychologists were still working out problems that had been set many years before by Wilhelm Wundt, the Wurzburg school, and the neo-Kantian philosophers. Psychologists were maintaining that the subject of psychology is immediate experience. To learn about immediate experience, they collected introspective accounts of people's immediate experience in laboratory settings under highly controlled conditions. These people's statements about their sensations were then analyzed to discover the basic elements of mind and the ways in which these elements combine.

The approach led to endless arguments, in part because there was no general agreement on what the basic mental elements are, no matter how carefully the experiments were conducted. For me, this kind of psychology was unattractive on other grounds as well. Classical German theories of how associations combined relied heavily on ideas about the laws of association that had orginated with the Greeks. I remember sympathizing with Harold Høffding, who argued that the laws of association could not account for memory. Høffding's argument was compelling: If two elements, $a$ and $b$, were associated because they occurred together, by what mechanism could a new experience $A$ evoke a memory of $b$? Wundt would say that $A$ was associated with $a$, which then evoked the memory of $b$. But if $A$ were occurring for the first time, why was it associated with $a$? The answer would be that $A$ and $a$ were somehow "similar." But there was no basis for establishing similarity in associationistic theory until after the associations between *A* and *a* had already been established!

Although Høffding's work found fault with the weaknesses of simple associationism, he accepted the currently popular methods of collecting and analyzing psychological data. I concurred with the criticism but felt it did not go far enough. I was depressed by how dry, abstract, and removed from reality all those arguments seemed. I wanted a psychology that would apply to real people as they live their lives, not an intellectual abstraction in a laboratory. I also found academic psychology terribly unattractive because I could see no way to connect such research to anything outside of the laboratory. I wanted a psychology that was relevant, that would give some substance to our discussions about building a new life.

Dissatisfied with the competing arguments over mental elements, I looked for alternatives in the books of scholars who were critical of laboratory-based psychology. Here I was influenced by the work of the German neo-Kantians, men like Rickert, Windelband, and Dilthey. Dilthey was especially interesting because he was concerned with the real motives that energize people and the ideals and principles that guide their lives. He introduced me to the term *reale Psychologie* in which man would be studied as a unified, dynamic system. He contended that a real understanding of human nature was the foundation for what he referred to as the *Geisteswissenschaften* or "social sciences." This psychology was not the psychology of the textbooks but a practical psychology based on an understanding of people as they live and behave in the world. It was a psychology that described human values but made no attempt to explain them in terms of their inner mechanisms, on the grounds that it was impossible to achieve a physiological analysis of human behavior.

While I was attracted to these ideas, the problems of implementing them became apparent to me as I read Windelband and Rickert's critiques of Dilthey. They raised the issue of whether psychology was a natural science, like physics or chemistry, or a human science, like history. In doing so, they made a distinction between the laws of the natural sciences and the human sciences. The laws of natural science were generalizations applicable to a multiplicity of individual events. Laws describing the acceleration of falling objects in general also describe any particular falling object. Such laws were referred to as "nomothetic," in contrast to "idiographic" thinking in which events and people were studied as individual cases, not as examples of some scientific or natural law. Events and people studied by history are good examples of the idiographic approach. For instance, a historian would study Peter I as a tsar who westernized Russia, not as a convenient representative of the entire class of tsars, or even of all progressive tsars.

Although I was excited by Dilthey's ideas of a realistic psychology, one that would reflect what I knew to be generally true of the complexities of real people, I was convinced that his descriptive approach was insufficient. I wanted a psychology that would overcome this conflict, that would simultaneously describe the concrete facts of the mental life of individuals and generate general explantory laws.

While I was struggling with this conflict, I came across the early writings of the psychoanalytic school. Sigmund Freud's *The Interpretation of Dreams* and several other of his early books had been translated into Russian, and other writings of his as well as of Alfred Adler and C. G. Jung (including his *Studies of Diagnostic Associations*) were available in German. Many of Freud's ideas seemed speculative and somewhat fantastic to me, but the study of emotional conflicts and complexes using the method of associations seemed promising. Here, I thought, was a scientific approach that combined a strongly deterministic explanation of concrete, individual behavior with an explanation of the origins of complex human needs in terms of natural science. Perhaps psychoanalysis could serve as the basis for a scientific *reale Psychologie,* one that would overcome the nomothetic-idiographic distinction.

At the age of twenty, as I was completing my formal education, I began to write a book about these "insights." The manuscript never advanced beyond the original handwritten copy which rests in my files today. Although this work had no scientific value, the fact that I even attempted such a task is worth mentioning because my ambitions were characteristic of the younger generation of the time.

Also characteristic was the way in which I plunged into psychoanalytic research. To begin with, I established a small psychoanalytic circle. I even ordered stationary with "Kazan Psychoanalytic Association" printed in Russian and German on the letterhead. I then sent news of the formation of this group to Freud himself, and was both surprised and pleased when I received a letter in return addressed to me as "Dear Mr. President." Freud wrote how glad he was to learn that a psychoanalytic circle had been founded in such a remote eastern town of Russia. This letter, written in a Gothic German script, as well as another letter authorizing the Russian translation of one of his smaller books, are still in my files.

In their early stages these efforts of mine led to no more than a few exploratory studies of psychiatric patients at the Kazan Psychiatric Hospital, which was part of the medical school. Curiously enough, one of the patients I worked with was the granddaughter of Fedor Dostoevsky. While I was able to fill notebooks with her free associations, I was in no position to carry out my plan to use such data to capture "the concrete reality of the flow of ideas." In fact, just posing the problem in this way makes it clear why such an approach could lead nowhere.

In later years, I published some papers based on psychoanalytic ideas and even wrote a draft of a book on an objective approach to psychoanalysis, which was never published. But I finally concluded that it was an error to assume that one can deduce human behavior from the biological "depths" of mind, excluding its social "heights."

My future course in science was by no means clear when I graduated from Kazan University in 1921. My father urged me to enter medical school. But my primary ambition was to become a psychologist. I wanted to take part in the creation of an objective approach to behavior that concentrated on real-life events. My compromise was to pursue both careers at the same time.

At that time it was possible to be enrolled simultaneously in more than one school. So I began taking medical classes and completed about two years of medical school before interrupting my studies, which were resumed only many years later. Simultaneously I spent time at the Pedagogical Institute and the Kazan Psychiatric Hospital.

Despite all these institutional affiliations, it was not a simple matter to obtain experience in the use of laboratory techniques. Neither at Kazan University nor in the Pedagogical Institute was there a working psychological laboratory. One of the first psychological laboratories in Russia, founded in the late 1880s by V. M. Bekhterev in the Psychiatric Hospital of Kazan University, had disappeared without a trace. The only experimental device I could find in the university was an old, unused Hipp chronoscope for measuring reaction time.

While casting around for an opportunity to learn laboratory methods, I continued to read every psychology book I could find. I was deeply impressed by Jung's *Studies of Diagnostic Associations,* which suggested entirely new ways of applying objective methods to the study of psychological processes. William James' work, especially *The Varieties of Religious Experience,* which I thought a brilliant example of the description of the concrete forms of psychological processes, also impressed me.

It was while I was working my way through these books that I came upon some papers by Bekhterev and by I. P. Pavlov. What immediately impressed me was that both men had objective approaches to problems that psychologists were able to discuss only in subjective terms. I was especially excited by Pavlov's conditioning experiments. Most of us have come to accept as commonplace his demonstration that it is possible to measure excitatory and inhibitory processes in the central nervous system which mediate the way in which peripheral stimulation produces salivary reflexes. At the time, however, they were revolutionary in their implications.

I seized the chance to put some of my ideas into practice by accepting a position as a laboratory assistant at the Kazan Institute for the Scientific Organization of Labor, which was established in the immediate postrevolutionary period. Using the old Hipp Chronoscope that I had found at the university, I started a study of the effect of hard work on mental activity. My subjects were workers at a foundry. I tried to measure the influence of verbal instructions on their reaction time. It was my first attempt to discover the role of speech in regulating reaction time. My results were sketchy and not very interesting, but in trying to find a way to get them published, I embarked on a course that eventually led me to Moscow.

Having read a good deal of Bekhterev's work and knowing the broad range of his interests, my colleagues and I decided to found a journal, in hopes that Bekhterev would be a member of the editorial board. The name we decided to give this enterprise was "Problems of the Psychophysiology of Labor," and I was selected to go to Petrograd (now Leningrad) to ask Bekhterev to participate.

My first visit to Petrograd was a great adventure. Bekhterev, then an old man with a long white beard, showed me around his Brain Institute, which still bears his name. I was impressed both by his great energy and by the different world from the one I knew in Kazan.

Bekhterev agreed to become a member of the editorial board of our journal on one condition. We had to add to the title the words "and Reflexology," the name he had given to his psychological system. We readily agreed, and Bekhterev became one of the editors-in-chief. The other was a venerable physiologist at Kazan University, N. A. Mislavsky, who actually had nothing to do with psychophysiology, labor, or reflexology. We were short of paper in those years, and I had to borrow some packages of yellow paper from a soap factory to print the first issue of the journal. This bit of academic entrepreneurship produced an outcome I had not anticipated: the end of my scientific "apprenticeship" in Kazan and an invitation to Moscow.

Throughout this period of my life I was naively groping. Still, after fifty years, I have the feeling that many of these activities were significant in my further development as a psychologist. In later years the surface appearance of my research changed a great deal. But the central themes that had guided my initial efforts remained.

# 2 ...

# MOSCOW

IT WAS 1923 when Professor K. N. Kornilov, who had just been appointed head of the Moscow Institute of Psychology invited me to join his staff. He selected me because he needed young, objectively oriented collaborators who would be involved in experimental psychology. My first soap-paper articles published in Kazan and using objective methods to study the effect of fatigue on motor reactions attracted his attention.

I arrived in Moscow to find a city that, like Kazan, was enthusiastically engaged in the work of reconstruction. Unlike my working conditions in Kazan, however, Moscow's psychologists had well-defined goals and specialized research facilities. I joined a small group of scholars who were charged with reconstructing Russian psychology in order to bring it into accord with the goals of the Revolution. But here a short digression is necessary so that the situation which greeted me in Moscow will be clear.

Russia's first psychology laboratories were created by Bekhterev in the 1880s, first in Kazan and then in St. Petersburg. It was not until 1911 that an institute of psychology was founded, by G. I. Chelpanov, a mentalistic philosopher and logician who had taught psychology as well. Familiar with the psychological research that had been under way for some time in the West, Chelpanov thought it would be useful to have such an institute in Moscow. A special building was erected on the grounds of Moscow University, and a fine collection of German experimental instruments (including my old friend the Hipp chronoscope) was set up. Chelpanov served as the institute's first director. In essence the work that went on there was an attempt to replicate the contents of Wundt's and E. B. Titchener's textbooks and even of Høffding's *Empirical Psychology* (which by that time, owing to its boring content, had accumulated a certain negative symbolic significance for me).

Chelpanov had published a psychology textbook for secondary schools which went through almost twenty printings prior to the Revolution. This large volume, entitled *Brain and Mind*, was devoted to a discussion of the relation between subjective experience and the material world. Here Chelpanov tackled the perennial problem of European psychology at the time: Do mind and matter interact in the brain, or do they merely work parallel to each other? Chelpanov adopted the position that a materialist approach to the study of mind was useless. So deeply ingrained was the idea of splitting the brain from the mind that even Pavlov welcomed Chelpanov's institute into the circle of Russian science. In a letter addressed to him in connection with the opening of the institute, Pavlov remarked that because the activities of the brain are so complex, they require both intensive and varied methods of study, and therefore "he who fully excludes any mention of subjective states from his laboratory sends his cordial congratulations to the Institute of Psychology and its founder." This letter, written in 1914, was not published until 1955.

If the institute's research had continued as it began, nothing much of importance would have been accomplished, save for additional evidence on visual thresholds or memory span, and descriptive studies of thinking. There appeared no way of linking psychology, in the academic style, to practical social problems. Research of this latter type existed, as in the case of the neurologist G. I. Rossolimo and the psychiatrist A. N. Bernshtein who were conducting important research in medical psychology, but there was none within the institute itself.

Following the Revolution, the work of the institute was re-evaluated. An isolated, ivory-tower psychology was found to be antithetical to the goals of the Revolution, and in 1922 changes that would link the activities of the institute to a scientific reconstruction of life were started.

Kornilov, one of Chelpanov's students, had developed a technique which he claimed could measure mental effort. Working with variations on the reaction time paradigm, Kornilov used a device to measure both the strength and the duration of motor reactions. He assumed that there was a fixed amount of energy in an organism that had to be shared by the mental and motor systems; the more energy expended on the mental component of an action, the less remained for its motor component. Kornilov naively assumed that his technique could measure this "energy." He predicted that motor strength would be maximum in simple reactions, less in reactions where the subject had to choose between two stimuli, and less still in complex, associative choice responses. Of course Kornilov never measured mental energy directly. He simply used his assumptions to claim he had measured it.

He also claimed to have created a materialist approach to the study of mind, which he supposed to encompass all of man's activity and to be consistent with Marx and Engels. Although his approach, which he dubbed "reactology," was naive, naturalistic, and mechanistic, it seemed to offer an alternative to Chelpanov's openly idealistic psychology. Chelpanov was removed as head of the institute in 1923, and Kornilov was appointed as the new director.

Marxist philosophy, one of the world's more complex systems of thought, was assimilated slowly by Soviet scholars, myself included. Properly speaking, I never really mastered Marxism to the degree I would have liked. I still consider this to have been a major shortcoming in my education. It should be no surprise, therefore, that although many discussions invoking Marxist thought took place in those early days, they were on rather shaky ground. Nonetheless, Kornilov's stated goal of reconstructing psychology along materialist lines was at this time a step forward. It enabled him to point the institute in a more productive direction and to rally a crowd of young scholars to help accomplish the necessary reconstruction of psychology. The reason my work was attractive to Kornilov should thus be clear: he saw in it a reflection of his own prejudices.

The situation in the institute when I arrived was peculiar indeed. All of the laboratories had been renamed to include the term *reactions*: there was a laboratory of visual reactions (perception), of mnemonic reactions (memory), of emotional reactions, and so forth. All this was meant to eliminate any traces of subjective psychology and to replace it with a kind of behaviorism.

The staff was young and inexperienced. No one was older than twenty-four years of age and few had proper training, but everyone was extremely enthusiastic, and the variety of work that was carried out on various reactions was broad indeed: White rats ran mazes, motor reactions of adult subjects were studied carefully, and problems of education were given attention.

Along with an active research program, there was teaching to be done, since the institute was also the training ground for future psychologists. The young scholars were a mixture of newcomers like myself and holdovers from Chelpanov's program. I was no older and knew no more than many of my students, so I spent the evenings preparing lectures and demonstrations for the next day's lessons, hoping I could stay at least one day ahead of my students. It was at this time that I met the young Alexei N. Leontiev, with whom my later life was closely connected. Among my other students were I. M. Soloviev and L. V. Zankov, both of whom went on to become important scholars in Soviet psychology.

It is difficult to characterize my feelings at the start of my professional life except perhaps to say that they were highly ambivalent. I was in full sympathy with the institute's efforts to develop objective methods of research. I did not think much of the efforts to measure mental energy; Kornilov's mechanistic scheme was clearly an oversimplification. But my former interest in psychoanalysis was helpful in overcoming my ambivalence and in finding something useful to do. I even found a use for the "dynamoscope," a U-shaped glass tube filled with mercury, which Kornilov used to record the strength of a movement on moving paper.

In my earliest experiments in Kazan I had used such an instrument to measure the strength of motor reactions, at which time I had noticed an interesting phenomenon. If conditions were created in which subjects were uncertain of what to do, such as whether or not to press a button, the line tracing their movements was disrupted; the smooth curve I usually obtained was distorted in a way that seemed to reflect the subject's uncertainty. I decided to see if I could expand these pilot observations into an objective, experimental study of conflict, stress, and strong emotions. In other words, I decided to initiate my own "experimental psychoanalysis," using the distortion of motor responses as an objective expression of inner, emotional conflicts.

Free associations as used by Jung in his *Studies of Diagnostic Associations* (1910) was one component of the technique we developed. We asked the subject to engage in a motor response *simultaneously* with each verbal associative response. I stress the word *simultaneously* because the logic of our approach required that the verbal and motor components of the response form a unitary functional system. Only when they were simultaneous could we be confident that an emotional reaction would be reflected in a break in the pattern established by the motor component of the system.

We began an intensive period of research that was to last many years. At first Leontiev and I conducted studies with students preparing to take their examinations. We instructed each subject to squeeze a small rubber bulb with his right hand while holding his left hand completely still on another rubber bulb, simultaneously giving us the first word that came to mind in response to our verbal stimuli.

We presented two kinds of verbal stimuli. First there were "neutral" stimuli, common words that we could assume had no special significance for someone taking an examination. Mixed in with these words were the "critical" stimuli, words such as "examination," "formula," and "passed," which were bound up with the difficult experience the students were about to undergo. When we looked at the students' free association responses or reaction times by themselves, we found it difficult to distinguish their responses to these two classes of words. But when we added the motor component, showing how the voluntary movement of squeezing a bulb was disrupted by the emotions evoked by certain stimuli, we could reliably distinguish the critical words for that subject.

We then decided to see whether we could use this technique to discover a person's "hidden complexes." We had in mind the kind of phenomena Freud and the psychoanalytic school were interested in, emotion-laden experiences that motivate and guide people's behavior far beyond the boundaries of the experience itself. We began by devising a laboratory model of the problem as we thought it would occur in real life situations. For this purpose we needed to be able to distinguish reliably between responses to critical and to neutral stimuli.

Our experimental model worked as follows. My research assistant constructed a story that was told to several subjects. For example, one story was about a thief who broke into a church by climbing through a window and stole a golden candlestick, an icon, and a crucifix. The subjects were instructed to remember the story but not to reveal that they knew it. Then they and other subjects who had not been told the story were asked to participate in an experiment in which they would respond to a list of about seventy words, ten of which were critical to the story, by squeezing a bulb with their right hand while free associating. My task was to determine from the combined record of their motor and verbal responses what the critical words were, who did and did not know the story, and what the story was. This laboratory model was quite successful. As events turned out, the most extensive application of this technique outside our laboratory was in connection with the criminal justice system.

In principle, psychologists interested in studying the emotions have always sought ways to produce emotional states that are of sufficient stability and duration to be studied. Various attempts prior to our studies, however, had not been successful. As a rule, acute emotional states such as fear or disgust were evoked artificially in the laboratory by shooting off a gun unexpectedly behind the subject's head or holding feces in front of his nose for inspection. These methods suffered two shortcomings. First, the emotion was in no way a part of the subject's real life situation but only an artificial incident unrelated to his ongoing purposes and motives. Second, acute states evoked in this way were quickly dissipated.

We decided that one way to overcome these kinds of inadequacy in our own and others' previous research was to work directly with people who were experiencing strong emotions in real life situations. The people we chose were actual or suspected criminals. We thought that if we could study criminals just after they had been arrested and at various times following the arrest, such as on the eve of trial, we might be able to observe the strong emotions that are very much a part of the person's real life. Such situations usually produce several intense emotions: those arising from the crime itself, those evoked by being apprehended and jailed, and those evoked by the fear of punishment. We also thought that if we had an opportunity to test subjects who were later judged to be innocent, we would have a contrasting group in whom fears of incarceration and the emotions arising out of the uncertainties of the situation were present, but who had no knowledge about the details of the crime. In these cases we could observe general stress but no specific "emotional complexes" related to the crime. Our laboratory model suggested that if we knew the details of the crime, they could be used as the critical stimuli in the combined motor test, and we could use the resulting data to reconstruct the events and determine who was guilty.

We were not the first, of course, to think of working with criminals in such a way, but previous researchers had been confined to working with convicted criminals only after they had been released. We were able to work with suspects from the time of arrest until after their trials. During several years of study, we were able to collect experimental material on more than fifty subjects, most of whom were actual or suspected murderers.

One of the first things we discovered in this work is that strong emotions prevent a subject from forming stable, automatic motor and speech responses, although subjects of equivalent intelligence, operating under normal circumstances, can form such responses after only a few trials. It appeared as if subjects influenced by strong emotions adapted to each new situation in a unique way and did not settle into a stable reaction pattern. Not only did the subjects have unstable motor and speech responses when considered separately, but they seemed unable to create a single functional system that included both motor and speech components, often delaying the speech components of their reactions.

This diffuse disruption of organized behavior was an impediment to discovering the presence or absence of a localized source of emotion that one would expect from a criminal who had specific knowledge of the crime; the baseline responding was too variable. In all cases we adopted a procedure of comparing the subject's responses to various stimuli: those that were fairly certain to be neutral, those that were doubtful, and those that were closely connected with the crime. Using this procedure of comparing responses to different stimuli within a single subject, we often found it possible to discriminate the actual criminal from other suspects. Since we were permitted to carry out this work prior to formal interrogation, we were able to use later criminal evidence to verify our hypotheses.

This work turned out to be of practical value to criminologists, providing them with an early model of a lie detector. For us, it represented the fulfillment of the goal that I had set myself when I came to Moscow: to apply objective methods to the study of emotional situations that were an integral part of people's real lives. Although the theoretical foundation for a lot of this work was naive, I found it far more appealing than Kornilov's "reactology," which remained unconnected with real life problems.

Perhaps because the style of this work was very much a part of the times, the research evoked interest outside of Russia. Max Wertheimer published one of my early papers in *Psychologische Forschungen*. Later this line of research came to the attention of American researchers, one of whom, Horsely Gantt, who had translated Pavlov's book on conditioned reflexes, translated my work under the title *The Nature of Human Conflicts*, which appeared in the United States in 1932. I was particularly pleased that the eminent psychiatrist Adolph Meyer wrote a preface in which he said of our work: "Luria offers us a true psychobiology and not largely neurologizing tautologies, in remarkably close contact with the sense of the work of Lashley and other American workers but definitely occupied with human problems. He shows a much greater applicability of laboratory methods to the human being than is generally expected in our environment, without surrendering to a sidestepping in merely physiologizing concepts." I met Meyer for the first time several years later. Now, forty-five years after the publication of this book, I remain grateful to this great psychiatrist for his moral support of my early work.

With the perspective provided by the distance of almost half a century, I can see both values and limitations in this research. It did accomplish my early goals and at the same time opened up new avenues of research, such as aphasia and child development, which were to assume central importance in my later work. Nevertheless, my initial applications of the combined motor method were of limited value. While they represented a synthesis of techniques and approaches that had existed in isolation prior to our studies, they did not lead to a basic reconstruction of psychology as a science. That enormous task, which was beyond my limited capacities, presented itself to me quite unexpectedly in 1924. In that year I met Lev Semionovitch Vygotsky. This event was a turning point in my life as well as in the lives of my colleagues in Soviet psychology.

# 3

# Vygotsky

IT IS NO exaggeration to say that Vygotsky was a genius. Through more than five decades in science I never again met a person who even approached his clearness of mind, his ability to lay bare the essential structure of complex problems, his breadth of knowledge in many fields, and his ability to foresee the future development of his science.

We met early in 1924 at the Second Psychoneurological Congress in Leningrad. This gathering was the most important forum at that time for Soviet scientists who worked in the general area of psychology. Kornilov brought along from the Institute of Psychology several of his younger colleagues, among whom I was included.

When Vygotsky got up to deliver his speech, he had no printed text from which to read, not even notes. Yet he spoke fluently, never seeming to stop and search his memory for the next idea. Even had the content of his speech been pedestrian, his performance would have been notable for the persuasiveness of his style. But his speech was by no means pedestrian. Instead of choosing a minor theme, as might befit a young man of twenty-eight speaking for the first time to a gathering of the graybeards of his profession, Vygotsky chose the difficult theme of the relation between conditioned reflexes and man's conscious behavior.

Only the previous year Kornilov had used this same podium to deliver an attack on introspective theories in psychology. His point of view had prevailed, and his objective, reactological approach was the dominant viewpoint in our institute. Both Bekhterev and Pavlov were well known for their opposition to subjective psychology, in which consciousness was a key concept. Yet Vygotsky defended the position that consciousness as a concept had to remain in psychology, arguing rather that it must be studied by objective means. Although he failed to convince everyone of the correctness of his view, it was clear that this man from a small provincial town in western Russia was an intellectual force who would have to be listened to. It was decided that Vygotsky should be invited to join the young staff of the new, reorganized Institute of Psychology in Moscow. In the fall of that year Vygotsky arrived at the institute, and we began a collaboration that continued until his death a decade later.

Prior to his appearance in Leningrad, Vygotsky had taught at a teachers college in Gomel, a provincial town not far from Minsk. By training he was a literary critic, whose dissertation on Shakespeare's *Hamlet* is still considered a classic. In this work, as well as in his studies of fables and other works of fiction, he revealed a striking ability to carry out psychological analysis. He was influenced by scholars who were interested in the effect of language on thought processes. He referred to the works of the Russian A. A. Potebnya and of Alexander von Humboldt, who first formulated the Sapir-Whorf hypothesis of linguistic relativity. Vygotsky's work at the teachers college brought him in contact with the problems of children who suffered from congenital defects—blindness, deafness, mental retardation—and with the need to discover ways to help such children fulfill their individual potentials. It was while searching for answers to these problems that he became interested in the work of academic psychologists.

When Vygotsky arrived in Moscow, I was still conducting studies by the combined motor method with Leontiev, a former student of Chelpanov's with whom I have been associated ever since. Recognizing Vygotsky's uncommon abilities, Leontiev and I were delighted when it became possible to include Vy-

gotsky in our working group, which we called the "troika."
With Vygotsky as our acknowledged leader, we undertook a
critical review of the history and current status of psychology in
Russia and the rest of the world. Our aim, overambitious in the
manner characteristic of the times, was to create a new, comprehensive approach to human psychological processes.

Our shared assumption at the outset was that neither the subjective psychology propounded by Chelpanov nor the oversim-
plified attempts to reduce the whole of conscious activity to simple reflex schemes would provide a satisfactory model of human
psychology. A new synthesis of the partial truths of previous approaches had to be found. It was Vygotsky who foresaw the
outlines of this new synthesis.

Drawing heavily on German, French, English, and American
writings, Vygotsky developed his analysis of what he called the
crisis in psychology. He discussed these ideas at various confer-
ences and actually wrote them down in 1926 when he was hos-
pitalized for the treatment of tuberculosis. Unfortunately, this
work was never published; the manuscript was lost during
World War II, and a copy was not discovered until 1960, when
it was placed in his archives.

According to Vygotsky's analysis, the situation in world psychology at the beginning of the twentieth century was extremely
paradoxical. During the second half of the nineteenth century,
Wundt, Ebbinghaus, and others had succeeded in turning psychology into a natural science. The basic strategy in their approach was to reduce complex psychological events to elementary mechanisms that could be studied in the laboratory by
exact, experimental techniques. The "sense" or "meaning" of
complex stimuli was pared away in order to neutralize the influence of experiences outside the laboratory which the experimenter could not control or properly evaluate. Isolated tones
and lights, or nonsense syllables, were the favorite stimuli that
served as the occasion for behavior. The goal of researchers became the discovery of laws of the elementary mechanisms that
gave rise to this laboratory behavior.

Acknowledging the success of this enterprise, Vygotsky pointed out that an essential consequence of this strategy was the exclusion of all higher psychological processes, including consciously controlled action, voluntary attention, active memorizing, and abstract thought. Such phenomena were either ignored, as in theories derived from reflex principles, or left to mentalistic description, as in Wundt's notion of apperception.

The failure of the natural science psychologists to incorporate complex human functions in their work provoked Dilthey, Spranger, and others to offer an alternative approach. They took as their subject matter exactly those processes that the natural scientists could not cope with: values, will, attitudes, abstract reasoning. But all of these phenomena were treated in a purely phenomenological, descriptive manner. They claimed that explanation was impossible in principle. To stress the difficulty, they would pose the question, "Can one ask *why* the sum of the angles of a triangle is 180°?"

Surveying this situation, Vygotsky pointed out that the division of labor between the natural science psychologists and the phenomenological psychologists had produced an implicit agreement that complex psychological functions, the very functions that distinguish human beings from animals, could not be studied scientifically. The naturalists and mentalists had artificially dismembered psychology. It was his goal, and our task, to create a new system that would synthesize these conflicting approaches.

It is probably impossible to assess all of the influences on us as we undertook a grand revision of psychology back in early 1925. But I know some of the resources on which we drew. For the natural science base we turned to Pavlov's study of "higher nervous activity." The basic structural units that produced adaptive adjustments to the environment were then being studied by Pavlov and his co-workers at their experimental station near Leningrad. Pavlovian psychophysiology provided a materialistic underpinning to our study of the mind.

Vygotsky was particularly impressed by the work of V. A.

Wagner, an eminent Russian specialist in the comparative study
of animal behavior. Wagner was a scientist who applied a broad
biological approach to animal behavior. His ideas on evolution
greatly impressed Vygotsky, and the two men carried on a
lengthy correspondence.

Within psychology proper we read widely. Though we disagreed with many of their theoretical ideas, we found a good
deal of merit in the work of our German contemporaries, especially Kurt Lewin, Heinz Werner, William Stern, Karl and Char-
lotte Buhler, and Wolfgang Kohler, many of whom are too
poorly known by my American colleagues. We accepted their
insistence on the emergent nature of the complexities of many
psychological phenomena. Pavlovian reflexes might serve as the
material foundation of mind, but they did not reflect the structural realities of complex behavior or the properties of higher
psychological processes. Just as the properties of water could
not be discovered directly from knowing that water consists of
two hydrogen and one oxygen atom, the properties of a psychological process such as voluntary attention could not be recov-
ered directly from knowing the way in which individual cells respond to novel stimuli. In both cases, the properties of the
"system"—water in one case, voluntary attention in the other—
must be understood as qualitatively different from the units that
compose them.

We also took to heart the point that similar looking behaviors
do not necessarily reflect similar psychological mechanisms.
When studying children of different ages or people from different cultures, we needed to examine carefully the nature and developmental history of the surface similarity in order to preclude
the very likely existence of different underlying systems.

When Piaget's *Language and Thought of the Child* became
known to us, we studied it carefully. A fundamental disagreement with the interpretation of the relation between language
and thought distinguished our work from that of this great
Swiss psychologist. But we found the style of his research, especially his use of the clinical method in the study of individual

cognitive processes, highly compatible with our goal of discovering the qualitative differences that distinguish children of different ages.

Vygotsky was also the leading Marxist theoretician among us. In 1925, when he published the lecture that brought him to Moscow, he included a citation from Marx which was one of the key concepts in the theoretical framework he proposed to us:

> The spider carries out operations reminiscent of a weaver, and the boxes which bees build in the sky could disgrace the work of many architects. But even the worst architect differs from the most able bee from the very outset in that before he builds a box out of boards, he has already constructed it in his head. At the end of the work process he obtains a result which already existed in his mind before he began to build. The architect not only changes the form given to him by nature, within the constraints imposed by nature, but he also carries out a purpose of his own which defines the means and the character of the activity to which he must subordinate his will. (*Capital*, Pt. 3, ch. 7, sec. 1)

This kind of general statement was not enough, of course, to provide a detailed set of procedures for creating an experimental psychology of higher psychological functions. But in Vygotsky's hands, Marx's methods of analysis did serve a vital role in shaping our course.

Influenced by Marx, Vygotsky concluded that the origins of higher forms of conscious behavior were to be found in the individual's social relations with the external world. But man is not only a product of his environment, he is also an active agent in creating that environment. The chasm between natural scientific explanations of elementary processes and mentalist descriptions of complex processes could not be bridged until we could discover the way natural processes such as physical maturation and sensory mechanisms become intertwined with culturally determined processes to produce the psychological functions of adults. We needed, as it were, to step outside the organism to discover the sources of specifically human forms of psychological activity.

Vygotsky liked to call his approach "cultural," "historical," or "instrumental" psychology. Each term reflected a different feature of the new approach to psychology that he proposed. Each emphasized different sources of the general mechanism by which society and social history mold the structure of those forms of activity that distinguish man from his animal neighbors.

"Instrumental" referred to the basically mediated nature of all complex psychological functions. Unlike basic reflexes, which can be characterized by a stimulus-response process, higher functions incorporate auxiliary stimuli, which are typically produced by the person himself. The adult not only responds to the stimuli presented by an experimenter or by his natural environment, but also actively modifies those stimuli and uses his modifications as an instrument of his behavior. We know some of these modifications through folk customs such as tying a string around one's finger in order to remember more effectively. Many less prosaic examples of this principle were uncovered in studies of changes in the structure of children's thinking as they grow from the age of three to ten years.

The "cultural" aspect of Vygotsky's theory involved the socially structured ways in which society organizes the kinds of tasks that the growing child faces and the kinds of tools, both mental and physical, that the young child is provided to master those tasks. One of the key tools invented by mankind is language, and Vygotsky placed special emphasis on the role of language in the organization and development of thought processes.

The "historical" element merged into the cultural one. The tools that man uses to master his environment and his own behavior did not spring fully developed from the head of god. They were invented and perfected in the long course of man's social history. Language carries within it the generalized concepts that are the storehouse of human knowledge. Special cultural instruments like writing and arithmetic enormously expanded man's powers, making the wisdom of the past analyzable in the present and perfectible in the future. This line of reasoning implied that if we could study the way the various thought operations are structured among people whose cultural history has not supplied them with a tool such as writing, we would find a different organization of higher cognitive processes but a similar structuring of elementary processes. I had the opportunity to evaluate these very ideas early in the 1930s.

All three aspects of the theory are applicable to the development of children. From the moment of birth, children are in constant interaction with adults who actively seek to incorporate them into their culture and its historically accumulated store of meanings and ways of doing things. In the beginning, children's responses to the world are dominated by natural processes, namely those provided by their biological heritage. But through the constant intercession of adults, more complex, instrumental psychological processes begin to take shape. At first, these processes can operate only in the course of the children's interaction with adults. As Vygotsky phrased it, the processes are interpsychic; that is, they are shared between people. Adults at this stage are external agents mediating the children's contact with the world. But as children grow older, the processes that were initially shared with adults come to be performed within the children themselves. That is, the mediated responding to the world becomes an intrapsychic process. It is through this interiorization of historically determined and culturally organized ways of operating on information that the social nature of people comes to be their psychological nature as well.

When we first began this work, the three of us—Vygotsky, Leontiev, and I—used to meet at Vygotsky's apartment once or twice a week to plan the research that would be required to develop his ideas. We reviewed each of the major concepts in cognitive psychology—perception, memory, attention, speech, problem solving, and motor activity. Within each of these areas we had to come up with new experimental arrangements which would incorporate the notion that, as higher processes take shape, the entire structure of behavior is changed.

At this time I held a position as director of the Laboratory of Psychology in the Krupskaya Institute of Communist Education, which was named for Lenin's wife, a woman who, following the Revolution, was extraordinarily supportive of educational work in the USSR. The institute was across the street from what was then called the Second Moscow University (now the Pedagogical Institute). Drawing on students from the university, I formed a student psychology circle where we discussed Vygotsky's ideas. Each of Vygotsky's students and colleagues undertook the task of inventing experimental models for the development of instrumental behavior.

The development of memory became the special province of Alexei Leontiev. Working with normal and retarded children of various ages, Leontiev devised a task in which auxiliary stimuli could be used by the subject to help him remember a series of stimuli presented by the experimenter. Further, Leontiev demonstrated that the process of mastering mediated remembering is long and difficult. At first the very young child, presented with clear reminders of a dozen or so common words, such as a picture of a sleigh to help him remember the word "horse," pays no attention at all to the reminders. Such a child might remember two, three, or four of the words, but not systematically and giving no evidence of engaging in any special activity to ensure the remembering. We called this kind of behavior "natural remembering," since the stimulus seems to be remembered through a process of direct, unmediated impression.

A little later the child might begin to take note of the reminders, or "auxiliary stimuli" as we called them. Although auxiliary stimuli sometimes helped the child, as often as not the reminder failed to remind him of the stimuli it was intended to evoke. Instead, the child would simply incorporate it into a chain of associations. Thus, if "sleigh" were the reminder, a child might end up recalling "snow" instead of "horse." Still later the child could use such ready-made reminders quite efficiently, but the process of using auxiliary stimuli was still external to the child in the sense that the connections between stimuli to be remembered and reminders were given by the conventional meanings of the words, that is, by the culture. Only somewhat later, at the age of nine or ten, did we begin to observe internalized mediation, when children began creating their own reminders so that virtually any auxiliary stimulus would be effective in aiding memory. The idea of using two sets of stimuli, one the primary set that has to be mastered and the other an auxiliary set that can serve as an instrument for mastering the primary set, became the central, methodological tool in all our studies.

Prior experiments on how complex choices are made employed trained adults who were required to press one or more telegraph keys when a stimulus was presented. By comparing the speed of a single response to a single stimulus with the time required to choose between two or more stimuli, many investigators hoped to be able to study the psychology of a single choice, and to distinguish the process of choosing from other processes, such as differentiating between stimuli and organizing a motor response. Vygotsky criticized this work severely, pointing out contradictions in typical results that suggested the need for a new way to treat the process of making choices.

Instead of relying on data from trained adults, Natalia Morozova studied the development of complex choices in small children. In her experiments a three or four-year-old child would be presented with a simple task: "Press the button when you see a red card." Then two or perhaps three cards were shown to the child simultaneously and three keys were made available for pressing. When these complications were introduced, the systematic flow of the child's responding disintegrated. The child often forgot which color went with which key. Even if the child remembered which keys to press in response to which stimuli, the entire method of responding was quite different from that typical of adults. As soon as a stimulus was shown, the child would begin to respond, but the response had no special direction. No choice had been made among the response alternatives. Rather, the child moved hesitantly, as if choosing among his own movements instead of among the stimuli.

Morozova's studies of choice soon shaded into research on memory of the sort that Leontiev was undertaking at the time. Since remembering which stimuli went with which responses was shown to be difficult for the young child, Morozova began to introduce auxiliary stimuli into the choice reaction experiment. Thus, a picture of a horse would be shown the child, with a picture of a sleigh pasted on the appropriate key. When Morozova traced the way in which children began to use the auxiliary stimuli to guide their choice responses, she found that the rules governing the acquisition of mediated remembering applied to the remembering that was required in the choice experiment as well.

R. E. Levina carried out studies on the planning role of speech. On the surface this work seemed quite different from the work of Leontiev and Morozova, but the underlying idea was exactly the same. Although Piaget had impressed us with his studies of the relation between language and thought in the young child, we disagreed fundamentally with his idea that early speech in the child plays no important role in thought. The phases in the development of speech-thought relations, according to Vygotsky, were roughly as follows. Initially, motor and speech aspects of the child's behavior are fused. Speech involves referential elements, object-oriented conversation, emotional expressions, and other kinds of social speech. Because the child is surrounded by his elders, speech begins to take on more and more demonstrative features, which permits the child to indicate what he is doing and what his needs are. After a while, the child, making distinctions for others with the aid of speech, begins to make distinctions for himself, internally. In this way, speech ceases to be solely a means for guiding the behavior of others and starts to serve the function of self-guidance.

Levina asked three-to four-year-old children to solve analogous problems to those that Wolfgang Köhler had posed for his chimpanzees: to obtain desired objects that were out of reach. For example, a piece of candy was placed in a cupboard out of reach of the children and a stick placed nearby on the floor. One child was observed to behave as follows, talking to herself the while:

"That candy is up so high. [Here the child climbs up on the divan and jumps up and down.] I have to call Mommy so she will get it for me [jumps some more]. There's no way to get it, it's so high. [Here the child picks up the stick, looking at the candy.] Papa also has a big cupboard and sometimes he can't reach things. No, I can't get it with my hand, I'm too small still. Better to stand on a stool [climbs on a stool, waves the stick around, which bangs the cupboard]. Knock, knock. [Here the child laughs. Glancing at the candy, she takes the stick and knocks it off the cupboard.] There! The stick got it. I'll have to take this stick home with me."

Vygotsky paid special attention to the way in which seemingly egocentric speech in tasks like this begins to play a role in carrying out the action and then in planning the action. At some point in the course of solving these problems, speech ceases merely to accompany action and begins to organize behavior. In short, it attains the instrumental function that he believed characteristic of all older children and adults.

This same fundamental idea was applied by Alexander Zaporozhets to the restructuring of motor behavior that occurs as the child grows older. In place of natural movements, controlled from outside, the child begins to gain voluntary control over his own movements. The change from natural, involuntary movements to instrumental, voluntary movement could be seen very clearly by placing the child in a situation where, in order to complete a task successfully, he was required to guide himself by an external rule.

For example, suppose we wanted to study the acquisition of jumping movements. In very young children, jumping occurs only when the immediate context, including the child's own desires, requires it. Jumping "just happens." We can not evoke it. Then, gradually, the child begins to use auxiliary stimuli to master his own movements. At first these auxiliary stimuli are of an external nature; a board is placed in front of the child to guide jumping or an adult gives a verbal command, "Jump." Later the child can attain the same level of proficiency by giving the command to himself, saying the word "jump" in a whisper. Finally, the child can simply think "jump," and the movements unfold in a voluntary way.

In a quite different example, L. S. Sakharov, a gifted collaborator of Vygotsky's who died at a young age, applied this same method to studies of classifying. He discovered that the naming function of words, which seems to be constant at different age levels because the surface features of the words remain the same, in fact undergoes deep changes in the course of development. At the very earliest stages, words designate whole complexes of referents, including not only the object named but also the child's feelings toward the object. Next, words refer to objects and their concrete contexts, and only later do they begin to refer to abstract categories. The block sorting technique upon which these observations rest was called the Vygotsky-Sakharov method when it was first invented, but over the years, as it began to take hold abroad, it came to be known as the Hanfman-Kasanin method, in honor of two investigators who translated Vygotsky's work and applied the method.

In 1929 our group devoted ourselves to a study of early "significative" activity, by which we meant the way in which children come to engage in activities that give significance to the stimuli that they are asked to master, thereby creating their own instrumental, mediated activities. We developed the idea of asking children to invent pictograms, pictures of their own choosing, to help them memorize a series of abstract words.

At a very early stage, children are really incapable of producing a pictorial stimulus that can guide later remembering. For example, a four-year-old, asked to draw something that would help her remember the phrase "The teacher is angry," responded by laughing and making a simple mark on the paper. She talked about her activity, but her talk and her movements were not guided by the task of remembering and bore no instrumental relation to each other. She forgot not only the phrase but the purpose of the entire task.

We saw the beginnings of useful productions in slightly older children. Not only did the children make pictures that captured an essential element of the phrase (a deaf boy was pictured by a head with no ears), but the children's descriptions had an interesting character. As Vygotsky pointed out, these children, having made a picture, would turn to the experimenter (although not required to do so) and formulate, as if for the adult, a feature of the stimulus. For example, for the phrase "sly old lady," one child drew an old lady with big eyes. Turning to the experimenter, he said, "Look at what big eyes they are." When we worked with older children, we found that this "attention-gathering" speech ceased to be addressed to the adult. Instead, it "went inside" and was used by the child to guide its own productions.

The individual studies that we carried out at this time, of which I have mentioned a few, must be considered banal in and of themselves. Today we would consider them nothing more than student projects. And this is exactly what they were. Nevertheless, the general conception that organized these pilot studies laid the methodological foundation for Vygotsky's general theory and provided a set of experimental techniques which I was to use throughout the remainder of my career. The students who carried out this work have gone on to play important roles in the development of Soviet psychology, generalizing these early efforts in a variety of sophisticated ways.

My own work was permanently changed by my association with Vygotsky and by the ingenious studies of our students. At the same time that we were carrying out this new line of work I was still conducting studies using the combined motor method, but as exemplified in *The Nature of Human Conflicts*, the focus in my work began to change. Although I had begun with an interest in studying the dynamic course of emotions, Vygotsky saw in my research a model for studying the relation between complex voluntary movements and speech. In particular, he emphasized the way in which speech served as an instrument for organizing behavior. As a result, in the later chapters of *The Nature of Human Conflicts* I included some of my earliest studies on the development of the regulatory role of speech. This topic became a central focus of my work only many years later.

It is extremely difficult, after the passage of so much time, to recapture the enormous enthusiasm with which we carried out this work. The entire group gave almost all of its waking hours to our grand plan for the reconstruction of psychology. When Vygotsky went on a trip, the students wrote poems in honor of his journey. When he gave a lecture in Moscow, everyone came to hear him.

His lectures were always a great occasion. It was in no way unusual for him to lecture for three, four, and even five hours at a stretch. Moreover, he did so with not so much as a scrap of notes. A good deal of the surviving material describing Vygotsky's work comes from stenographic notes of these lectures.

In the early years of our collaborative work, our theoretical stance met with little understanding or enthusiasm. People would ask: "Why cultural psychology? Every process is a mixture of natural and cultural influence. Why historical psychology? One can deal with psychological facts without being interested in the history of the behavior of primitive peoples. Why instrumental psychology? We all use instruments in our experiments."

In the course of time, as the result of many heated discussions and exchanges in scientific and social journals, the isolation of our small group came to an end. Our methods became more sophisticated, our theories more thorough and robust. In a few years, the concepts formulated by Vygotsky became widely accepted, and eventually they formed the basis for the main school of Soviet psychology.

One of the many characteristics of Vygotsky's work that was important in shaping my later career was his insistence that psychological research should never be limited to sophisticated speculation and laboratory models divorced from the real world. The central problems of human existence as it is experienced in school, at work, or in the clinic all served as the contexts within which Vygotsky struggled to formulate a new kind of psychology. It is significant that, when Vygotsky got his first job as an instructor in the teachers college in Gomel, he devoted his attention to the special problems of educating retarded children. He did not forget this interest. During the 1920s he founded the Experimental Defectological Institute (EDI) which is now called the Institute of Defectology in the Academy of Pedagogical Sciences.

Unlike many previous investigators of handicapped children, Vygotsky concentrated his attention on the abilities that such children had, abilities that could form the basis for developing their full potential. It was their strengths, not their defects, that interested him most. Consistent with his overall approach, he rejected simple quantitative descriptions of such children in terms of unidimensional psychological traits reflected in test scores. Instead, he relied on qualitative descriptions of the special organization of their behavior. His diagnostic protocols analyzing children with various forms of deficiency were preserved by his collaborator, L. Geshelina, but many were destroyed during the war, and others were lost after Geshelina's death. Nonetheless, this work has been carried on by many able people, including his early students, Morozova and Levina.

A second and equally important area of applied work for Vygotsky was psychiatry. At this time, psychiatry shared in the crisis that characterized psychology. Its theories, such as they were, were largely descriptive and highly speculative. With a few notable exceptions, its methods were subjective and unsystematic. Vygotsky was strongly opposed to Freud's "depth psychology" with its overemphasis on man's biological nature. Instead he proposed a psychology from the "heights" of man's socially organized experiences, which, he maintained, determines the structure of human conscious activity. From a theoretical perspective, the psychiatric clinic provided an additional setting in which to study the higher psychological functions. He applied a series of experimental tasks—some of them borrowed from developmental research, some invented for the special population —in order to be able to evoke pathological behavior under experimentally controlled circumstances. He was joined in this work by Bluma Zeigarnik, who had returned to the USSR in the late 1920s after studying for a number of years with Kurt Lewin in Germany.

Perhaps one of the most fruitful applied areas studied by Vygotsky, and certainly the one that had the greatest influence on my own career, was his work in neurology. This interest led us both to take courses in medical school. For me, it was the return to a medical career that my father had wished for me a decade earlier. For Vygotsky, it was the beginning of a road that time did not allow him to travel.

The neurology that we knew in the 1920s derived primarily from the achievements of German neurology in the latter half of the nineteenth century. Certain major "centers" controlling psychological functioning had been identified, such as the speech center discovered by Paul Broca, and neurologists were busy constructing maps of the cerebral cortex. This work proved important in formulating the cortical basis of psychological functions. But Vygotsky did not consider it sufficient because the neurological evidence was not closely linked to an adequate psychological theory. What the enterprise called for was the creation of a neuropsychology.

Vygotsky had two early models of such a compound discipline in the work of two Russian scientists. Bekhterev had applied experimental psychological methods in the neurological clinic, although Vygotsky could not accept reflexology as a theory of higher, specifically human psychological functions. At the Moscow Neurological Institute, Rossolimo had constructed a battery of tests for clinical diagnosis, rather similar to the battery developed some years later by David Wechsler. But the tasks that made up this battery failed to give a clear picture of the psychological mechanisms that were disrupted by neurological disorders.

Having surveyed previous versions of neuropsychology, Vygotsky proposed an approach based on his own analysis of the structure of psychological functioning. He sought first to specify the relation between elementary and higher psychological functions and their brain organization in the normal adult. He then proposed general principles to explain the changes in the structure of psychological functioning that characterized various pathological states and early ontogeny.

Vygotsky's observations in the neurological clinic began with aphasia, a language disorder. This choice reflected his conviction that the acquisition of language plays a decisive role in the development of higher psychological processes. Aphasia promised to be a condition that could be shown to affect specific aspects of mediated forms of cognitive activity in association with specific neurological damage. While the specific hypotheses related to aphasia proved simplistic, the general proposition that neurological explanations of human behavior required a sophisticated psychological theory of that behavior proved central to the later development of neuropsychology in the USSR.

Vygotsky's approach to the study of aphasia served as a model for all our later investigations in neuropsychology. Beginning with prior evidence concerning both the neurology and the psychology of the disturbance, he used clinical examinations of individual patients to gain a clearer picture of the qualitative differences between normal and aphasic functioning. The qualitative picture of the syndrome then led in two directions, toward a deeper understanding of both the brain structures intimately involved in the disorder and the psychological features of the disorder. Because in this case the psychological disorder was both organized by and reflected in language, we undertook a study of linguistics to supplement our psychological research.

In the brief decade between the time Vygotsky arrived in Moscow and his death from tuberculosis in 1934, his intelligence and energy created a psychological system that has by no means been fully explored. Virtually every branch of Soviet psychology, both its theory and its practical applications, have been influenced by his ideas. These same ten years altered forever the course of my own work. Without destroying the basic impulses that had attracted me to psychology in the first place, Vygotsky provided me with an incomparably broader and deeper understanding of the enterprise into which my early research fit. By the end of the 1920s the future course of my career was set. I was to spend my remaining years developing various aspects of Vygotsky's psychological system.

From 1928 to 1934 my energy was concentrated on demonstrating the social origin and mediated structure of higher psychological processes. The studies evolved from Vygotsky's belief that human beings' higher psychological functions come about through the intricate interaction of biological factors that are part of our physical makeup as *Homo sapiens* and cultural factors that have evolved over the tens of thousands of years of human history. At the time of his death, my colleagues and I had developed two complementary strategies for discovering·the interplay of biological and social factors in the structure of higher psychological functions. The first strategy was to trace the development of such functions out of the natural, biologically determined functions which preceded them. The second strategy was to study the dissolution of higher psychological functions as the result of some kind of insult to the organism.

During the period 1928–1934 and again in the late 1940s I concentrated my work on the first class of strategies, those that emphasize developmental change. From 1936 to 1945 and again from the mid 1950s to the present day I emphasized the study of dissolution and restoration of higher psychological functions in terms of the brain mechanisms that control them.

The developmental research was further divided into three lines of work, each of which addressed the relation of biological and cultural factors in human cognition in a different way. First, in an attempt to demonstrate the social origins of the particular forms that higher psychological functions assume in differently organized cultural circumstances, we undertook a study of adults who had been raised in different cultural circumstances from those that prevailed in the industrial centers of European Russia. Next, we carried out a longitudinal study of identical and fraternal twins. Here we, like others who have been concerned with the relative roles of "nature" and "nurture" in human development, made use of the differences between identical and fraternal twins, in that identical or monozygotic, twins have identical genetic material, whereas fraternal twins do not. By calculating the difference in performance of twins of the two kinds, we hoped to separate "natural" and "cultural" factors in development. Working from Vygotsky's theory, we added our own refinements to the techniques then available to us. Finally, we undertook a study of the comparative development of normal and mentally retarded children of various kinds. Here we used biological distortion in the course of development to aid us both in understanding the structure of normal functioning and in developing means of compensating biologically disabled children to the greatest extent possible using carefully designed educational curricula.

The work that emphasized the dissolution of higher functions was always seen as a natural complement to the developmental work. In fact, in the late 1920s we drew no really clearcut distinction between the two approaches; our work went on simultaneously on all fronts. The kindergarten and the clinic were equally attractive avenues of approach to the difficult analytic problems. But when war broke out in 1941, there was no room for choice. All of our efforts were concentrated on the study of the cortical foundations of higher functions, and in the trying years that followed, we put our limited theory into practice, developing both the theory and its applications.

# 4

# Cultural Differences
# in Thinking

WE WERE by no means the first to realize that comparisons of intellectual activity in different cultures could yield important information about the origin and organizations of man's intellectual functioning. For many decades before I met Vygotsky there had been widespread debate on the question of whether people growing up under different cultural circumstances would differ in the basic intellectual capacities they developed as adults. As early as the beginning of the century Durkheim assumed that the basic processes of mind are not manifestations of the spirit's inner life or the result of natural evolution; mind originates in society. Durkheim's ideas formed the basis of a number of studies and discussions. Prominent among those who furthered the debate was the French psychologist Pierre Janet. Janet proposed that complex forms of memory, as well as complex ideas of space, time, and number, had their sources in the concrete history of a society and were not intrinsic categories of mind as classical, idealist psychology believed them to be.

In the 1920s this debate centered on two questions: whether the contents of thought, the basic categories used to describe experience, differ from culture to culture; and whether the basic intellectual operations people perform on information differ from one culture to another. Lucien Levy-Bruhl, who influenced many psychologists of the period, argued that the thought of primitive, nonliterate people employs a different set of rules and operations from those employed in the thought of modern people. He characterized primitive thinking as "prelogical" and "loosely organized." Primitive people were said to be indifferent to logical contradiction and dominated by the idea that mystical forces control natural phenomena.

His opponents, such as the English ethnographer-psychologist W. H. R. Rivers, proposed that the intellect of people in primitive cultures is fundamentally identical to that of contemporary people living in technological societies. Rivers suggested that people living in primitive conditions think in accordance with the same logical laws we do. The basic difference in thinking is that they generalize the facts of the external world into different categories from those we are accustomed to use.

Various Gestalt psychologists also applied their ideas to the question of "primitive" thinking. Heinz Werner emphasized the differences in thought that distinguish the modern adult from the primitive. He speculated on the "structural similarity" of thinking among primitive people, children, and deranged adults. He saw undifferentiated, "syncretic" thinking as the characteristic feature of cognitive activity in all these groups. Other Gestalt psychologists emphasized the common properties of mind in all cultures. They promoted the idea that principles of perception and thought such as "closure" or "good form" are universal categories of mind.

These and other proposals were understandably of great interest to us. But the discussion was being conducted without the benefit of any appropriate psychological data. The data relied upon by Levy-Bruhl as well as by his anthropological and sociological critics—in fact, the only data available to anyone at that time—were anecdotes collected by explorers and missionaries who had come in contact with exotic people in the course of their travels. Professional anthropological field work was still in its infancy, so appropriate data of the observational sort were virtually nonexistent. Only a few studies on sensory processes, carried out by trained psychologists at the turn of the century, were available. These did not address the issues under debate, which concerned higher, not elementary, cognitive functions.

Things were no better in the area of psychological theory. The long-standing division of psychology into its natural (explanatory) and phenomenological (descriptive) branches had robbed psychologists of a unifying framework within which to study the effects of culture on the development of thought. Vygotsky's theory provided us with the needed framework, but we lacked the data to which we could apply our ideas.

We conceived the idea of carrying out the first far-reaching study of intellectual functions among adults from a nontechnological, nonliterate, traditional society. Moreover, by taking advantage of the rapid cultural changes that were then in progress in remote parts of our country, we hoped to trace the changes in thought processes that are brought about by social technological change. The early 1930s were especially suitable for carrying out the necessary experiments. At that time many of our rural areas were undergoing rapid change with the advent of collectivization and mechanization of agriculture. Although we could have conducted our studies in remote Russian villages, we chose as our research sites the hamlets and nomad camps of Uzbekistan and Khirgizia in Central Asia where great discrepancies between cultural forms promised to maximize the possibility of detecting shifts in the basic forms, as well as in the content of people's thinking. With Vygotsky's help I planned a scientific expedition to these areas.

Uzbekistan could boast of an ancient high culture which included the outstanding scientific and poetic achievements associated with such figures as Uleg Bek, a mathematician and astronomer who left behind a remarkable observatory near Samarkand, the philosopher Al-Biruni, the physician Ali-ibn-Senna (Avecenna), the poets Saadi and Nezami, and others. However, as is typical of feudal societies, the peasant masses remained illiterate and for the most part separated from this high culture. They lived in villages that were completely dependent on wealthy landowners and powerful feudal lords. Their economy was based mainly on the raising of cotton. Animal husbandry prevailed in the mountainous regions of Khirgizia adjacent to Uzbekistan. The conservative teachings of the Islamic religion were profoundly influential among the population and acted to keep women isolated from the life of society.

Following the Revolution these areas underwent profound socioeconomic and cultural changes. The old class structure was dissolved, schools were set up in many villages, and new forms of technological, social, and economic activities were introduced. The period we observed included the beginnings of collectivization of agriculture and other radical socioeconomic changes, as well as the emancipation of women. Because the period was one of transition, we were able to make our study comparative to some extent. Thus we could observe both underdeveloped nonliterate groups living in villages and groups already involved in modern life who were experiencing the influences of the social realignment that was occurring.

None of the populations we observed had received any higher education. Even so, they differed markedly in their practical activities, modes of communication, and cultural outlooks. Our subjects came from five groups:

1. Women living in remote villages who were illiterate and who were not involved in any modern social activities. There were still a considerable number of such women at the time our study was made. Their interviews were conducted by women, since they alone had the right to enter the women's quarters.

2. Peasants living in remote villages who were in no way involved with socialized labor and who continued to maintain an individualistic economy. These peasants were not literate.

3. Women who attended short-term courses in the teaching of kindergarteners. As a rule, they had no formal schooling and almost no training in literacy.

4. Active kolhoz (collective farm) workers and young people who had taken short courses. They were involved as chairmen running collective farms, as holders of other offices on the collective farm, or as brigade leaders. They had considerable experience in planning production, distributing labor, and taking

stock of output. By dealing with other collective farm members, they had acquired a much broader outlook than isolated peasants. But they had attended school only briefly, and many were still barely literate.

5. Women students admitted to teachers school after two or three years of study. Their educational qualifications, however, were still fairly low.

We assumed that only the final three groups, who by participating in the socialist economy had gained access to the new forms of social relations and the new life principles accompanying the changes, had experienced the conditions necessary to alter radically the content and form of their thought. These social changes had brought them into contact with technological culture and with literacy and other forms of knowledge. The first two groups had been exposed to a much lesser extent to the conditions that we assumed necessary for any fundamental psychological shift. Accordingly, we expected that they would display a predominance of those forms of thought that come from activity that is guided by the physical features of familiar objects. We also expected to find that the communication requirements of people doing planned, collectivized farming would have an impact on their thinking. Furthermore, we assumed that we could observe the changes caused by cultural and socioeconomic realignment through a comparison of the mental processes of these groups.

Adequate research methods had to include more than simple observation, and our methods approached a full-fledged experimental inquiry. But such a study inevitably encountered a number of difficulties. Short-term psychological experiments would have been highly problematic under the field conditions we expected to encounter. We were afraid that if, as strangers, we posed unusual problems that were unrelated to our subjects' habitual activities, they might become perplexed or suspicious. Administering isolated "tests" in such circumstances could yield data that misrepresented the subjects' actual capabilities. Therefore we began, as most field work with people does, by emphasizing contact with the people who would serve as our subjects. We tried to establish friendly relations so that experimental sessions seemed natural and nonthreatening. We were particularly careful not to conduct hasty or unprepared presentations of the test materials.

As a rule, our experimental sessions began with long conversations which were sometimes repeated with the subjects in the relaxed atmosphere of a tea house, where the villagers spent most of their free time, or in camps in the field and in mountain pastures around the evening campfire. These talks were frequently held in groups. Even when the interviews were held with one person, the experimenter and other subjects made up a group of two or three who listened attentively to the person being interviewed and who sometimes offered remarks or comments on what he said. The talk often took the form of a free-flowing exchange of opinion between participants, and a particular problem might be solved simultaneously by two or three subjects, each proposing an answer. Only gradually did the experimenters introduce the prepared tasks, which resembled the "riddles" familiar to the population and therefore seemed like a natural extension of the conversation.

Once a subject proposed a solution to a problem, the experimenter conducted a "clinical" conversation to determine how the subject had arrived at the solution and to gain more information about what he meant by it. A subject's response usually led to further questions and to some debate. To reduce confusion in the free discussion that followed, which was conducted in Uzbek, the experimenter left the actual recording of the results to an assistant, who usually sat near the discussion group and took care to avoid attracting attention. He made notes throughout the session. Only later did he prepare a clean copy and process the data. Although this laborious procedure required half a day for a brief session, it was the only practice adequate to the field conditions.

We also tried to make the content of the tasks presented to the subjects as natural as possible. It would have been foolish to give our subjects problems they regarded as pointless. Thus we used no standard psychometric tests. Instead we worked with specially developed tests that the subjects found meaningful and which were open to several solutions, each of which indicated some aspect of cognitive activity. For example, we contrived our categorization studies so that they could be solved either in a functional-graphic way, based, for example, on how things look or work, or in an abstract, categorical way. A subject could solve deductive reasoning problems either by using what he knew about the world or by using the terms of the information given in the problems to go beyond his experience and deduce the answer.

We also introduced some learning tasks into our sessions. By offering to help subjects in certain ways, we tried to show them how and to what extent they could use our assistance in solving a given problem and go on to solving others like it by themselves. This procedure allowed us to explore how people incorporate new ways of problem solving into their repertoire of intellectual activities.

Our basic hypothesis was tested using techniques that assessed the way people cognitively reflect their experience at several levels of analysis. We began with the way people linguistically code such basic categories of their visual experience as color and shape. Next we studied classification and abstraction. And finally we turned our attention to such complex cognitive activities as verbal problem solving and self-analysis. In each of these areas we discovered a shift in the organization of people's cognitive activity that paralleled the changes in the social organization of their work lives.

A basic change in perceptual categories that recurred in all of our observations was encountered in the way that subjects from our different groups named and grouped geometric stimuli such as those shown in the accompanying figure, which are numbered for ease of identification:

| 1 | 2 | 3 | 4 | 5 | 6 | 7 |
|---|---|---|---|---|---|---|
| ○ | △ | ◡ | ⬚ | □ | ◮ | △ |

A typical list of names given by nonliterate women living in remote villages was as follows:

1. a plate
2. a tent
3. a bracelet
4. beads
5. a mirror
6. a clock
7. a kettle stand

As subjects had more experience with literacy classes or organized collective farming techniques, abstract geometric names became predominant, and women at a teachers training school used such names exclusively.

This difference in naming was accompanied by a distinct difference in the figures that were classified as the same or similar. For the more traditional peasants, concrete likeness was the dominant mode of grouping. So, △ and ◿ were considered to be alike because "they are both window frames"; ◮ ⬚ were both watches, but ◡ ● □ were not alike in any way.

We were particularly interested in our subjects' rejection of our suggestions that such pairs as ● and ◡ were alike. These figures closely resemble the kind of stimuli that our Gestalt colleagues had used to demonstrate what they considered to be universal laws of perception. In their experiments, which as a rule had used well-educated subjects, they found that such figures were normally grouped together because they were both "representatives" of the abstract class of circles. Their subjects ignored the "individual" feature of each of the figures, isolated the major feature of "geometrical class," and made a decision on this basis. But when we asked traditional peasants whether these figures were alike, they answered no. They perceived the figures as similar to objects in their environment and classified them accordingly. "No, they cannot be alike," one peasant said, "because the first is a coin and the second a moon." To be sure, slightly educated subjects classified these stimuli on the basis of their general configuration, but we could no longer attribute this mode of classification to any "universal law of perception." This kind of categorical perception reflects historically developed and transmitted ways of classifying objects in the world around us. More educated subjects may classify such stimuli on the basis of a single "ideal" property, but this is not a natural and inevitable achievement of the human mind.

Man can perceive three million different hues, but there are only sixteen to twenty names for colors. Does this mean that the perception and classification of hues vary with the names of different colors themselves? Or do language and practical attitudes toward different colors evoke any changes in how people perceive and classify them? We studied the perception and classification of colors of various groups in our subject population and obtained results that were analogous to those in our studies of the perception of geometric figures.

We asked subjects in our basic groups to name and classify colored skeins of wool. Uneducated subjects, especially the women, many of whom were excellent weavers, used very few categorical color names. Instead they labeled the colored pieces of wool by the names of similarly colored objects in their environment. For example, they called various hues of green by the names of different plants: "the color of grass in the spring," "the color of mulberry leaves in the summer," "the color of young peas." When these subjects were asked to group together different strings that were similarily colored, many refused outright, claiming that each string was distinct. Others ordered them into a continuous series of colors which increased in hue or saturation. This pattern of responding to the individual skeins of wool on a visually dominated, particularistic basis disappeared in our other experimental groups, whose responses were dominated by the categorical color names and who readily classified similar colors together.

Our next series of studies concerned the way in which people categorize and make generalizations about objects in their everyday world. Unlike a set of different-colored strands of wool or two-dimensional geometric figures, the objects in our daily life are rarely categorized on the basis of some common physical attribute. Rather, they can be categorized in a variety of ways, and it was the nature of this variety in which we were interested.

On the basis of his developmental research Vygotsky made a number of distinctions between the types of categories that children were found to use at different ages. During the early stages of a child's development, words are not an organizing factor in the way that he categorizes his experience. Having no logical principle for grouping objects, the small child perceives each object in isolation. During the next stage of categorization the child begins to compare objects on the basis of a single physical attribute, such as color, form, or size. But in making these comparisons, the child quickly loses sight of the attribute he originally singled out as the basis for selecting objects and shifts to another attribute. As a result, he often assembles a group or chain of objects that reflects no unified concept. The logical structure of such groupings in fact often suggests a family in which one individual is included as the "son" of a central figure, a second as the "wife," and so on. This type of group structure can be detected when objects are incorporated into a general situation in which each participates on an individual basis. An example of such a grouping would be a "meal" in which the chair is used to sit on at the table, a cloth is used to cover the table, a knife to cut the bread, a plate to put the bread on, and so on.

This way of grouping objects is not based on a word that allows one to single out a common attribute and denote a category that logically subsumes all the objects. Rather, the determining factor in classifying objects into situational complexes of this sort is called functional-graphic perception or remembering of the real life relations among objects. Vygotsky found that grouping objects according to their relations in actual situations is typical of older preschoolers and elementary school children.

By the time children reach adolescence, they no longer generalize on the basis of their immediate impressions. Instead they categorize by isolating certain distinct attributes of objects. Each object is assigned to a specific category by relating it to an abstract concept. After establishing a system for including diverse objects in a single category, adolescents develop a hierarchical conceptual scheme that expresses increasingly greater "degrees of community." For example, a rose is a flower, a flower is a plant, a plant is a part of the organic world. Once a person has made the transition to this mode of thought, he focuses primarily on the "categorical" relations between objects, not on the concrete way in which they interact in real situations.

It is easy to understand that the psychological laws governing such taxonomic thinking differ entirely from the process at work when a person is making generalizations on the basis of concrete experience. Categorical thinking is not just a reflection of individual experience but a shared experience that society can convey through its linguistic system. This reliance on society-wide criteria transforms functional-graphic thinking processes to a scheme of semantic and logical operations in which words become the principal tool for abstraction and generalization.

Since all activity is initially rooted in graphic, practical operations, we believed that the development of taxonomic, conceptual thinking would hinge on the theoretical operations which a child learns to perform in school. If the development of taxonomic thinking did depend on formal schooling, then we would expect to see taxonomic forms of abstraction and generalization only in those adult subjects who had been exposed to some kind of formal schooling. Because most of the subjects in our studies had attended little or no school, we were curious about the principles that they would apply to grouping objects encountered in their everyday life.

Almost all the subjects listened to the instructions attentively and set to work eagerly. Yet often, even at the beginning, instead of trying to select similar objects, they proceeded to choose objects that were "suitable to a specific purpose." In other words, they rejected the theoretical task and replaced it with a practical one. This tendency became apparent early in our experimental work when subjects began to evaluate objects in isolation and to name their individual functions. For example, "this one" was needed to do such and such a job, and "that one" for a different job. They saw no need to compare and group all the objects and to assign them to specific categories. Later in the experimental sessions, as a result of our discussion and of the various probe questions asked, many of the subjects overcame this tendency. Even then, however, they tended to deal with the task as a practical one of grouping objects according to their role in a particular situation rather than as a theoretical operation of categorizing them according to a common attribute. As a result, each subject grouped the objects in an idiosyncratic way depending on the particular graphic situation he had in mind. The concrete groups that our subjects created on the basis of this "situational" thinking were extremely resistant to change. When we tried to suggest another way to group the objects based on abstract principles, they generally rejected it, insisting that such an.arrangement did not reflect the intrinsic relations among the objects and that a person who had adopted such a grouping was "stupid." Only in rare instances did they concede the possibility of employing such a means of classification, and even then they did so reluctantly, convinced that it was not important. Only classification based on practical experience struck them as proper or important.

The following example illustrates the kind of reasoning we encountered. Rakmat, a thirty-year-old illiterate peasant from an outlying district, was shown drawings of a hammer, a saw, a log, and a hatchet. "They're all alike," he said. "I think all of them have to be here. See, if you're going to saw, you need a saw, and if you have to split something, you need a hatchet. So they're all needed here."

We tried to explain the task by saying, "Look, here you have three adults and one child. Now clearly the child doesn't belong in this group."

Rakmat replied, "Oh, but the boy must stay with the others! All three of them are working, you see, and if they have to keep running out to fetch things, they'll never get the job done, but the boy can do the running for them . . . The boy will learn; that'll be better, then they'll all be able to work well together."

"Look," we said, "here you have three wheels and a pair of pliers. Surely, the pliers and the wheels aren't alike in any way, are they?"

"No, they all fit together. I know the pliers don't look like the wheels, but you'll need them if you have to tighten something in the wheels."

"But you can use one word for the wheels that you can't for the pliers—isn't that so?"

"Yes, I know that, but you've got to have the pliers. You can lift iron with them and it's heavy, you know."

"Still, isn't it true that you can't use the same word for both the wheels and the pliers?"

"Of course you can't."

We returned to the original group, including hammer, saw, log, and hatchet. "Which of these could you call by one word?"

"How's that? If you call all three of them a 'hammer,' that won't be right either."

"But one fellow picked three things—the hammer, saw, and hatchet—and said they were alike."

"A saw, a hammer, and a hatchet all have to work together. But the log has to be here too!"

"Why do you think he picked these three things and not the log?"

"Probably he's got a lot of firewood, but if we'll be left without firewood, we won't be able to do anything."

"True, but a hammer, a saw, and a hatchet are all tools?"

"Yes, but even if we have tools, we still need wood. Otherwise, we can't build anything."

The subject was then shown drawings of a bird, rifle, dagger, and bullet. He remarked, "The swallow doesn't fit here . . . . no, this is a rifle. It's loaded with a bullet and kills the swallow. Then you have to cut the bird up with the dagger, since there's no other way to do it. What I said about the swallow before is wrong! All these things go together!"

"But these are weapons. What about the swallow?"

"No, it's not a weapon."

"So that means these three go together and the swallow doesn't?"

"No, the bird has to be there too. Otherwise, there'll be nothing to shoot."

He was then shown drawings of a glass, saucepan, spectacles, and a bottle. He observed, "These three go together, but why you've put the spectacles here, I don't know. Then again, they also fit in. If a person doesn't see too good, he has to put them on to eat dinner."

"But one fellow told me one of these things didn't belong in this group."

"Probably that kind of thinking runs in his blood. But I say they all belong here. You can't cook in the glass, you have to fill it. For cooking, you need a saucepan, and to see better, you need the spectacles. We need all four of these things, that's why they were put here."

This tendency to rely on operations used in practical life was the controlling factor among uneducated and illiterate subjects. Subjects whose activities were still dominated by practical labor, but who had taken some school courses or had attended training programs for a short time, were inclined to mix practical and theoretical modes of generalization. The somewhat more educated group of subjects employed categorical classification as their method of grouping objects even though they had had only a year or two of schooling. For example, when we asked them which of the following three objects go together—a glass, saucepan, spectacles, and a bottle—they immediately responded, "The glass, the spectacles, and the bottle go together. They are made of glass, but the saucepan is metal." Similarly, when given the series of camel, sheep, horse, and wagon, they responded, "The wagon doesn't belong. All the others are animals." I could give more examples, but they are all the same: the individual picked out single attributes to make his generalization (such as "glass") and used a category name to subsume the different objects (such as "animals").

A somewhat different way of characterizing these results is to say that the primary function of language changes as one's educational experience increases. When people employ a concrete situation as a means of grouping objects, they seem to be using language only to help them recall and put together the components of the practical situation rather than to allow them to formulate abstractions or generalizations about categorical relations. This raised the question of whether abstract terms in their language, such as "tool," "vessel," or "animal," actually had more concrete meaning for them than for better educated subjects. The answer turned out to be yes.

For example, we presented three subjects (1–3) with drawings of an ax, a saw, and a hammer and asked, "Would you say these things are tools?"

All three subjects answered yes.

"What about a log?"

*1*: "It also belongs with these. We make all sorts of things out of logs—handles, doors, and the handles of tools."

*2*: "We say a log is a tool because it works with tools to make things. The pieces of logs go into making tools."

"But" we remarked, "one man said a log isn't a tool since it can't saw or chop."

*3*: "Some crazy fellow must have told you that! After all, you need a log for tools, together with iron it can cut."

"But I can't call wood a tool?"

*3*: "Yes, you can—you can make handles out of it."

"But can you really say wood is a tool?"

*2*: "It is! Poles are made out of it, handles. We call all the things we have need of 'tools.'"

"Name all the tools you can."

*3*: "An ax, a mosque [light carriage on springs], and also the tree we tether a horse to if there's no pole around. Look, if we didn't have this board here, we wouldn't be able to keep the water in this irrigation ditch. So that's also a tool, and so is the wood that goes to make a blackboard."

"Name all the tools used to produce things."

*1*: "We have a saying: take a look in the fields and you'll see tools."

*3*: "Hatchet, ax, saw, yoke, harness, and the thong used in a saddle."

"Can you really call wood a tool?"

*2*: "Yes, of course! If we have no wood to use with an ax, we can't plow and we can't build a carriage."

The answers of these subjects were typical of the group of il-literates with whom we worked, and they indicate that in at-tempting to define the abstract, categorical meaning of a word, subjects began by including things that in fact belonged to the designated category. But they soon exceeded the limits of the category and added objects that were simply encountered to-gether with items that were members of the designated class, or objects that could be considered useful in an imagined situation in which such items were used. Words for these people had an entirely different function from the function they have for edu-cated people. They were used not to codify objects into concep-tual schemes but to establish the practical interrelations among things.

When our subjects had acquired some education and had par-ticipated in collective discussions of vital social issues, they read-ily made the transition to abstract thinking. New experiences and new ideas change the way people use language so that words become the principal agent of abstraction and generaliza-tion. Once people are educated, they make increasingly greater use of categorization to express ideas about reality.

This work on word definition, when added to work on classi-fication, led us to the conclusion that the modes of generaliza-tion which are typical of the thinking of people who live in a society where rudimentary practical functions dominate their activities differ from the generalization modes of formally educated individuals. The processes of abstraction and generalization are not invariant at all stages of socioeconomic and cultural development. Rather, such processes are themselves products of the cultural environment.

On the basis of the results showing a shift in how people categorized the objects encountered in their daily lives, we speculated that when people acquired the verbal and logical codes that allowed them to abstract the essential features of objects and assign them to categories, they would also be able to do more complex logical thinking. If people group objects and define words on the basis of practical experiences, one might expect that the conclusions they draw from a given premise in a logical problem would also depend on their immediate practical experience. This would make it difficult, if not impossible, for them to acquire new knowledge in a discursive and verbal-logical fashion. Such a shift would represent the transition from sensory to rational consciousness, a phenomenon that the classics of Marxism regard as one of the most important in human history.

The presence of general theoretical concepts to which more practical ones are subordinated creates a logical system of codes. As theoretical thought develops, the system becomes more and more complicated. In addition to words, which take on a complex conceptual structure, and sentences, whose logical and grammatical structure permits them to function as the basis of judgment, this system also includes more complex verbal and logical "devices" that make it possible to perform the operations of deduction and inference without reliance on direct experience.

One specific device that arises in the course of cultural development is syllogistic reasoning, in which a set of individual judgments give rise to objectively necessary conclusions. Two sentences, the first of which makes the general proposition and the second of which gives a specific proposition, comprise the major and minor premises of the syllogism. When educated adults hear the two premises of a syllogism together, they do not

perceive them as two isolated phrases in juxtaposition. Rather, they "hear" the premises as a logical relation implying a conclusion. For example, I may say:
"Precious metals do not rust.
Gold is a precious metal."
the conclusion "Gold does not rust" seems so obvious that many psychologists were inclined to regard the drawing of such a logical conclusion as a basic property of human consciousness. The phenomenologists or adherents of the Wurzburg school, for instance, spoke about "logical feelings" and implied that such feelings existed throughout the history of mankind. Piaget raised doubts about the ubiquitousness of such "logical feelings" in his studies of the development of intellectual operations. But at the time we did our studies no one had bothered to determine whether or not such logical schemas are invariant at different stages of social history and social development. We therefore set out to study the responses of our subjects to syllogistic reasoning problems.

To determine whether people's judgments were being made on the basis of the logic of the major and minor premises or whether they were drawing conclusions from their own practical experience, we created two types of syllogism. First, we included syllogisms whose content was taken from the immediate practical experience of the people. Second, we created syllogisms whose content was divorced from such experience so that conclusions could be drawn only on the basis of logical deduction.

We were afraid that if the subjects did not perceive the major and minor premises as parts of a single problem, they might forget or distort either element of the problem, in which case their conclusion would be based on evidence other than that which we had presented. To guard against this possibility, we developed a procedure in which we first presented the major and minor premises and then asked subjects to repeat the entire syllogism. We paid particular attention to distortions in the premises and to any questions of the subjects. These distortions would be important evidence of the extent to which syllogisms were perceived as a unified system. After a subject was able to repeat a syllogism correctly, we went on to see whether he could draw the proper deduction.

One of the first things we found was that the nonliterate subjects often failed to perceive the logical relation among the parts of the syllogism. For them, each of the three separate phrases constituted an isolated judgment. This was manifested when subjects attempted to repeat the separate sentences of the problem, because they recalled them as if they were unrelated and separate, frequently simplifying them and modifying their form. In many cases the sentences virtually lost all syllogistic character.

This can be demonstrated with examples from subjects who were presented the syllogism:

"Precious metals do not rust.
Gold is a precious metal.
Does it rust or not?"

The recall of three subjects (1–3) was as follows:

1: "Do precious metals rust or not?
Does gold rust or not?"

2: "Precious metals rust.
Precious gold rusts.
Does precious gold rust or not?
Do precious metals rust or not?
Does precious gold rust or not?"

3: "These are all precious.
Gold is also precious.
Does it rust or not?"

These examples show that the syllogisms were not perceived by the subjects as a unified logical system. The different parts of the syllogism were remembered as isolated, logically unrelated phrases. Some subjects grasped the interrogative form of the last sentence, which they then transferred to the formulation of both premises. In other instances, the question formulated in the syllogism was repeated regardless of the preceding premise. Thus,

the question was perceived as unrelated to the two intercon-
nected premises.

These results made us realize that further study of logical operations required us to do preliminary work on syllogisms with
our subjects in order to stress the universal nature of the premises and their logical interrelations so that subjects would focus
their attention on these relations and better recall the basic
problem when it came time to make a deduction. In this later
work, we contrasted reasoning from syllogisms with familiar
and unfamiliar content. When the syllogisms were drawn from
the subject's practical experience, our only transformation was
to change the particular conditions to which they applied. For
example, a syllogism of this type would be:

"Cotton grows well where it is hot and dry.

England is cold and damp.

Can cotton grow there or not?"

The second type of syllogism included material unfamiliar to the
subjects so that their inferences had to be purely theoretical. For
example:

"In the far north, where there is snow, all bears are white.

Novaya Zemlya is in the far north.

What color are the bears there?"

Subjects living under the most backward conditions often refused to make any inferences even from the first kind of syllogism. In such cases, they were likely to declare that they had
never been in such an unfamiliar place and did not know
whether cotton grew there or not. Only after extended discussion, when they were requested to answer on the basis of what
the words suggest, would they reluctantly agree to draw a conclusion: "From your words, it should be that cotton can't grow
there, if it's cold and damp. When it's cold and damp, cotton
doesn't grow well."

Such subjects refused almost entirely to draw inferences from
the second type of syllogism. As a rule, many refused to accept
the major premise, declaring, "I've never been in the north and
never seen bears." One of our subjects told us, "If you want an

answer to that question, you should ask people who have been there and have seen them." Frequently they would ignore the premise that we gave and replaced it with their own knowledge, saying such things as, "There are different kinds of bears. If one is born red, he'll stay that way." In short, in each case they would avoid solving the task.

These reactions were demonstrated in our discussion with a 37-year-old villager. We posed the syllogism: "Cotton can grow only where it is hot and dry. In England it is cold and damp. Can cotton grow there?"

"I don't know."

"Think about it."

"I've only been in the Kashgar country. I don't know beyond that."

"But on the basis of what I said to you, can cotton grow there?"

"If the land is good, cotton will grow there, but if it is damp and poor, it won't grow. If it's like the Kashgar country, it will grow there too. If the soil is loose, it can grow there too, of course."

The syllogism was then repeated. "What can you conclude from my words?"

"If it's cold there, it won't grow. If the soil is loose and good, it will."

"But what do my words suggest?"

"Well, we Moslems, we Kashgars, we're ignorant people; we've never been anywhere, so we don't know if it's hot or cold there."

Another syllogism was presented: "In the far north, where there is snow, all bears are white. Novaya Zemlya is in the far north, and there is always snow there. What color are the bears there?"

"There are different sorts of bears."

The syllogism was repeated.

"I don't know. I've seen a black bear; I've never seen any others . . . Each locality has its own animals: if it's white, they will be white; if it's yellow, they will be yellow."

"But what kind of bears are there in Novaya Zemlya?"

"We always speak only of what we see; we don't talk about what we haven't seen."

"But what do my words imply?" The syllogism was again repeated.

"Well, it's like this: our tsar isn't like yours, and yours isn't like ours. Your words can be answered only by someone who was there, and if a person wasn't there, he can't say anything on the basis of your words."

"But on the basis of my words, 'in the north, where there is always snow, the bears are white,' can you gather what kind of bears there are in Novaya Zemlya?"

"If a man was sixty or eighty and had seen a white bear and had told about it, he could be believed, but I've never seen one and hence I can't say. That's my last word. Those who saw can tell, and those who didn't see can't say anything!"

At this point a young Uzbek volunteered, "From your words it means that bears there are white."

"Well, which of you is right?"

The first subject replied, "What the cock knows how to do, he does. What I know, I say, and nothing beyond that!"

The results from many interviews of this kind seem particularly clear: the process of reasoning and deduction associated with immediate practical experience dominates the responses of our nonliterate subjects. These people made excellent judgments about facts of direct concern to them, and they could draw all the implied conclusions according to the rules of logic revealing much wordly intelligence. However, as soon as they had to change to a system of theoretical thinking, three factors substantially limited their capability. The first was a mistrust of initial premises that did not arise out of their personal experience. This made it impossible for them to use such premises as a point of departure. Second, they failed to accept such premises as universal. Rather, they treated them as a particular statement reflecting a particular phenomenon. Third, as a result of these two factors, the syllogisms disintegrated into three isolated, particular propositions with no unified logic, and they had no way in which to channel thought into the system. In the absence of such a logical structure, the subjects had to answer the problems by guessing or by referring to their own experience. Although our nonliterate peasant groups could use logical relations objectively if they could rely on their own experience, we can conclude that they had not acquired the syllogism as a device for making logical inferences.

As in all of our other research, the picture changed sharply when we turned our attention to the educated subjects, who responded to these logical syllogisms much as we would. They immediately drew the correct, and to us obvious, conclusion from each of the syllogisms presented, regardless of the factual correctness of the premises or their application to a subject's immediate experience.

I have briefly described only three kinds of experiments from a much larger set that we conducted in the course of our two expeditions. These were followed by careful analyses of problem solving and reasoning, imagination and fantasy, and the ways in which informants evaluated their own personalities. We dubbed these later observations "anti-Cartesian experiments" because we found critical self-awareness to be the final product of socially determined psychological development, rather than its primary starting point, as Descartes' ideas would have led us to believe. I will not repeat all the details of these experiments because the pattern remained constant across experiments. In all cases we found that changes in the practical forms of activity, and especially the reorganization of activity based on formal schooling, produced qualitative changes in the thought processes of the individuals studied. Moreover, we were able to establish that basic changes in the organization of thinking can occur in a relatively short time when there are sufficiently sharp changes in social-historical circumstances, such as those that occurred following the 1917 Revolution.

# 5

# Mental Development
# in Twins

THE IDEA of studying identical and fraternal twins in order to separate the contributions of heredity and environment to a particular human characteristic was by no means original with us. At the time we undertook this work in the early 1930s, we were familiar with the work of K. J. Holzinger, Cyril Burt, and others who had begun to exploit the possibilities for exploring the origins of human intellectual functions that were inherent in the existence of identical and fraternal twins.

The logic of this approach is by now sufficiently familiar that a sketchy review is all that is needed to show the foundations on which we built. The simplest comparisons involve identical and fraternal twins raised at home. Here one can assume that the social environment for each member of a twin pair is more or less homogeneous, although among pairs there may be a great deal of environmental homogeneity as well, depending on the particular life circumstances of the families, such as educated versus non-educated parents, urban versus rural settings. However, the biological similarity between two twins in the same family will differ according to whether they are monozygotic (identical) or heterozygotic (fraternal). With constant environmental influences, one can assume essentially identical intellectual abilities for identical twins since both environmental and biological causes are more or less identical. For fraternal twins one can assume greater variability owing to differences in genetic makeup. More complex comparisons involving twins separated shortly after birth, which would vary the environmental as well as the biological antecedents of behavior, are also possible, but in practice such work will be complicated by the many unknown factors arising from differences of the environments in which these children are placed.

In the early 1930s an extremely propitious opportunity to investigate these issues arose as a result of research on genetics that was then going on at the Medico-Genetic Institute in Moscow. It was proposed that we set up a research program at the institute, which had outstanding boarding facilities, a fine educational program, and virtually unlimited access to twins from all over the USSR.

We undertook this work from our own theoretical perspective. The logic of varying environmental and biological factors using twins was clear enough, but we felt that previous research had been severely handicapped, not only in the limited numbers of subjects that were usually included from each of the crucial groups, but also in the weak measures of intellectual function that were used to assess environmental and biological influences. We were particularly unhappy with the use of standardized IQ tests as the indicators of intellectual development. These tests, which were developed on a purely pragmatic basis to predict school performance, seemed to us then, as now, to be a hopelessly atheoretical and opaque means of observing the structure of higher psychological functions.

Drawing on the many pilot studies of the late 1920s, we conceived a more complex set of relations between the performance of identical and fraternal twins which depended jointly on the nature of the specific task presented, the theoretical contributions of natural (biological) and environmental (cultural) factors to each kind of task performance, and the age of the child.

Natural and cultural processes not only arise from different sources but also change in different ways in the course of development. As a child grows older, natural processes change *quantitatively*. His muscles become larger, his brain grows more myelinated, his limbs change in size; analogously, his mental processes increase in power. But the basic principles of their action remain unchanged. Testing memory span, for example, is a means of gauging natural memory, because the child simply has to reproduce the stimuli without changing any of the information presented. Involuntary remembering also shares the property that the child does nothing special to accomplish recall; the material simply "impresses itself" on him.

Cultural processes, on the other hand, change *qualitatively*. To use memory as an example again, it is not just that the growing child's natural capacity to register and retrieve information increases; as a result of the increasing influence of the social environment, changes occur in the principles whereby the information is registered and retrieved. Instead of remembering naturally by retaining impressions and involuntarily reproducing them, the child gradually learns to organize his memory and to bring it under voluntary control through use of the mental tools of his culture.

Our research assumed that genetic contributions to behavior will be more directly reflected in tasks that call for natural cognitive processes than in ones that evoke culturally mediated processes. Drawing on our ideas concerning the developmental course of natural processes, we assumed a stable relation between heredity and behavior in natural cognitive tasks as the child matures. But for cultural processes we assumed a changing relation. We reasoned that among young children, in whom cultural processes still play a subordinate role, children who are genetically similar will behave similarly because their behavior is based on natural processes. But as culturally determined forms of information processing come to be relied on more and more, the children's environment will have a greater effect on behavior than does their genotype. Thus in older children, a similar environment will lead to similiar performance in tasks that require mediated, culturally influenced modes of cognition, even if the children differ genetically.

The logic of our approach required us to arrange that children be exposed to tasks that varied in the extent to which natural and cultural psychological processes were brought into play. We also wanted to work with children whose ages ranged from the period in which natural processes are dominant (5–7 years) up to the period where cultural processes are normally dominant. (11–13 years). Finally, we needed a way to vary genetic factors while holding environmental factors constant. Comparing identical and fraternal twins seemed the ideal technique.

Our previous research helped us to determine the age range of the children needed. Our younger group was composed of five- to seven-year-olds. Although we had been able to see the early stages of the emergence of culturally mediated information processing in children of this age under specially arranged conditions, we knew they were unlikely to apply cultural processes in most tasks. Our older group was made up of eleven- to thirteen-year-olds, who we knew were likely to use cultural processes if the task permitted. Within each age group we had approximately fifty pairs of twins, half identical and half fraternal.

One series of experiments consisted of three memory tasks studied extensively by Leontiev in his research on the development of memory. In the first task we presented nine geometric figures to the children and later asked them to recognize these figures from a set of thirty-four. We considered the visual recognition required by this study a good example of natural, direct remembering.

In our next task fifteen difficult-to-remember words were presented one at a time to each subject. The subject was asked to recall them all following presentation of the entire set. This task could be done either by simply remembering the words directly or by using complicated mediated processes to remember the words. For example, the subject could think of a word to help him remember each word presented or could conjure up an image to help him recall the necessary word. Because words could be recalled either directly or in a mediated way, we believed that this task allowed either natural or cultural processing. However, the difficulty of the task made it seem likely that natural processes would dominate in all but the oldest, most sophisticated children.

In the third task we asked each child to remember another set of fifteen words. As we presented each word to the child, we showed him a picture that he could use as an auxiliary sign to help him remember the word. The pictures were not connected with the words in any obvious way, so the child had to establish artificial links between them in order for them to be effective aids in helping him to remember. As in the second study, we presented the words and their associated pictures repeatedly until the child could remember all the words on the list. Then, when the child had memorized all the words in this way, we showed him the pictures one by one and asked him to recall the word that went with it.

It would have been difficult to ascertain anything like a structural change in the way that remembering was carried out if we had considered a quantitative analysis of the data alone. There were the usual age-related increases in remembering associated with each of these three tasks. But a qualitative analysis of the data revealed some important facts.

We found that the structure of visual memory for geometric figures was as elementary and natural in the older group as in the younger group. Almost none of our subjects used indirect or logical processes to any noticeable degree in memorizing the geometric figures. By contrast, a qualitative analysis of the results of the third task, in which each word presented to the children was accompanied by a picture, yielded quite different results. Most of the younger children remembered the words in the same direct way that they remembered either the visual figures in the first task or the orally presented words in the second. They were unable to use the auxiliary stimuli to build a logical connection between the picture and the words to be remembered. In many cases the memorized word was recalled in the absence of any connection between the word and the picture cue. The children were unable to give any information at all about the connection between the words recalled and the pictures being seen. When we questioned these children, they usually answered, "I simply remembered it." I do not think that their answers reflected a lack of introspection. Their remembering simply had not been mediated by the pictures.

We also found that the picture was a good auxiliary device for remembering for some of the children, not because of any logical connection between the words and the picture, but because of visual similarity. When using the picture as a cue to help them to remember, such children did not form a logical connection but tried to see the word in the picture. For instance, one child remembered the word "sun" when presented the picture of an ax. When we asked how he remembered the word, the child pointed to a small yellow spot on the picture of the ax and said, "Look, here is the sun." In one form or another, natural processes dominated.

When we studied the qualitative features of the recall of older children, we found the process of remembering by establishing similarities between the word and the picture changed to remembering by creating logical connections between the word and the picture. In these children we rarely found a word that had been remembered in an elementary, direct manner or by means of visual connection with the picture. They remembered the word "sun," for example, when using the auxiliary picture ax by creating such logical connections as, "We work with an ax and the sparks glitter in the sun" or "A man worked with an ax on a sunny day."

These observations established that our tasks were successful in evoking both cultural, mediated responding in some cases and direct, natural responding in others. These results provided the background for the next step in our analysis, to see if we could demonstrate that natural remembering is most closely related to the genetic makeup of the child, whereas the cultural form is related to his environment.

We reasoned as follows: the genetically determined, natural process should be similar in identical twins; that is, the difference in performance for such twins ought to be small. In particular, it ought to be smaller than the difference in scores for fraternal twins who share a similiar environment but relatively dissimilar genetic makeup. If we call the difference in scores for a given test $D$, we can calculate two different $D$ scores: $D_i$ is the difference between scores of identical twins, and $D_f$ is the difference between fraternal twins. Our reasoning led us to concentrate on the ratio of these differences. In particular, we expected $D_f > D_i$ for natural processes, and $D_f = D_i$ for cultural processes, since genetic similarity is not influential and the environments of the different kinds of twins ought to be equally susceptible to cultural influences.

The quantitative results in terms of the difference scores $D_f$ and $D_i$ for the natural and mediated tasks in the two age groups were as follows:

| Age | Natural task (geometric figure recognition) | | Mediated memory task (words and pictures) | |
|---|---|---|---|---|
| | $D_f$ | $D_i$ | $D_f$ | $D_i$ |
| 5–7 years | 18.0 | > 5.4 | 4.4 | > 1.9 |
| 11–13 years | 14.0 | > 5.6 | 1.2 | = 1.5 |

The pattern of results fitted our prior expectations rather neatly. For the task where natural, direct remembering dominated, the identical twins performed almost three times more similarly than the fraternal twins at both age levels (e.g. $D_f > D_i$). In the mediated task, the same pattern emerged for the younger children, although the superiority of $D_f$ over $D_i$ was much less; but among the older children, $D_f$ and $D_i$ were almost identical. This is exactly what we had predicted would happen on the assumption that for this task the older children would come to use mediated, culturally patterned forms of remembering. A report of this research was published in the American journal *Character and Personality* in the late 1930s.

Psychologists for the most part have been interested in twins in order to separate environmentally influenced processes from those influenced by heredity, as we attempted to do in the study just described. But twins are of enormous importance for psychological research over and above that set of questions. Because identical twins usually share a very similar home environment, more so than that of other siblings by virtue of their identical ages, and because their physical similarities often induce adults to treat them alike, identical twins also represent an interesting opportunity to study the effects of environmental variation because psychologists can introduce such variation in a planned manner against an unusually constant background, thus making their studies maximally sensitive to detecting environmental influences.

V. N. Kolbanovsky, A. N. Mirenova, and I collaborated on a second series of studies to see if we could design educational games that would develop children's ability to engage in constructive activity. We chose to concentrate our study on constructive play because games designed to develop such activity are widely used in preschool. They usually consist of a set of blocks of various shapes which the child can use to build different kinds of structures. Most educators argue that in addition to being entertaining, constructive play helps develop a child's imagination and elementary mental processes, including the ability to discriminate shapes and to estimate visually.

We began by surveying the kind of educational material used to stimulate constructive activity in preschoolers and the way these materials were used by teachers. We distinguished two main methods of inducing children to engage in constructive activity. In the first, the teachers required the children to construct block structures using a model. On occasion these models were drawings of structures in which outlines of all the elements necessary to build the structure were shown, so the children could copy the model by putting the blocks together step by step. This kind of construction was supposed to teach the child to pursue specific goals, to concentrate on the task, and to analyze the patterns of the model and to discriminate its component parts.

However, we found that it rarely held the attention of pre-schoolers. The work of putting the blocks in place according to a preselected pattern was often so boring that the teacher had to coax children to complete the task.

Perhaps as a result of the shortcomings of this highly structured method, many teachers allowed preschoolers to play freely with blocks, building whatever they wanted. While this free play may be conducive to the development of children's creative imagination, we doubted that it had any further educative effects.

In fact, our analysis suggested that both these educational strategies had shortcomings. From our point of view, real constructive activity should give the child a carefully defined goal. This goal should be either stated verbally or presented in the form of a model which the child has to copy. In carrying out this goal, the child should have to analyze the problem and find ways to solve it by selecting blocks which match the distinctive features of the particular structure and by rejecting those not suited to the task. Neither of the two forms of constructive activity we had observed met all of these conditions. A child who is given a detailed model to copy does not really need to analyze the problem. All the child has to do is select the blocks that are in the drawing or the model one by one and put them in place. There is nothing in the task presented in this way that requires reasoning. About the best we can hope from it is that it gives the child an opportunity to make elementary discriminations, which most children of this age have already practiced extensively.

Free block building gives the child an appealing goal to work toward, but it does not tell the child how to achieve it. The child has to find his own way by selecting those building blocks and procedures suited for the task. Both the task and the means used to complete it are flexible. As the child builds, the task often becomes more subtle and refined, and new details are added. Because of these features, free building activity is usually interesting to the child and holds his attention for a relatively long time.

Despite these positive features, free building activity also has a number of drawbacks from a pedagogical point of view. In formulating a construction task in free play situations, the child usually is not concerned with whether he can actually build the structure with the materials at hand. Another drawback of the free play situation is that it often drifts from true constructive activity into ad hoc creative play. By ad hoc creative play I mean that the child assigns meanings to things on the spur of the moment for the purposes of the game, like putting down a block and calling it a car. To some extent, such play can get along without any analysis of the objective properties of the materials with which the child is playing. He can put a block out and say, "Let this be a tree." Another block may be a car, and a third, smaller block, a dog. Using the blocks, children, especially the younger preschoolers, give free reign to their creative imaginations. This kind of play is often entertaining, but it does not develop the child's observational skills or his ability to analyze the problem and determine the elements and combinations of elements that are best suited for the constructive task.

With these objections in mind, Mirenova and I developed the following constructive task. We presented the child with a model which he was asked to copy with a set of blocks. The models we presented differed from those normally used in preschools in that the contours of the individual elements needed to build the structure were hidden (see figure). This was accomplished either by giving the child a two-dimensional outline of the model he was to construct or by presenting him with a three-dimensional model covered with thick white paper so that the general contours were visible but the individual components

A model with all elements visible (left) and a model with only the outline visible

were not. The typical model, in which each of the individual blocks in the structure are visible, can be copied by the child simply by matching, visually, the blocks before him with the individual blocks in the structure he is trying to copy. But the outline model gave the child a specific goal without giving him explicit information on how to accomplish this goal, because he could not see how the components were put together. In contrast to the normal type of constructive task, the outline model required that the child himself figure out which of many possible blocks were best suited to the task. This challenge made the work interesting and helped to hold his attention.

Our construction task also differed from free play block building by requiring the child to remain within the framework provided by the model, against which he could continually monitor his progress. Even slight discrepancies in dimensions or shapes were noticeable when the child compared the structure he had built to the model. This requirement kept the child within the framework of constructive thinking and prevented him from drifting off into ad hoc play.

We felt that play of this sort would develop complex forms of perceptual activity in children. Their direct, unanalyzed perception of the building model would not suffice; they had to organize their examination of the model to distinguish critical elements and relations. They had freedom of choice in ordering some parts of the task, but they also had to work within definite constraints.

We tested these ideas about constructive play on five pairs of identical twins attending school at the Medico-Genetic Institute. We began by conducting a number of psychological tests to determine if the twins' perceptual and cognitive development was in the normal range expected for children of this age. We also observed their visual constructive thinking. After these examinations, the two groups were given control tasks to perform. In one control task the child was asked to build from diagrams showing individual elements that made up the structure; in another control task he was asked to build from diagrams that showed only the general outline; and in the last task he was asked to play freely with the blocks. These control tasks gave us a baseline against which we could later measure the psychological changes brought about by our training program.

We gave one twin of each pair a training regimen based on the model in which all of the elements were clearly depicted. This group was designated the "build-from-elements group." The second group of twins was given a training regimen using the outline model, in which the elements making up the model were not visible. This group was called "the build-from-model group."

To ensure that all the children had the same level of experience with the kind of constructive activities we had designed for them, we chose children who were living at the Medico-Genetic Institute and attending the special kindergarten there. The two groups of children lived in different rooms, attended different kindergartens, and met each other only on walks or at times when play materials were not available. Each group of children was given training sessions with their respective construction tasks twice a day for two and a half months. In all, each twin completed a total of about fifty building sessions.

At the beginning, both groups of children had considerable difficulty with their constructive activity. They would often use the wrong size or the wrong shape of blocks and end up with structures that markedly diverged from the models they had been given to copy. One of the main difficulties exhibited by all the children was to chose a block arbitrarily and announce that it was going to represent a certain feature of the model without checking to see if it actually did resemble that feature. For example, if the model had a pointed roof, a child might use a pyramid or lean two elongated blocks against each other and call it a pointed roof without looking to see if his construction was like the pointed roof of the model. As a result, the children's buildings often bore little resemblance to the models they had been given to copy. Yet the children described these structures as if they were indeed replicas of the model and showed little or no awareness of the discrepancies.

After two months of training, we gave each of the groups some tests to determine whether the two training programs had differentially affected the development of their visual thinking and constructive activity. In the first test we gave all the children a model to copy whose elements were concealed as in the three-dimensional model. We found that the children who had trained using such models could build identical structures far more successfully than could children who had constructed their buildings from models in which all the elements were depicted. At first it seemed possible that this difference merely reflected a specific practice effect. However, when we presented both groups with new models depicting all the elements and asked the children to copy them, we found that those children who had practiced on models which gave only the general outlines were still superior.

What was it about the practice in the build-from-model group that had produced differences in the children's behavior? We tried to answer this question by analyzing the mistakes made by the children in the course of constructing the different models. We found that the children who had been trained in the build-from-model group planned their structures. Their first response to the task was to stop and analyze the overall pattern, whereas the children trained in the build-from-elements group just plunged ahead. We also found the build-from-model-group superior in the way in which they related elements of the structure to the whole, and they were more articulate in describing the way in which their structure differed from the model when they reached the stopping point. When the children in the build-from-elements group had completed their structures, they often maintained that their structures were identical to the model even when discrepancies were apparent. They seemed to be referring to the fact they had picked the correct elements and seemed not to notice that these elements did not bear the proper relation to the whole.

After completing an analysis of the children's performance on the training tasks, we designed a variety of new problems to try to explore the basis of the initial differences observed. One such task was to present the children with a model that had one or two pieces missing. The children in the build-from-model group seemed to have little difficulty picking out the proper elements and putting them in their places. But the children who had learned to rely on models that specified all the elements could not deal with the task at all.

This result led us to consider the possibility that the training program for the build-from-elements group had only exercised the children's elementary perception, so that they had difficulty when trying to apply these perceptual skills to more complex problems. When we tested the two groups of children on their ability to discriminate elementary figures, we found no difference between them. We also tested the children's ability to concentrate by asking them to study the difference between pairs of blocks in order to determine which were necessary to complete the next steps in a task. The children showed no difference in the amount of time they were able to concentrate.

From these observations we concluded that the differences in their performance on the criterion construction task were not the result of differences in elementary skills or attention span. Rather they were located in the children's ability to analyze complete models into their component elements and to relate these elements to the whole. We further tested this notion by presenting the children with complex figures and asking them to reproduce them from memory. The figures were made of irregularly shaped blocks which, when put together, formed a recognizable whole (see figure). We found that the children who had trained in the build-from-model group were able to reproduce

A model with irregularly shaped elements

the general shape of the figures using the correct elements, whereas the children trained in the build-from-elements group were able to reproduce only the individual elements in the task and could not grasp the whole.

We then presented the children with what we called the honeycomb task (see figure). To do this task, the children had to rec-

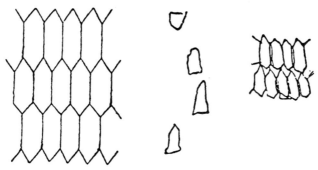

A honeycomb model (left) and the attempts of two children—the first with training in building from elements, the second with training in building from outline models—to reproduce the honeycomb

ognize that the side of each diamond making up the honeycomb was also the side of the adjacent diamond. Like all five- to six-year-olds, the twins with whom we were working found this task difficult. However, the children in the constructive modeling group showed that they could generate rules for reproducing the honeycomb in their copies even though they made errors, while the children in the build-from-elements group were completely unable to handle the problem.

To determine how general was the analysis of the relationship between objects and their spatial configuration, we asked each child to imitate the movements of the experimenter who was facing him. If the experimenter raised his right hand, the child was supposed to raise his right hand, although the hand nearest the experimenter's right hand was the child's left. In other words, in order to respond correctly, the child had to transpose the movement in space. Consistent with our analysis, the children who had been trained in the build-from-model group were better able to do the spatial transpositions than were the children in the build-from-elements group.

Finally, we examined the quality of both groups of children's free constructions. We found that the children in the build-from-elements group had not progressed at all in their free constructive play. They often became distracted in the middle of building something and wandered off into fantasies which transformed the meanings of the elements and of the task itself. The children in the build-from-model group first formulated a plan for the building and than carried it out. We saw this as reflecting a general change in their ability to plan and execute a constructive task. In follow-ups on this work we found that there was a significant difference between the children in the two groups as much as six months later. This research was interesting not only for its general theoretical and educational implications but also for its demonstration that identical twins could serve as especially useful subjects in intensive work with small groups of children.

The special attraction of working with twins in the two series of studies described so far rested on the opportunities they offered for controlling environmental and genetic influences on intellectual development. A third study of ours with twins was based on the special social relation that sometimes arises between twins and its effect on their language and subsequent intellectual development.

It is not unusual for twins to spend most of their waking hours together. When they are very young, a great many of these hours are spent in semisupervised play; an adult is present to see that no harm comes to the children, but they are left to amuse themselves. In the course of their time together twins commonly develop figures of speech that are "private," that is, words or phrases that have a special meaning to them but to no one else. In its simple form such private speech is common in any social group, but it is usually restricted in scope. Occasionally, however, special circumstances that further isolate twins can lead to a special "twin situation" in which the two children begin to rely heavily on the shared meanings of private words which have no identifiable significance to the adults around them.

In the course of our work we encountered such a pair of twins. Yura and Liosha, identical twin boys, had a complex phonetic impairment. They did not speak at all until they were two years old. At two and a half their only identifiable words were "mama" and "papa". At four they made only a few additional sounds when playing together. These sounds did not seem to be related in any systematic way to objects or actions; at least their mother could not detect any patterns. By the time the boys were five years old they could say a few conventional words when speaking to adults, but their play with each other did not involve much talk, and when they did speak, the sounds they made (*aga, nu, ntsa, a, bulbul*) seemed to be guided not by grammar but by actions and gestures. Some stable names were detectable: their own slightly distorted, made-up words, such as *pi pi* for "chicken," and a small store of Russian words for common objects, for parts of the body, and for elementary actions. The twins could also understand common speech that referred to them. But when the speech did not refer to them directly or when it was grammatically complicated, it seemed to pass them by.

At home the twins spent most of their time playing together. They were not read to or intellectually stimulated in any special way. Despite their anomalous speech, they appeared to be intellectually normal. They were mischievous, energetic, and friendly. They dressed themselves, ate at the table, and helped with small chores.

The facilities of the Medico-Genetic Institute offered a unique opportunity to study these twins and the relation of speech to the development of cognitive activities. The children were enrolled in the institute's residential kindergarten and quickly adjusted to their new setting. In comparison with their classmates, both Yura and Liosha's constructive play was somewhat retarded. They never made buildings or complex structures. When playing with large blocks, they spent most of their tiime hauling them around the room. They played together most of the time, rarely playing with or speaking to other children. When they did play with others, it was usually in simple chasing games. They never played with other children in creative activities such as drawing or modeling, or in role play.

During their initial period in the kindergarten we were able to record a great deal of their speech. Although by this time, at five and a half years old, their vocabulary had grown some, their speech was still agrammatical. They were never seen initiating conversations with adults, and attempts to draw them into conversation usually failed, although they would sometimes point to an object mentioned or use some idiosyncratic word to name it.

Their speech with each other was closely bound to action and marked the emotional character of the activity. An analysis of their speech during eight play sessions showed that about 80 percent of all their talk was made up of amorphous expression sentences that were incomprehensible if you could not see what the children were doing. Even though they used many common words, the meaning of the words remained unstable and resembled the speech of normal two-and-a-half to three year olds. These characteristics of Yura and Liosha's speech contrasted sharply with that of their peers, who had progressed far in their mastery of the semantics and grammar of Russian.

On the basis of our belief that speech is the mechanism for constructing and maintaining culturally determined, mediated cognitive activities, we saw the situation-bound, undifferentiated character of the twins' speech as the primary cause of their primitive play. Furthermore we expected to observe other differences in the children's intellectual activities as well. So long as the twins' speech remained diffuse and action-bound, it could not serve to regulate their behavior effectively. Without adult word meanings they were, in a sense, shut off from the culture's tools of thought. This feature of the children's speech was apparent in the virtual absence of narrative speech and of speech that served a planning function, that is, could guide the children's actions. The most sophisticated planning or regulative speech we heard during this initial period consisted of a few short phrases, such as, "Liulia (Yura), throw here, you here," and even these examples were connected with what they were doing at the time.

Once the children were accustomed to the kindergarten and we had made these baseline observations, we undertook an experiment to determine if we could modify the level of the children's speech in a short time and by so doing produce a change in their mental functions. We began with a ten-month program during which time the twins lived apart, a circumstance which in itself helped to break up the twin situation and promote the rapid acquisition of more adult speech and the parallel development of mental functions in both children. In addition, we gave Yura, the weaker and less developed twin, special speech training which was designed to help him discriminate and articulate sounds and to master adult speech. The lessons were as follows: first the child was encouraged to answer questions, then required to name objects, and finally to answer questions actively, repeat complicated phrases, and describe pictures. The instruction continued for three months and then, after a two-month break, resumed for another six months.

Following are two examples of such dialogues taken from the beginning and end of Yura's training program:

| Instructor | Yura |
|---|---|
| "Good morning, Yura." | Silently stretches his hand. |
| 'Well, good morning Yura." | Silent. |
| "Did you come by tram?" | Silent. |
| "Did Yura come in the tramcar?" | Silent. |
| "Who did Yura come with?" | Silent. |
| "With Uncle Vania?" | Shakes head negatively. |
| "Who did Yura come with? "With Fania Yakovlevna?" | Nods head silently. |
| "Yes, Yura came with Auntie Fania?" | Same reaction. |

"What is Yura wearing today? Boots?" (*Points.*)

Silently looks on.

. . . . . . .

"What is this?" (Holds out a picture.)

"A squirrel [*pelotska*, for *belochka*]."

"How do you know it is a squirrel?"

"The tail is so bushy [*pusistyi*, for *pushistyi*]."

"Where does she live?"

"The forest."

"In the forest?"

"In the forest."

"But where does she live in the forest?"

Silent.

"Does she have a house?"

"She does."

"Where?"

"On the tree [*delevo*, for *dereve*]."

"How on the tree?"

"In a hole [*dilke*, for *dirke*]."

"In a hole?"

Silent.

In the first of these examples Yura responded silently or not at all to the adult. Ten months later his speech, although somewhat distorted phonetically, had acquired the adult form semantically, grammatically, and functionally.

We tested the children at three months into the program and again at ten months to see if separating them had produced changes in their speech and in their mental functions. We also wanted to see if the special training that we had given Yura made an appreciable difference over and above the experience of being separated from his brother. At first the boys remained silent most of the time. But nonverbal communications were inadequate for communicating with the children and teachers in the kindergarten, and as the boys began to participate in the general life of the group, they began to speak in order to express their wishes, to participate in play, and to avoid being excluded. By the time we made our first systematic evaluation of the experimental program at three months, speech bound tightly to the specific situation and agrammatical speech had become less common than forms of speech that were appropriate for children of their age. Now, although they still made errors in grammar and pronunciation, the children could produce utterances that were extended phrases, such as, "I wanted a house, didn't get it" or "Liosha's making a table."

After three months the verbatim records of the children's speech showed that both boys had made great progress, but Yura had advanced more than Liosha. About 40 percent of their talk was devoted to planning functions, as in, "May we have the cubes?" or "I am going to get the truck." But Liosha's speech was rarely narrative—this is, he rarely described his own actions or those of others—and more of it was situation bound and agrammatical. Speech referring to future or past events was virtually absent. This pattern suggested that the development of planning speech grows out of the activities and interactions that normally occur in kindergarten, but the development of narrative speech seems to need special training at this stage in the child's language development.

We discovered a second, more subtle difference in the twins' speech at this time. Although both twins used planning speech in about 40 percent of the phrases recorded, Yura was more likely to formulate plans that applied to objects and actions that were not in the immediate environment. After ten months we found that Liosha had increased the amount of his planning speech, but he continued to be less able to plan things that were not immediate.

This difference was also evident in the twins' narrative speech. Yura learned to use narrative speech before Liosha did, but after ten months of separation the total percentage of narrative speech phrases was greater for Liosha (28 percent) than for Yura (21 percent). However, even here Liosha demonstrated a continued dependence on the immediate context. For the most part, his narrative speech described his own actions and immediate perceptions, in contrast to Yura whose narration was usually about events that were not connected to the immediate situation. From these findings, I formulated the respective roles of normal experience and of special practice as follows. The necessity to communicate led to the development of objective speech, but special training was required for the children to produce differentiated, well-developed sentences.

Examining the development of the twins' ability to understand adult speech, we could see an analogous pattern of development. In normal discourse it was virtually impossible to tell the twins apart because the immediate circumstances reinforced the meaning of their speech. But in special interviews we found that Yura's ability to analyze complex grammatical constructions and inflections, which are so important in Russian, was more developed than his twin's, who experienced some difficulty in comprehension.

Although these changes in speech behavior were of no small significance, our basic concern was to determine how changes in speech affected the structure of the children's thought processes. In particular, we were interested in determining whether the same qualitative changes that we had seen in the pilot studies by Vygotsky's students would occur in the short time span of our experimental intervention with the twins. At the beginning of our intervention the twins engaged in primitive play in which they attached conditional or play meanings to objects. But their play never integrated such objects into a system that incorporated verbally formulated rules, such as, "You be driver, I'll be passenger," or "Let's build a castle." When the twins were allowed to play together after three months of separation, there were remarkable changes in the structure of their play. The children began by singling out a project and verbally formulating it. Object meanings no longer changed in the course of the game. At last the game had an agreed-upon objective toward which the children oriented as they played.

Next we observed how the children constructed objects of their own choosing out of clay. In contrast to their earlier behavior, each child announced what he intended to build as he began, and he more or less kept to his plan. The architectural accomplishments of our twins were remarkable not for their beauty but for the forethought that guided their creation. Being able to plan, or to preconceive, the building also made the children less distractable and more actively determined to carry the activity to its conclusion.

While both twins improved, there were divergences in their intellectual development that corresponded to the linguistic differences between them. Before they were separated, Liosha generally initiated their joint activity. While he continued to lead their games based on motor activity after their separation, Yura became the acknowledged leader in activities requiring verbal formulation.

Yura's advantage in such situations was clearly demonstrated in a game in which objects were given play names and the children had to make up a story using the objects. For example, we called a pencil "mama," a vase "the tree," and a spoon "the wolf." We then played out a little game with "the tree," "the wolf," and "mama." Yura, using the pencil, the vase, and the spoon to represent characters in the story, immediately caught on and played the game. But even with gestural cues from the adult, Liosha did not participate and refused to call the objects by their play names. He simply could not use the labeling function of words in a flexible way. The conflict between the words' meanings and the objects' conventional names prevented him from entering the game. Liosha also had difficulties when asked to classify objects or to point out the absurdities in a picture, while Yura quickly mastered these tasks. In each case Yura demonstrated that he had learned to use culturally assimilated schemes to organize his thinking, while Liosha's behavior resembled that of younger children. I could provide many other examples to substantiate these conclusions, but the generalizations can easily be verified simply by referring to the monograph that I wrote with F. Y. Yudovich entitled "Speech and the Development of Mental Processes in the Child."

6 . . .

# Verbal Regulation
# of Behavior

IN THE LATE 1940s and early 1950s we worked on the role of speech in the formation of normal behavior in young children and on the failure of speech to assume normal regulative functions in retarded children. The role of human language in the formation and regulation of human activity has fascinated me from the very beginnings of my career. It is an issue to which I have returned again and again, each time in a different form. I have described, albeit briefly, the experiments I did while still a young man in Kazan which attempted to use verbal suggestion to influence reaction time. At that period in my life I was interested in modifying states of fatigue among workers. A little later I designed studies where overt motor responses to meaningful verbal stimuli were used to investigate the dynamics of hidden psychological complexes. In the mid-1920s, when we were just beginning to do clinical work, Vygotsky and I began to explore ways in which language could be used to reorganize the mental processes of patients suffering from neurological disorders, such as Parkinson's disease, so they could compensate for some of the symptoms. In the next decade our studies focused on the development of higher mental processes in children, especially twins, and the role of language in the formation of these processes.

In the years following World War II there was a great resurgence of interest in the use of Pavlovian physiology as a means of explaining *all* forms of human and animal behavior. This trend influenced my work for a number of years. The main strengths of the Pavlovian school lay in its extensive use of laboratory models of behavior and the sophisticated forms of experimentation that it had evolved through the years. Although my use of laboratory models was in many ways similar to that of Pavlovian scholars, I had several reservations about Pavlovian methods as they were then applied. In particular, I thought they offered an overly mechanistic and simplified explanation of human behavior which relied too heavily on the concepts of reinforcement and conditioning, that is, on the formation of temporary connections between stimuli and responses. The most dogmatic Pavlovians applied these concepts as if the behavior of children at different ages represented only the quantitative complication of simple stimulus-response principles, whereas I and others who had worked with Vygotsky believed that children's behavior underwent qualitative changes as they grew older.

In the early 1950s I moved my base of operations to the Institute of Defectology which Vygotsky had founded many years before. There I initiated a series of experiments in which the child's own speech was used to organize simple movements in response to arbitrary physical stimuli. We were interested in how the verbal regulation of behavior develops. To improve our understanding of the way in which the organization of behavior in normal children changes from being natural and unmediated to being instrumental and mediated as they grow older, we made our experiments comparative. We compared the influence of speech on the organization of behavior of normal children at different ages, as well as comparing normal behavior with that of children who were suffering from various forms of mental retardation.

When we began this work, the major Pavlovian theorist in the area, A. G. Ivanov-Smolensky, was using a version of the combined motor method which I had employed in my early research as summarized in *The Nature of Human Conflicts*. Ivanov-Smolensky used the technique as follows: a child would be presented a long series of trials in which he had to learn to press or to refrain from pressing a rubber bulb when one of a set of lights came on. The child, who was not told ahead of time what the task was, had to discover it through what Pavlovian theorists claimed was a kind of "verbal reinforcement" in the form of the instructions "press" or "don't press." Ivanov-Smolensky drew a strong parallel between the words "press" and "don't press" and the presentation of food to a dog following a signal of one type or another, and he viewed the child's mastery of this problem as a form of Pavlovian conditioning.

It should come as no surprise that I rejected this interpretation of the child's behavior and was not particularly happy with the way in which the experiments were conducted. In my opinion, Pavlovian scholars neglected the fact that each stimulus given to the child, especially a stimulus of the sort "press" or "don't press," evoked a conceptually derived generalization. Following as few as one or two trials, most human beings began to formulate a general rule of the sort, "I have to press whenever there's a red light" or "I have to refrain from pressing whenever the light is green." If my guess about the subject's reaction to this situation was correct, then the child was not reacting to the separate verbal reinforcements in these conditioning experiments. Rather, he was trying to discover a general strategy appropriate to the particular experiment. Believing that these kinds of experiments with verbal reinforcement were misguided, I decided to make a study of the real mechanisms underlying the formation of such motor responses.

While using a general methodological framework that was compatible with Pavlovian techniques, we developed an experimental method which, in my opinion, was more appropriate to an understanding of the psychological system with which we were concerned. We began each experimental session by giving the subject a set of verbal instructions that were meant to evoke a simple motor reaction. Then the limits within which the child was able to follow these instructions were studied, and the tasks were modified in various ways so that we could learn how children of different ages and different neurodynamic characteristics came to master or failed to master problems of this kind.

We found that normal children of two to two-and-a-half years of age are unable to follow even the simplest direct verbal instructions if the instructions are given prior to the task itself. When we instructed children of this age, "When the red light appears, squeeze," they reacted to the verbal instruction itself and began to press the bulb at once instead of waiting for the red light to appear. The first part of the verbal instruction—"When the red light appears"—evoked what we, using Pavlovian terminology, called an "orienting reflex." That is, the child began to search for the light. The second part of the verbal instruction— "squeeze"—evoked an immediate motor reaction, and the child pressed the bulb. The intended stimulus, the red light, actually became a distracting factor, and children who had already begun to press the bulb at the mention of the word "squeeze" often stopped responding altogether when the light came on. In addition, each verbal command "squeeze" evoked, not a unitary bulb-squeeze, but a whole series of involuntary motor reactions which only gradually exhausted themselves. Even the direct negative instruction "stop," frequently led to excitation and to stronger, less controlled motor responses.

This picture began to change when we observed normal children between the ages of three and four. They could follow the instruction "squeeze" with only a few, if any, extraneous responses. In the course of the most simple experiments they learned to listen to the instructions and to wait until the appropriate stimuli appeared. We called this ability to withhold a response and to organize it in terms of preliminary verbal instructions a "functional barrier." We believed that the children were verbally formulating a general rule for themselves which served as a barrier against the tendency to respond directly to the verbal instruction.

Although there is a clear improvement at this age, the verbal regulation of the three to four-year-old's motor responses are still easily disorganized. In order to produce such disorganization, we needed to change the conditions of the experiment only slightly. Instead of asking the child to respond to a single stimulus—to squeeze or not squeeze when a red light came on—we asked him to make a choice: "When you see a green light, do nothing. When you see a red light, squeeze."

We found two kinds of disorganization in the performance of children between the ages of three and three-and-a-half when they were asked to make such a choice. One group of children continued to respond when a negative stimulus, the green light, followed a positive stimulus, the red light. That is, the negative stimulus evoked an impulsive motor reaction which in Pavlovian terms could be explained as "irradiation of excitation." This is another way of saying that the initial verbal instruction was no longer controlling the children's actions because the first part of the response, pressing a button when a red light came on, spilled over into the response to the green light.

Another group of children failed to respond when a red light, the positive stimulus, followed a green light, the negative stimulus. Again, using Pavlovian terminology, we spoke of this as "irradiation of inhibition," evoked by the preceding negative stimulus. An analogous phenomenon appeared when we asked children to react with their right hand to a red light and their left hand to a green light. After pressing the button with their right hand, the children continued to use their right hand to respond to any stimulus even when the left hand was specified by the preliminary instructions.

None of these mistakes occurred because the children forgot the instructions. Following each experimental session, we asked the children to repeat the verbal instructions. All were able to do so adequately, even though they were still unable to do what they said they were supposed to do. The behavior of these normal children began to be brought under verbal control only after the age of four. By the age of six they had no difficulty at all with these kinds of tasks. Then they made mistakes only when we asked them to react as quickly as possible, or when fatigue set in. We summarized this pattern of age-related changes in response to verbal instruction in Pavlovian terms by speaking of the gradual development of selectivity and plasticity in the nervous processes. Within the theory developed by Vygotsky we spoke of the gradual formation of complex models of verbally controlled programs of motor behavior.

When we began to conduct similar experiments with mentally retarded children, we found that even at the age of seven, when Russian children normally start school, severely feeble-minded children could not follow the simplest direct instructions. If we presented our single stimulus experiment in which children had to press or refrain from pressing when a single light came on, we found that saying the words "When the red light appears" prompted them to try and find the light, while the order "squeeze" evoked an immediate motor response and they squeezed the bulb. Each link of these instructions evoked a direct orienting or motor response. In fact, the children's uncontrolled motor impulses evoked by the word "squeeze" often did not stop after the order "stop" was given. In some cases the second command increased the excitation in the child's motor system, and he responded more intensely.

These feeble-minded children were completely unable to create the more complex programs of behavior required by the second task, in which the child had to choose between responding and not responding. They could not shift between the required negative and positive motor responses and continued to react to the second stimulus as they had to the first. Thus, if a positive red light came on following a negative green light, they continued not to respond. In the situation where they were told to change hands when the light changed, they continued to use whatever hand they had begun with. Mildly retarded children were able to respond correctly in the simplest version of this kind of problem. Their symptoms were sometimes less clearly expressed and appeared only in the more complex versions of the task.

Explaining these phenomena within a Pavlovian framework

was not at all a simple matter. At first glance there seemed to be two possibilities. Perhaps the children's difficulties were caused by an imbalance between excitation and inhibition, or perhaps they were caused by insufficient plasticity of the nervous processes. Although these explanations arose in connection with Pavlovian physiological concepts, the terminology should not obscure the main ideas. By speaking of a balance between excitatory and inhibitory processes, psychophysiologists were referring to the possibility that the nervous system might have a general bias so that either excitation or inhibition would tend to be pervasive. If inhibition were dominant, the child would fatigue rapidly and would be unable to respond; if excitation prevailed, the child would over-respond to the verbal instructions.

Although in our opinion the notion that mental retardation is caused by an insufficient balance between excitatory and inhibitory neural processes does not explain the phenomena we observed, we could not rule it out as a factor. A lack of balance between excitation and inhibition was long ago described by Pavlov as the basic symptom of neurosis and was studied in a number of experiments by B. M. Teplov and V. D. Nebylitsen, and its applicability to phenomena of immature children's behavior and mental retardation was a distinct possibility when this work began.

Of the two explanations, we much preferred the one that focused on the lack of plasticity and the inertia in the neural processes of feeble-minded children. As experienced teachers of the retarded know, changing from one lesson to another is not easy for feeble-minded pupils. After an hour of spelling, retarded children often continue to spell even when the lesson changes to arithmetic. We thought that the same kind of explanation might apply in our experiments. However, unlike several of the more dogmatic Pavlovian physiologists, who thought that a combination of a lack of plasticity and an imbalance between inhibitory and excitatory processes explained mental retardation, we thought that such an explanation was insufficient and that a more sophisticated approach to the problem was necessary.

As might be anticipated, we used the line of reasoning advanced by Vygotsky to discriminate between different forms of behavioral retardation and to provide a firmer basis for experiments on the neurodynamic basis of retardation. The primary distinction was between behavior organized on the basis of higher, mediated processes and behavior based on natural processes. We acknowledged that while it was possible for the neurodynamic mechanisms posited by Pavlovian theory, such as the interplay between excitation and inhibition, to operate equally at both levels, it was also possible for a pathological condition to be present predominantly at either the higher or lower level. We hypothesized that in cases where the lower level has suffered, it is possible to compensate for the difficulties by changes in the organization of the activity using the higher, better preserved levels. In other cases we supposed that the psychophysiological situation is reversed. The higher level of organization of behavior is itself disturbed and hence cannot be used to compensate for behavioral defects. In such cases only compensation that uses lower functions would have a chance of working. To confirm this hypothesis, we needed techniques that would allow us to carry out studies of the neurodynamic features of children's behavior at both the lower and higher levels.

Although our approach was theoretically sound, to prove the correctness of our general formulation would be no easy matter. The unity of lower and higher levels of behavior in human beings does not allow a full separation of the two levels. Rather, the best we could hope for would be to construct experimental situations that would allow us to vary the relative importance of the two levels with respect to any particular activity.

My co-worker E. D. Homskaya and I used the combined motor method in a series of three experiments to study the controlling functions of speech on motor and verbal processes. We hoped that by using speech responses in one case and motor responses in the other, we would achieve the desired differentiation between levels of behavioral organization. In one situation the children were told to respond to a verbal instruction with a simple motor response, squeezing a recording device, as in the previous studies. In the second situation they had to respond by saying the word "yes" to the red stimulus and "no" to the green one. By comparing the children's responses in these two modalities, we could see if there were differences in the plasticity of the nervous system at the higher, verbal level of behavior and at the lower, motor level. In a third experimental situation the verbal and motor responses were combined: the children had to say "yes" and press a recording device at the same time or say "no" and refrain from pressing the device.

The exact psychological consequences of each kind of task had to be analyzed carefully. In the first experimental condition, where only motor reactions were required, the child needed both a well-balanced relation between excitatory and inhibitory processes and a high degree of plasticity in the motor system to complete the task successfully. When only a verbal reaction was required, excitatory-inhibitory balance and plasticity in the motor system were irrelevant. The required reaction would be hindered only if the higher level at which verbal behavior is organized were disturbed. The last experimental arrangement was of course more complex. In order to cope adequately with this problem, it was necessary for the child to establish a functional system coordinating both motor and verbal components. If such a functional system were not formed, the verbal and motor components would represent no more than parallel actions, and it was entirely possible that they would interfere with each other.

We found that normal children from two to two-and-a-half years of age were unable to respond appropriately in any of these experimental situations. Excitation of their motor impulses was so generalized that they were unable to carry out the required program of motor activity. Their verbal reactions were also disorganized. They inertly repeated "yes, yes" or "no, no," depending on the initial stimulus. And it was totally impossible for them to combine motor and verbal responses. As a rule these two actions inhibited each other.

I hasten to caution that in natural situations when a two to

two-and-a-half year old's actions are meaningful to him and are
bolstered by relevant previous experience, he will not behave inertly. A two-year-old child who stretches out his hand for candy
will not continue to stretch out his hand once the candy is in it.
But under artificial laboratory conditions, when pressing a button or saying "yes" is not accompanied by immediate rewards
and occurs in response to an arbitrary verbal instruction, there is
a certain inertia of both motor and verbal systems.

A different picture emerges when three to three-and-a-half
year olds engage in these experiments. At this age the child's
motor system in the artificial laboratory situation becomes more
plastic and loses its earlier inertia. The verbal system also begins
to become more flexible. The child who responds by saying
"yes" or "no" to the conditioning stimuli no longer keeps on
repeating these words. Combining the verbal and motor responses usually only slightly improves the child's performance
on the motor component of the task. In a few cases we observed
a definite improvement in the child's performance when these
two response modes were combined. Saying "yes" or commanding himself "go," the child's motor responses begin to be better
organized and controlled, and he overcomes the inertia that has
been typical of his motor responses at an earlier age.

We noted a remarkable phenomenon in children between
three-and-a-half and four years of age. Although saying "yes" or
"go" and pressing a button is a double response, it shares a single positive direction. Both motor and verbal response systems
are excited. However, when a child has to say "no" or "stop"
and simultaneously must block a motor reaction, the excitation
of the verbal system is positive while the meaning is negative.
Since every vocal response tends to produce a motor response,
even though the meaning of the response "no" is negative, a psychophysiological conflict is evoked when the negative is used.
We noted a certain degree of disassociation between verbal and
motor reactions during this three-and-a-half to four year old
transitional stage. While saying "no," the child often presses the
button and does not inhibit his movements. When the child is a

few months older, or if we institute special training in which the meaning of the verbal response is emphasized by explicit rewards, a new functional system is formed which begins to regulate the child's motor reactions. His motor activity comes under the control of word meaning rather than the primitive response to the mere sound produced by speech. I viewed this result as an indication that we had created a model of how the child's language comes to control his behavior under special laboratory conditions.

This transition from impulsive responses to responses controlled by the meaning of an utterance occurred in children somewhere between the age of three-and-a-half and four, although the exact timing differs greatly, depending on subtle features of the experiment and the particular children involved. It is difficult to specify exactly when and under what conditions the newly organized functional system can be observed, because it is initially quite fragile. Numerous studies conducted in various countries have both supported our findings and come up with conflicting results. The discrepancies can be explained only by careful analysis. In this kind of experiment, using children between the ages of three-and-a-half and four, even the slightest differences in the morphology of the verbal responses, such as between the instruction "go" and "no" or "press" and "don't press," can be important. But the essential point is that each set of deficiencies can be observed at a particular period in the child's development and will disappear during subsequent periods. As I see it, the sequence of changes is the important factor and not the precise age at which the new functional system appears. It is also important to emphasize again that these experiments are no more than experimental, laboratory models of the development of control in children's behavior.

When we were carrying out this work, we knew that specialists distinguished two basic forms of mental retardation in children, excluding retardation caused by local brain lesions and the still unclear group usually labeled "minimal brain disorders." We called one type "general asthenia." This type of retardation is usually caused by undernourishment and some somatic diseases. The other form is true feeble-mindedness or retardation, and it is caused by intrauterine brain intoxication, congenital traumas, or in some cases genotypic factors. Because the two forms of retardation often share similar symptoms, it is not an easy task to distinguish between them. We attempted to use our general characterization of the development of verbal self-regulation as a means of providing a differential diagnosis of these two forms. We hypothesized that in retardation of the sort associated with general asthenia, the symptoms of the disorder were the result of a dysfunction in lower, somatic processes. If this were the case, the neurodynamic features associated with excitation and inhibition in the motor system would be more deficient than the neurodynamic features of the higher, verbal system. It followed that the better preserved verbal system could be used to help overcome the neurodynamic insufficiencies of the motor system.

The situation would be different for children suffering from essential feeble-mindedness. We hypothesized that their higher functions, including their verbal system, would suffer more than their lower functions. Therefore the children's speech would be of little help in reorganizing their behavior or in compensating for their defects.

Our work on this kind of differential diagnosis began in the early 1950s and took many years to complete. It is summarized in a two-volume monograph, *Problems in the Higher Nervous Activity of Normal and Abnormal Children,* published in Russian in 1956 and 1958. [English summaries of this work appear in A. R. Luria, *The Role of Speech in the Regulation of Normal and Abnormal Behavior* (Pergamon Press, 1960).] In this work E. D. Homskaya observed that although children with an asthenic syndrome showed marked disturbances when required to make motor responses to verbal instructions, they did not show similar difficulties when asked to make only verbal responses. They could respond "yes" and "no" in an appropriate way, but they over-reacted when required to make a movement in response to a light. They failed to respond if a positive stimulus followed a negative one. They also showed inertness in the face of an initial positive stimulus, continuing to respond even when given the negative stimulus. Since their defects seemed to be localized in their motor system, we hypothesized that it would be possible to use the verbal system to help bring the motor system under control.

We were correct. We found that when we combined the verbal and motor responses, children who suffered from general excitation began to respond more regularly and more appropriately to the instructions. They stopped responding impulsively to negative stimuli altogether. And children whose behavior was inert began, with the help of their own verbal responses, to make stable motor responses to positive stimuli.

Our study of truly retarded children yielded totally different results. Members of our research group, including Dr. A. I. Meshcheryakov, Dr. V. I. Lubovsky, and Dr. E. N. Martsinovskaya, showed that the neurodynamic disturbances in the verbal processes of these children were far more pronounced than their motor processes. The difficulties that we had associated with an imbalance between excitatory and inhibitory processes or with the problem of pathological inertia were evident in both the motor and the verbal systems of these children. Since the same difficulties appeared in the same form in both the verbal and motor systems, we could confidently predict that combining verbal and motor responses would not improve the performance of the truly retarded children.

All these observations were made under artificial laboratory conditions. Although they are useful both as experimental models of the development of verbally controlled behavior and as diagnostic aids, they should not be overgeneralized. To establish the generality of the laws, we knew that we had to investigate children's natural behavior in order to understand the distortions that the laboratory conditions might have introduced. In the late 1950s we conducted a series of special observations in nurseries.

We found generally that one to one-and-a-half year olds cannot follow verbal instructions if they are not linked to feeding. And even in the feeding situation the intonational components of the stimulus and their place in the situation as a whole, rather than word meaning, are clearly decisive in regulating the children's behavior. The behavior of a child crawling on the floor is almost wholly determined by his orienting reactions to the physical characteristic of commands, no matter what the verbal instructions. This same phenomenon can be seen when a child is next to a table on which there are several toys. The verbal instruction, "Please give me the fish," may start a reaction, but it does not yet program the child's behavior. The child's gaze may turn to the fish, and his hand may start to move toward it, but both his eyes and his hand easily wander off the instructed course. The child, when he orients, is attracted by nearer, brighter, newer, or more interesting objects. Only by singling out the object named and moving it can one make it more attractive to the child. In short, the child is under the control of the physical features of the situation. What we wanted to discover were ways in which we could describe how verbal instruction comes into conflict with the influence of the immediate physical environment in very young children and finally comes to dominate it.

Our experiments were really quite simple. Two objects, a wooden cup and a small wooden wine glass, were placed on a table. A coin was put in the cup as the child watched. Then, asking the child, "Where's the coin?" we instructed him to find it. The youngest children, of one to one-and-a-half years old, reached for the cup, but their orienting response was still so strong that they usually grasped both the cup and the wine glass at the same time. Only somewhat later did children grasp the cup and find the coin. Verbal instructions became decisive only with children who were about two years old.

Next we wanted to know whether those children who correctly did as they were told would continue to remember the command after a short delay and whether it would still control their behavior. We introduced a delay of about ten to fifteen seconds between the time in which we put the coin in the cup and asked the children to find it and the time that they were free to begin their search. We found that the youngest children could not do the task at all. Although they could follow the verbal instruction immediately, the instruction lost its controlling function when there was a delay, and they resorted to grasping both objects at once. Children who were slightly older were able to retain control of their behavior despite the delay.

In both these cases our observations dealt with a combination of verbal commands and immediate stimulation: the child observed where the coin was placed and heard the instructions. What would happen if we isolated these factors from each other? Could the child follow the verbal command if it was not supplemented by the immediate visual stimulus? A screen was placed between the child and the containers on the table so that the child could not see where the coin was placed. Then the command was given: "The coin is in the cup. Please find the coin."

Children one-and-a-half to three years of age who easily performed the task in the previous series were unable to follow the "pure" verbal command unaided by the visual stimulus. They became confused and frequently picked up both the cup and the wine glass. Around the age of three and a half the pure verbal command began to assume a controlling role.

After we had gotten a glimpse of the early stages of the way in which verbal commands assume a controlling function, we began to investigate the stability of that function. We did so in two ways. First we created a situation in which the verbal command was in conflict with the child's prior experience. Second, we created a situation in which the verbal command conflicted with the immediate information in the visual environment. To create the first kind of conflict, the coin was placed in the cup three to four times to establish a set of expectations in the child. Then the pattern was broken and the coin was placed in the wine glass. In both the visually aided and the screened series, this complication made children who had previously been able to follow the verbal commands unable to do so. In this situation the children continued to grasp the cup. Only after a few months were they able to overcome this complication and complete the task.

The second kind of conflict that we introduced turned out to be even more complicated. We instructed children two-and-a-half to three years of age, "If I lift my fist, you lift your finger" or "If I lift my finger, you lift your fist." The youngest children had some difficulty repeating these verbal instructions and sometimes simplified them. The three to three-and-a-half year olds had no difficulty with this part of the task. But when the children tried to follow their own commands, they had a hard time. Observing the experimenter's fist, the younger children imitated him rather than following the verbal instruction. They showed no signs of being aware that there was a discrepancy between what they were doing and the verbal instructions. The older children, however, displayed some signs of conflict. In response to the experimenter's fist, they correctly raised their fingers, expressed doubts, and then replaced their fingers with their fists. Only after some months, when the children were nearly four years old and older, were they able to follow verbal instructions that conflicted with what they saw.

I am aware that this work constituted no more than a series of pilot studies and that additional extensive observations must still be made. Nonetheless, a strategy that combines artificial laboratory models with more natural kinds of observations and with quasi experiments is extremely fruitful.

# 7

# Disturbance of
# Brain Functions

WE HAD two strategies for discovering and describing the nature of higher psychological functions. The first was to trace their development; the second was to follow the course of their dissolution under conditions of localized brain damage. In the mid-1920s Vygotsky first suggested that an investigation of localized brain damage could provide a way to analyze the cerebral structure and development of the higher psychological processes. At that time neither the structure of the higher psychological processes themselves nor the functional organization of the brain was clear.

Two diametrically opposed principles then prevailed for explaining how the brain worked. On the one hand, there were the localization theorists who attempted to relate each mental function to a specific cortical area; on the other, there were the holistic theorists who assumed that the brain functions as a whole to produce the psychological functions expressed in behavior. According to this view, the amount of brain tissue damaged, rather than the location of a lesion, determines the nature of the resulting defects.

The scientific investigation of disturbances of the complex mental processes began in 1861 when the French anatomist Paul Broca described the brain of a patient who for many years had been kept in the Salpêtrière Hospital because he was unable to speak, although he could understand speech. When the patient died, Broca was able to obtain precise information about the area of his brain that had been damaged. Broca was the first to demonstrate that speech production, that is, the motor coordinations which produce speech, are associated with a localized region of the brain, namely the posterior third of the left inferior frontal gyrus. Broca postulated that this location is the "center for the motor images of words" and that a lesion in this region leads to a distinctive type of loss of expressive speech, which he originally called "aphemia" and which later came to be called "aphasia," the term still used today. Broca's discovery represented the first time that a complex mental function like speech was localized on the basis of clinical observation. It also led Broca to the first description of a marked difference between the functions of the left and right cerebral hemispheres.

Broca's discoveries were followed by those of Carl Wernicke, a German psychiatrist. In 1873 Wernicke published descriptions of cases in which lesions of the posterior third of the left superior temporal gyrus resulted in a loss of the ability to understand audible speech. He claimed to have found "the center for the sensory images of words," or the center for understanding speech.

The discovery that a complex form of mental activity can be regarded as the function of a local brain area aroused unprecedented enthusiasm in neurological science. Within a short time many other brain centers for intellectual functions were found, including a "center for concepts" in the left inferior parietal region and a "center for writing" in the posterior part of the left middle frontal gyrus. By the 1880s neurologists and psychiatrists were able to draw "functional maps" of the cerebral cortex. They thought that they had settled the problem of the relation between brain structure and mental activity. Such research persisted well into the 1930s.

From the beginning some scientists disapproved of this kind of theorizing. Prominent among them was the English neurologist Hughlings Jackson. He maintained that the cerebral organization of mental processes differs according to the complexity of the process in question and the representation in the brain for processing that complexity.

Jackson's ideas grew out of observations that seemed to defy the kind of localization theory advocated by Broca. In studies of motor and speech disturbances Jackson noted that circumscribed lesions of a particular area never caused complete loss of function. A paradox occurred: sometimes the patient moved or spoke in ways that, according to a strict localization position, ought to be impossible. For example, the patient might be instructed, "Say the word *no*," and would be unable to do so. Yet a little later in the same interview the patient might, in response to some quite different request, say, "No, doctor, I can't do that."

Jackson resolved paradoxes of this sort, where "no" is both possible and impossible, by suggesting that all psychological functions have a complex "vertical" organization. Each function has a "low" level representation in the spinal chord or brain stem, is also represented in the "middle" or sensory and motor levels of the cortex, and finally is represented at a "high" level, presumably in the frontal lobes.

He advocated careful study of the level at which a particular function is carried out, not its localization in particular areas of the brain.

Jackson's hypothesis, which greatly influenced our work, was not taken up and developed until fifty years later when it reemerged in the writings of such neurologists as Anton Pick (1905), von Monakow (1914), Henry Head (1926), and Kurt Goldstein (1927, 1944, 1948). Without denying that elementary psychological "functions" such as vision, hearing, cutaneous sensation, and movement are represented in clearly defined areas of the cortex, these neurologists expressed doubts about the applicability of the principal of narrow localization to the brain mechanisms of complex forms of human mental activity. However, forgetting Jackson's teaching, they approached complex mental activity from the opposite extreme of the strict localizationists. Pointing to the complex character of human mental activity, Monakow attempted to describe its specific features with as vague a term as the "semantic character of behavior"; Goldstein talked about "abstract sets" and "categorical behavior" to emphasize the same idea. They either postulated that complex mental processes—which they termed "semantics" or "categorical behavior"—are the result of activity of the brain as a whole, or divorced complex processes from brain structure altogether and emphasized their special "spiritual nature."

From our point of view neither of these two positions seemed to provide the necessary basis for further scientific research. We rejected the holistic theories because we felt it was absurd to maintain an obsolete separation between "spiritual life" and the brain and to deny the possibility of discovering the mind's material basis. Uncritical "mass potential" ideas revived what we considered to be equally unacceptable notions of the brain as a primitive, undifferentiated nervous mass. Our reasons for rejecting the strict localization theories were arrived at over the course of many years of work and are somewhat more complicated.

Most investigators who have examined the problem of cortical localization have understood the term *function* to mean the "function of a particular tissue." For example, it is perfectly natural to consider that the secretion of bile is a function of the liver and the secretion of insulin is a function of the pancreas. It is equally logical to regard the perception of light as a function of the photosensitive elements of the retina and the highly specialized neurons of the visual cortex connected with them. However, this definition does not meet every use of the term *function.*

When we speak of the "function of respiration," this clearly cannot be understood as a function of a particular tissue. The ultimate object of respiration is to supply oxygen to the alveoli of the lungs to diffuse it through the walls of the alveoli into the blood. The whole of this process is carried out, not as a simple function of a particular tissue, but rather as a complete functional system, embodying many components belonging to different levels of the secretory, motor, and nervous apparatus. Such a "functional system," the term introduced and developed by P. K. Anokhin in 1935, differs not only in the complexity of its structure but also in the mobility of its component parts. The original task of respiration—restoration of the disturbed homeostasis—and its final result—transportation of oxygen to the alveoli of the lung, followed by its absorption into the blood stream—obviously remain invariant. However, the way in which this task is performed may vary considerably. For instance, if the diaphragm, the principal group of muscles working during respiration, ceases to act, the intercostal muscles are brought into play, but if for some reason those muscles are impaired, the muscles of the larynx are mobilized and the animal or person begins to swallow air, which then reaches the alveoli of the lung by a completely different route. The presence of an invariant task, performed by variable mechanisms, which bring the process to a constant invariant conclusion, is one of the basic features distinguishing the work of every "functional system."

The second distinguishing feature is the complex composition of the functional system, which always includes a series of afferent (adjusting) and efferent (effector) impulses. This combination can be illustrated with reference to the function of movement, which has been analyzed in detail by the Soviet physiologist-mathematician N. A. Bernshtein. The movements of a person intending to change his position in space, to strike at a certain point, or to perform a certain action can never take place simply by means of efferent, motor impulses. Since the locomotor apparatus, with its movable joints, has many degrees of freedom because different groups of articulations participate in the movement, and since every stage of the movement changes the initial tonus of the muscles, movement is in principle uncontrollable simply by efferent impulses. For a movement to take place, there must be constant correction of the initiated movement by afferent impulses, which give information about the position of the moving limb in space and the change in muscle tone. This complex structure of locomotion is required to satisfy the fundamental conditions preserving the invariance of the task and its performance by variable means. The fact that every movement has the character of a complex functional system and that the elements performing it may be interchangeable in character is clear because the same result can be achieved by totally different methods.

In Walter Hunter's experiments a rat in a maze achieved its goal by running a certain path, but when one element of the maze was replaced by water, the rat achieved its goal by swimming movements. In some of Karl Lashley's observations a rat, trained to follow a certain movement pattern, radically changed the structure of its movements after removal of the cerebellum. The rat was unable to reproduce the movements learned through training, but still it was able to reach its goal by going head over heels. The same interchangeable character of movements necessary to achieve a required goal can be clearly seen if any human locomotor act is carefully analyzed, such as hitting a target, which is done with a different set of movements depending on the initial position of the body, manipulating objects, which may be performed by different sets of motor impulses, or writing, which can be performed with either pencil or pen, by the right or left hand, or even by the foot, without effecting the meaning of what is written.

This "systemic" structure is characteristic of complex forms of mental activity as well as of simple behavioral acts. Although elementary functions like the registration of sensations from the retina could legitimately be said to have precise localization in particular groups of cells, it seemed absurd to us to think that complex functions could be regarded as the direct function of limited cell groups or could be localized in particular areas of the brain. Our approach to the structure of functional systems in general, and of the higher psychological functions in particular, led us to believe that the ideas on localization provided by the theorists of the early part of the century had to be radically revised.

Applying what we knew and surmised about the structure of

higher psychological functions based on our work with children, Vygotsky reasoned that higher psychological functions represent complex functional systems which are mediated in their structure. They incorporate historically accumulated symbols and tools. Consequently, the organization of higher functions must differ from anything seen in animals. Furthermore, since the human brain took millions of years to evolve but human history is limited to thousands of years, a theory of the cerebral organization of higher functions must account for processes, such as those involved in writing, that depend in part on external, historically conditioned mediators. In other words, Vygotsky assumed that his historical approach to the development of such psychological processes as active memory, abstract thought, and voluntary actions would also hold for the principles of their organization on a cerebral level.

His theory of the development of higher psychological functions in children also led to the conclusion that the role played by a cerebral region in the organization of a higher psychological process would change during the course of an individual's development. Our research had shown that all complex, conscious activities are initially carried out in an expanded way. In its early stages, complex thinking requires a number of external aids for its performance. Not until later in the life of the child or in the course of mastering a particular form of activity does thinking become condensed and converted into an automatic skill. It seemed logical to suppose that in the course of development not only the functional structure of thinking changes but its cerebral organization as well. The participation of auditory and visual areas of the cortex, essential in the early stages of the formation of many cognitive activities, no longer plays the same role in their later stages when thinking begins to depend on the coordinated activity of different systems of cortical zones. For example, in the child the sensory areas of the cortex provide the basis for the development of cognitive processes, including speech. But in adults, in whom speech and complex cognitive processes are already developed, the sensory areas lose this function, and cognition becomes less dependent on sensory input. Reasoning in this way, Vygotsky explained why circumscribed lesions in cortical areas can have opposite effects depending on whether the lesion takes place in early childhood or in adulthood. For example, a lesion of the visual sensory areas of the cortex in early childhood results in an underdevelopment of cognition and thought, while in an adult an identical lesion can be compensated for by the influence of the already developed higher functional systems.

Our initial observations were strongly influenced by the English neurologist Head, who summarized a great deal of nineteenth and early twentieth century research on aphasia and provided us with a tempting interpretation of the relation between disturbance of speech and disturbance of thinking. In his classic monograph on aphasia, Head concluded that disturbances in language function produced disturbances in thinking. Aphasia caused a reduction of intellectual power, Head would have us believe, because thinking was no longer mediated by language but must depend on primitive, direct relations between objects and actions, on the one hand, and language on the other.

For example, Head pointed out that an aphasic patient who could easily match an object shown to him with a similar one lying on a table might fail if the task were complicated by adding another object to the one held up for inspection and asking the patient to select the two objects on the table that matched them both. Head attributed this difficulty to the possibility that, when presented with two objects, the patient tried to register them in words and to make his choice on the basis of their remembered names. In this case, Head noted, "A symbolic formula has been interjected and the act is no longer one of direct matching" (p. 518). Elsewhere Head made the point, in a manner completely consistent with our own theorizing, that "an animal, or even man under certain conditions, tends to react directly to the perceptual or emotional aspects of a situation; but symbolic formulation enables us to subject it to analysis and to regulate our behavior accordingly" (p. 525).

This testimony of a leading expert in the study of the brain fitted so closely with our own distinction between mediated and natural processes that at first we thought it possible that aphasia, by disturbing language—man's primary means of mediating his experience—acted to force the injured individual to operate on a natural, unmediated basis. We were reinforced in this presupposition by evidence presented by Guillaume and Meyerson, who claimed that their aphasic patients solved problems in a manner characteristic of young children. This position turned out to be incorrect, as many subsequent investigations have shown. We were greatly oversimplifing both the nature of aphasia and the psychological processing in brain-injured patients. At the beginning, however, these ideas were a strong motivation for assuming that the study of brain injury would lead us to an understanding of the nature of man's higher psychological functions and would provide us a means for understanding their material basis in the brain as well.

We were more successful when we began to observe patients suffering from Parkinson's disease. Parkinson's disease affects the subcortical motor ganglia so that the flow of involuntary movements is disturbed. We observed that tremors occurred shortly after patients suffering from this disease started to carry out an action. When we asked them to walk across a room, they could take only one or two steps before a tremor set in and they could walk no further.

We noted the paradoxical fact that patients who could not take two successive steps when talking on a level floor were able to climb stairs without difficulty. We hypothesized that in climbing stairs, each step represented a signal to which the patient's motor impulses responded. When climbing stairs, the successive, automatic flow of movement in walking on a level surface is replaced by chains of separate motor reactions. In other words, the structure of the motor activity is reorganized, and a conscious response to each link in a chain of isolated signals replaces the subcortically organized, involuntary system that guides ordinary walking.

Vygotsky used a simple device to construct a laboratory model of this kind of reorganization of movement. He placed a series of small paper cards on the floor and asked a patient to step over each one of them. A marvelous thing happened. A patient who had been able to take no more than two or three steps by himself walked through the room, easily stepping over each piece of paper as if he were climbing a staircase. We had helped the patient to overcome the symptoms of his disease by getting him to reorganize the mental processes he used in walking. He had compensated for his defect by transferring the activity from the subcortical level where his nerves were damaged to the cortical level which was not affected by the disease.

We then tried to use the same principle to construct an experimental model of self-regulating behavior, but our experiments were very naive and the results obtained were somewhat inconclusive. We asked a patient suffering from Parkinson's disease to tap sequentially for half a minute. This was impossible for him to do. In less than half a minute a muscle tremor set in, and his movements were blocked. But we found that if we asked the same person to tap in response to the experimenter's cues "one," "two"—standing for "tap once," "tap twice," and so on —he could tap for a short time.

We wondered what would happen if a patient were to produce his own cues that would act as stimuli for his actions. We chose blinking as a signal because it was a physical system that seemed to be less affected by the disease than either walking or hand movements. We asked each patient to blink and after every blink to press a rubber bulb which recorded his movements. We discovered that the blinks served as a reliable self-regulating device. Patients who could not keep up a steady stream of squeezing movements under ordinary circumstances, could blink on command and then squeeze a rubber bulb in response to their blink.

Our final series of experiments with Parkinsonian patients used the patient's own speech to regulate his behavior. Our first attempts failed. The patients listened to the verbal instructions and started to press, but muscle hypertension and the concomitant tremors set in almost immediately, preventing them from completing their actions.

We found that we needed to reorganize the Parkinsonian patient's motor act so that the decisive stimulation for it would come from his higher cortical processes. We accomplished this by arranging matters so that a motor reaction was produced as an answer to an intellectual problem that the patient had solved mentally. We asked patients to give us their answers to problems by tapping their solutions. The questions were of the following sort: "How many angles occur in a square?" "How many wheels does a car have?" "How many points are there on the red stars of the Kremlin?"

We found that although the limitations of movement associated with muscular hypertonicity remained, the structure of the patient's motor act changed under these conditions. When we had instructed the patient simply to "press five times," his first movements were strong but his subsequent movements diminished in intensity and muscular hypertension and tremors took over. Now when the patient signaled his mental solutions through movements, he showed no signs of exhaustion.

These early pilot studies were encouraging, but they also showed us how much we needed to learn if we were to make the study of the dissolution of higher psychological functions an integral part of our effort. We realized that we needed to undertake a study of the brain and its functional organization and to conduct clinical investigations in place of the experimental approach on which we had been relying. We also knew that the success of our work depended on a far better understanding of the structure of higher psychological functions, a line of investigation that was still in its infancy.

Undaunted, we decided to enter medical school. I resumed medical training in the late 1920s, beginning where I had left off many years before in Kazan. Vygotsky also began medical training. Professors in one school and students in another, we simultaneously taught, studied, and conducted our research.

In the early 1930s, a promising base for our work appeared

when we were asked to set up a psychology department in the Ukrainian Psychoneurological Academy of Kharkhov. I began commuting between Kharkhov and Moscow, while Vygotsky commuted on a triangular route between Moscow, Leningrad, and Kharkov. It was in Kharkov that I first began to create new methods for the psychological analysis of the consequences of local brain lesions. But my time was still heavily occupied with other work. I lived this double existence until 1936 when I entered medical school on a full-time basis.

Immediately after passing my examinations at the First Moscow Medical School in 1937, I approached N. N. Bourdenko, a neurosurgeon who was head of the Neurosurgical Institute (now named in his honor), to ask him if I could intern at the institute. My plan was to train as a practical neurologist and at the same time to develop psychological methods for the diagnosis of local brain lesions. I do not know if Professor Bourdenko understood or approved of my plans. But he must have thought it worthwhile to have a psychology professor as an intern on his staff, because he accepted me.

My two years as an intern at the Neurosurgical Institute were the most fruitful of my life. I had no staff and no scientific responsibilities except routine medical work. In my free time I turned to my own research. It was during this period that I began to devise my own approach to the neuropsychology of local brain injuries.

In 1939 I moved to the Neurological Clinic of the Institute of Experimental Medicine, which later became the Neurological Institute of the Academy of Medical Sciences, to become head of the Laboratory of Experimental Psychology. With the hindsight of many years I can see that the move was a mistake. It would have been much more productive to remain as a staff member at the 300-bed Bourdenko Neurological Institute with patients whose local brain lesions had been verified by operations or post mortem. As events would have it, this error was corrected in the fullness of time, for as I write these lines I once again have a laboratory at the Bourdenko.

The period from 1937 to 1941 was taken up by my first serious work in neuropsychology. I soon found that in order to accumulate adequate clinical data I had to revise the basic style of my research. In experimental work a scholar usually begins by choosing a specific problem. Then he constructs a hypothesis and selects methods for testing his hypothesis. He arranges matters so that he can more easily focus his attention on those facts that will prove or disprove it. He is able to ignore all data that do not contribute to his analysis of the problem and to the proof of his hypothesis. By contrast, in clinical work, the starting point is not a clearly defined problem but an unknown bundle of problems and resources: the patient. The clinical investigator begins by making careful observations of the patient in an effort to discover the crucial facts. In the beginning, he can ignore nothing. Even data that on first glance seem insignificant may turn out to be essential. At some point the vague contours of factors that seem important begin to emerge, and the clinician forms a tentative hypothesis about the problem. But it is still too early for him to say definitely whether the facts he has picked out are important to the problem or extraneous. Only when he has found a sufficient number of compatible symptoms that together form a "syndrome" does he have a right to believe that his hypothesis about the patient might be proved or rejected.

At first I found it difficult to change from the logic of ordinary experimental investigation, which was imprinted on me, to the logic of clinical work. It took a while to learn to pay attention to those small events that can become a turning point in such investigations. The procedures and reasoning of such investigations seemed more like those used by detectives solving a crime than like the problem-solving behavior that prevails among psychologists and physiologists. In addition to giving up my reliance on experimental methods, I also felt it necessary to reject any use of the psychological tests of the era that had been created for the evaluation of an individual's intellectual level and which some investigators employed in the clinic. I found such test instruments as the Simon-Binet and other "measures of intellect" inadequate either to the task for which they had been designed or to the new applications that we had in mind.

The first problem to which I turned my attention was the tangled knot of disorders that were and still are referred to under the general rubric "aphasia." At the time I began this work, three general classes of aphasia were recognized—sensory, motor, and semantic or amnestic—although there was great disagreement about the specific localization of each class and the character of the different capacities associated with each location. The first syndrome that we singled out for careful study, called "sensory aphasia," was a form of speech disturbance associated with damage to the left temporal lobe, predominantly in secondary zones. This disability was termed sensory aphasia because the patient's ability to comprehend speech was disturbed, an observation that had led Wernicke to say that the "sensory images of speech" were decoded in this area. Our observations soon showed that the basic difficulty which underlay the other symptoms associated with sensory aphasia was an inability to discriminate the distinctive features of phonemes, the basic units of word sounds. Difficulties in understanding words, in naming objects, in retrieving words while speaking spontaneously, and in writing were secondary, or system-related, consequences of the primary defect in phonemic hearing.

The second form of aphasia that we tackled, called "motor aphasia," was the disorder initially studied by Broca. Again we found that we were dealing not with a single syndrome, namely a center housing the motor images of speech, but with a variable set of symptoms within which we were able to distinguish two fundamentally different classes. Since our research on the motor aphasias illustrates neatly the basic logic of virtually all of my work, I shall digress somewhat to explain the distinctions we were forced to make and the broader approach to understanding the brain and its relation to psychological processes that resulted.

Speaking is only one of many voluntary acts that an individual performs. We therefore supposed that speaking would have a great deal in common with all kinds of complex, voluntary movements but would, like any other kind of movement, also have components that are specific unto itself. Thus, in order to understand motor aphasia, we needed to know more about voluntary motor responding in general and about the specific aspects which apply to speaking in particular.

Here we had the important advantage of being able to draw on the work of Bernshtein, who pointed out that movements require innervation not only by efferent nerve impulses that get muscle neurons to fire, but also by afferent nerve impulses that yield information about the state of the limbs. These afferent signals indicating the position of the limbs and the tension of the muscles are essential to restrict the infinite number of innervations that can occur and to reduce the degrees of freedom of movement. In cases where this system of afferent impulses is defective, no organized movement can take place. On the assumption that what was true of movement in general would be true of speech-related movement in particular, we hypothesized that motor aphasia would consist of two distinct varieties—one associated with disturbance of the efferent motor system, as Broca had surmised, and one associated with afferent defects.

True to our speculations, we found that there exists a kind of afferent motor aphasia, which I term "kinesthetic aphasia," in which the principal symptom is the mispronunciation of individual speech sounds called "articulemes." If the disturbance is severe, the patient may say *k* in place of *kh* and *t*, which are different with regard to articulation. Less severe lesions produce more localized substitutions, such as *b* for *p*. The basic cause of this difficulty is that the brain does not register feedback from movements producing the articulemes, articulatory actions lose their selectivity, and the patient cannot assume correct positions of the tongue and lips.

Another form of motor aphasia concerns the serial organization of movements that are needed in pronunciation. In order to speak normally, it is necessary that the links between individual articulemes be organized so that smooth transitions are possible.

In our terminology, the entire kinetic melody that links words must be intact. However, when the lower parts of the premotor cortex of the speech areas are damaged, although the articulemes themselves remain intact, the patient cannot provide the required transition from one articuleme to the next. This "kinetic motor aphasia" is what Broca was referring to in his early observations.

The third classical form of aphasia that I began to study at this time was termed "semantic" or "amnestic aphasia," after the word *amnesia*, "a state of forgetfulness." Amnestic aphasia was supposed to be a special form of speech disorder, in which neither the sensory nor the motor defects are present, but patients find it difficult to remember the names of objects. Some neurologists of the period had speculated that this defect was caused by sensory disorders which destroyed presumed "sensory word traces." Others hypothesized that the disorder reflected impairment of a special center where traces of language were stored. Still others, who generally favored the mass action approach to brain function, assumed that semantic aphasia was a result of deterioration in categorical thinking and the abstract attitude.

As in other classes of aphasic disorders, we were skeptical about hypotheses which assumed that all of the symptoms included under the rubric of semantic aphasia were really a single disturbance that could be precisely localized in a single area. We first satisfied ourselves that we were not dealing with some variety of motor or sensory aphasia, because patients with one or another of the semantic aphasia symptoms rarely showed signs of disturbed articulation or phonemic hearing. Their lesions also tended to occur in the parieto-temporal area, above and behind the lesions characteristic of the aphasias studied so far.

Next we searched the literature to see what kinds of symptoms arose in connections with semantic aphasia. In previous research and in our own observations we found that these patients had no difficulty grasping the meaning of complex ideas such as "causation," "development," or "cooperation." They were also able to hold abstract conversations. But difficulties developed when they were presented with complex grammatical constructions which coded logical relations. As Head pointed out in his work, these grammatical constructions require the coordination of details into a coherent whole. Such patients find it almost impossible to understand phrases and words which denote relative position and cannot carry out a simple instruction like "draw a triangle above a circle." This difficulty goes beyond parts of speech that code spatial relations. Phrases like "Sonya is lighter than Natasha" also prove troublesome for these patients, as do temporal relations like "spring is before summer."

Analysis shows that all of these logical-grammatical relations share a common feature: they are verbal expressions of spatial relations, although in some cases the spatial factor is more obvious than in others. The examples involving "above" and "to the right of" are clear, but on closer examination we found that in addition to linear relations expressed in such words as "before," there are also spatial factors in such expressions as "the master's dog" or "brother's father." As one patient put it in a particularly diagnostic manner, "Of course I know what *brother* and *father* are, but I can't imagine what the two mean together."

All these examples demonstrate the error in assuming that semantic aphasia is a single, unitary syndrome. We found no evidence for uniform intellectual dissolution. What we did find was that a variety of mental operations requiring a component of spatial comparison and synthesis are disturbed.

My initial work on the three basic types of aphasia posited by neurologists in the 1920s and 1930s brought me to the end of my *schuljahren*. At that time I tried to summarize my ideas in what was intended to be a three-volume work, with one volume devoted to each kind of aphasia. I completed the first volume on sensory aphasia and defended it for my second higher degree, Doctor of Medicine. Although I began the second volume on semantic aphasia, analyses were too fragmentary, and this volume, like the first, remained unpublished. I also began to write about the forms of motor aphasia, but here too I found that I had no more than begun my work. All of these manuscripts remain in my desk. I can remember feeling that if only Vygotsky had lived, he would have penetrated far more deeply into the complex problems I had encountered. Not until the appearance of my *Traumatic Aphasia* in 1947 was a full treatment of these ideas brought together in print.

In June of 1941 the course of my work was permanently altered. World War II began.

# 8

# Neuropsychology in
# World War II

WORLD WAR II was a disaster for all countries, and it was particularly devastating for the Soviet Union. Thousands of towns
were destroyed, tens of thousands of people died from hunger
alone. Many millions, both civilian and military, were killed.
Among the wounded were thousands who suffered brain injury
and who required extended, painstaking care.

The unity of purpose of the Soviet people so clearly felt during
the great Revolution and the subsequent years reemerged in new
forms. A sense of common responsibility and common purpose
gripped the country. Each of us knew we had an obligation to
work together with our countrymen to meet the challenge. We
each had to find our place in the struggle—either in the direct
defense of our country, in the preservation and expansion of industry, which was removed to remote regions of the country, or
in the restoration of the health and abilities of the wounded. My
institute was assigned to the latter task.

The medical corps of the Soviet army was superbly organized,
earning great respect during the war and afterward. The aging
Bourdenko, former head of the Institute of Neurosurgery, was
by then totally deaf. But he retained his acute clearness of mind
and was named surgeon general. Under his guidance and
through the efforts of a group of able physicians headed by
H. Smirnov, a superb system of medical care was organized.

The care of those with brain injuries was organized by N. I.
Graschenkov, head of the Neurological Clinic in the Institute of

Experimental Medicine and later deputy minister of health in the USSR, a neurologist as well as a neurosurgeon. He saw to it that soldiers with brain and peripheral nerve injuries received emergency medical care at the front during the first hours after being wounded. They were then sent to the Institute of Neurology in Moscow, which had been transformed into a neurosurgical hospital. Patients who required further care and special treatment were transported under careful supervision to rehabilitation hospitals in the southern Urals.

I was commissioned to organize such a hospital in the opening months of the war. I chose as the site for our hospital a newly established 400-bed sanitarium in a small village near Cheliabensk. I organized the construction of laboratories and therapeutic training rooms and recruited a team of former colleagues from Moscow to work with me. Within a month the hospital began its work.

We had two major tasks. First, we had to devise methods of diagnosing local brain lesions and of recognizing and treating complications such as inflammation and secondary infection that were caused by the wounds. Second, we had to develop rational, scientifically based techniques for the rehabilitation of destroyed functions.

Although our team of thirty researchers began with a general idea of how to carry out the work, we realized that specific solutions to the incredibly complex problems we faced could emerge only from the work itself. I personally brought to the task a small store of practical experience from my five or six years of work in neurology and on neurosurgical wards as well as the beginnings of an experimental approach to brain lesion study. The hospital was modestly supplied with neurophysiological devices, neurosurgical apparatus, and the basic equipment of a histology laboratory. Our most important resource was our dedication to the task. We were required to diagnose and treat a full complement of disturbed mental functions, ranging from defective sensation, perception, and movement to disturbances of intellectual processes.

We worked in the Urals for three years and then were transferred back to Moscow, where we continued this work after the end of the war. Paradoxically, this period of disaster provided an important opportunity for advancing our understanding of the brain and of psychological processes. It was during the war and its aftermath that neuropsychology became a full-fledged science.

My prewar studies proved to be an invaluable base from which to begin. But we had to broaden our general approach both to include the many new and terrible brain injuries made common by modern explosives and to provide a rational basis for restoring psychological functions. Although on their face these two needs appeared to be different, the logic of our approach made the procedures for diagnosing and describing the nature of cerebral dysfunction entirely compatible with the therapeutic techniques that were called for by different forms of damage.

In some cases we found chemical agents that disinhibited traumatized functions of certain kinds. When applicable, chemical therapy was particularly useful in speeding recovery. The basic phenomenon in such cases seemed to be a kind of "state of shock" which rendered part of the brain inoperative. As a rule, however, our basic methods of restoring function required us to combine chemical therapy with a program of retraining and functional therapy. One area in which we developed training methods for the reorganization of a functional system was writing.

The work of Bernshtein illustrated the way in which organized movement, or locomotion, constitutes a complex functional system, depending on the particular constellation of muscles used and the particular kind of motion involved. Walking, running, and playing soccer all involve leg muscles, but the system of activities is clearly different in each case. Moreover, if some of the muscles, or one of the systems of muscles, ordinarily involved in locomotion is disrupted, it is possible to compensate by using other muscles and systems of muscles that remain.

When there is severe damage, it is possible to supplement existing muscles by the addition of prosthetic devices which can be included as part of a functional system to permit adequate, if not normal, locomotion.

It should be apparent that if the operation of intellectual processes is thought of in terms of functional systems instead of discrete abilities, we have to reorient our ideas about the possibility of localizing intellectual functions. It is easy enough to reject both the holistic notion that every function is distributed equally throughout the brain and the idea that complex functions are localized in narrowly specified areas of the brain, but it is difficult to find an intermediate position. Our solution has been to think of the functional system as a working constellation of activities with a corresponding working constellation of zones of the brain that support the activities. An excellent example of such an activity, which clearly could not have been coded in the human brain in a purely organic fashion because it involves the use of man-made tools, is writing.

The task of writing a particular word, whether independently or from dictation, begins with the process of analyzing its phonetic composition. In other words, the activity begins by breaking down the sound stream of living speech into its individual phonemes. This process of phonetic analysis and synthesis is unnecessary only in the few languages, like Chinese, that use ideographic transcription, which represent concepts directly by means of symbols. In other cases those areas of the brain responsible for analysis of acoustic-verbal information play a decisive role in the analysis of normal speech into stable phonemes. When these parts of the cortex are injured and the isolation of stable phonemes from the flow of speech becomes impossible, as often occurs in sensory aphasia, writing is disturbed. In such cases, the disturbance takes the form of the substitution of similar phonemes, such as *b* for *p* or *d* for *t*, the omission of certain letters, and other indications that the speech flow has been inadequately analyzed. Substitutions of meaningless combinations of letters like *gar* for *car* illustrate this kind of disturbance.

In cases of kinesthetic, or afferent, motor aphasia a slightly different kind of disturbance in writing is apparent. In such patients "articulatory" analysis, which is involved in the pronunciation of a required phoneme and which helps the speaker to distinguish it from other phonemes, thereby clarifying the phonetic structure of the word, is disturbed. In the first stages of learning to write, saying a word often helps the writer to write it correctly. By pronouncing the word, he has analyzed its articulation. By the same token, when an individual can no longer correctly articulate a word, there are articulatory errors in his writing. Common errors in such cases are substitutions of letters that are similar in their articulation, such as *b* for *m*, and *n* for *l* or *t*, so that for the Russian word *stol* one gets the word *slot*, and instead of the Russian word *slon* one gets *ston*.

Once the speech stream has been correctly analyzed, the writer must translate the isolated phonemic unit into its proper visual or graphic unit. He must choose the necessary visual sign from the large number available, matching it and its spatially organized strokes with the auditory stimulus. These requirements of the task of writing involve the tempero-occipital and parietal-occipital regions of the cortex, which are responsible for spatial and temporal analysis. If these zones of the cortex are injured, the spatial organization of graphemes is disturbed. Similar letters are substituted for one another, there are mirror image mistakes, and even though the phonemic analysis of sound may be intact, writing is distorted.

The steps described so far are only preparatory to the actual act of writing. In the next stage, visual images of letters are transformed into motor acts. In the early stages of learning to write the motor process of writing consists of an extended series of steps, and the changes from one step to another occur as discrete acts. As the process of writing becomes more automated, the motor units increase in size, and the person begins to write whole letters at once, or sometimes firmly established combinations of whole letters. This can be seen in the work of an experienced typist who types established combinations of sounds with a single group of movements. When writing has become an automatic habit, some words, particularly those that are familiar, come to be produced by a single, complex movement and lose their link-to-link sequential nature. When writing reaches this stage, different parts of the cortex play a decisive role in the process, notably the anterior portions of the "speech zone" and the lower portions of the premotor area. A lesion in this part of the cortex interferes with transference from one movement to the next, and consequently writing becomes deautomatized; sometimes the correct order of letters in a word is lost or certain elements of a word are repeated. This syndrome is often linked with kinetic motor aphasia.

Finally, writing, like any activity, requires the maintenance of a constant purpose or plan and continuous feedback concerning the results of the action. If the patient cannot maintain a constant purpose and if he is not receiving continuous feedback concerning his actions, he loses his stability of purpose and also loses track of what he is doing. Under these conditions, writing also becomes defective, but here the defect becomes apparent in the meaning and content of what is written. Irrelevant associations and stereotypic expressions intrude in the writing processes. Such mistakes are commonly seen in patients with frontal lobe lesions. From this description one can see that many different regions of the brain are involved in the complex functional system that underlies writing. Each area is responsible for a particular part of the process under normal conditions, and a disturbance in any one area will have distinctive effects on subsequent writing.

There are several questions to ask and basic principles to apply in diagnosing and treating disruptions of complex psychological functioning by brain lesions. In making a diagnosis, we ask which link, or links, in the normal system of the working constellation of brain zones is disturbed in the patient. Once our analysis has indicated the area of disturbance, we can undertake treatment. Treatment and diagnosis are not as separate as they seem. In the course of trying to treat a particular disturbance we often modify our diagnosis. After determining which links of the activity are disturbed, we try to determine which links remain untouched. In treating the disturbance, we try to use the remaining links, which we supplement with external aids to reconstruct the activity on the basis of a new functional system. A considerable period of retraining may be necessary to build and maintain the new functional system, but at the end of the period it should be possible for the patient to engage in the activity without external assistance. During this process we try to find ways to give the patient as much feedback as possible concerning both the defect and its effect on the patient's actions. This feedback gives the patient information that is crucial to the reorganization of the required functional system.

These principles are stated here in a rather abstract manner, but in practice they are anything but abstract. Both to illustrate the basic principles of using the reorganization of functional systems as a way of restoring damaged functions and to show how the analyses and treatment of such functional systems provide information about the brain and the organization of psychological processes, I will describe some of the work we did during the war and immediately afterward.

Afferent motor aphasia, in which a lesion of the posterior portion of the motor speech area has disturbed the kinesthetic basis of speech articulation, was one subject of study. Essentially this aphasia consists of a disturbance of the act of articulation, resulting in an inability to find the articulation required to make a particular sound. Disturbances of articulated speech can of course be caused by a great variety of different local lesions. Before a program of rehabilitiation can be organized for a patient, a careful analysis must be made to determine the fundamental factors underlying the particular disturbance. It must be clear that the symptoms are caused by kinesthetic aphasia and not by kinetic or another kind of aphasia that sometimes involves similar individual symptoms. The aim of our retraining program is to reconstruct the functional system of articulated speech by replacing the disintegrated kinesthetic schemes, using new, extra-kinesthetic afferent systems. By raising the articulatory processes, which are automatic and unconscious in their natural states, to the level of consciousness, we can provide the patient with a new basis for restructuring articulation.

Usually not all levels involved in the construction of movements of the articulatory apparatus are injured to the same extent in afferent motor aphasia. It is often the case in patients with brain injuries that the imitative or symbolic movements of the articulatory apparatus disintegrate while the elementary "instinctive" and "purposive" movements of the tongue and lips remain intact. Thus a patient who cannot touch his upper lip with his tongue or spit when the doctor asks him to can do so easily in real, spontaneously arising situations. Consequently the most effective method of rehabilitation is one in which the therapist first begins by discovering the residual movements of the lips, tongue, and larynx. These are used in training the patient to produce sounds. For example, to get the patient consciously to produce the sound of the letter *p*, the therapist gives the patient a lighted match, which he instinctively blows out when the flame reaches his fingers. This is repeated many times in all sorts of varied circumstances. In the course of such practice, the patient's attention is gradually concentrated on the components that make up the movement. The therapist shows the patient how to position his lips so as to pronounce the corresponding sound and how to coordinate his movements with the puff of air. To make the patient aware of the components of the movement, the therapist presses and rapidly releases the patient's lips while applying pressure to his chest to produce the coordinated puff of air.

Other sounds are formed in similar ways. The sounds of *b* and *m* are produced by a coordinated set of bodily acts which are similar to the *p* sound, except that the regulation of the puff of air that produces them requires a slightly different position of the soft palate and the degree to which the lips are compressed. The sounds *v* and *f* are formed from another complex set of coordinated movements which have in common biting the lower lip. To pronounce the sound *u*, the patient forms a round, narrow opening by placing his mouth around a pipe. For the sound *a*, his mouth is opened wider. Based on this kind of analysis of the articulatory requirements of every sound, each program for relearning to articulate speech sounds begins by drawing on some real, purposeful movement of the lips, tongue, and larynx that has been left intact. The patient is then made aware of this movement and with the help of various external aids is taught to reproduce them consciously.

Among the external aids we have found useful are diagrams, mirrors, and even the printed letter. A patient can be taught to articulate a sound by reading the structure of the sound from a diagram that depicts the relative positions of the motor elements required to make the sound. A mirror is also helpful. Sitting beside the therapist and observing in a mirror the articulations that lead to the pronunciations of a particular sound, the patient begins to construct his own articulations. For a long time the visual scheme and the mirror are the patient's principal aids in learning to pronounce different sounds. Then the written letter begins to be used. Writing is a powerful auxiliary device because it allows the patient a means both for placing different variants of the same sound in the same category (all *p*'s are like *m*'s, *v*'s are like *f*'s) and for differentiating sounds closely related in their articulatory compositon (*b* versus *p*). The use of these auxiliary devices, especially the written letter, leads to the radical reconstruction of the entire functional system of articulation so that it is carried out by completely different mechanisms. Such reconstruction, using a complex, culturally mediated, external system of signs, is one illustration of the principle that higher functions can be used to replace lower ones in the restoration following brain injury.

This type of reconstruction is difficult and demands painstaking work. Every operation that the patient normally carries out automatically without thought must become conscious. As a rule, once the articulations of the required sounds are found, the patient easily passes on to the articulation of syllables and words. For a long time, however, the restored speech sounds very artificial, and the conscious character of each movement clearly reveals the difficult path of reconstruction. Only gradually does the patient begin to speak more automatically and normally.

The course of retraining in cases of semantic aphasia differs greatly from that in motor aphasia. Semantic aphasia occurs in patients who suffer damage to some part of the parietal zone. They have difficulty perceiving certain kinds of relations and combining certain kinds of details into a single whole. Underlying these difficulties is a disturbance of their spatial functions.

In contrast to those suffering from motor or kinetic aphasia, patients with this type of lesion have no difficulty articulating words. They also retain their ability to hear and understand most spoken language. Their ability to use numerical symbols and many different kinds of abstract concepts also remains undamaged. They can repeat and understand sentences that simply communicate events by creating a sequence of verbal images, such as: "One sunny day it was absolutely quiet in the forest. The fir trees were not stirring. Flowers were sprinkled through the fresh, green grass.

Their particular kind of aphasia becomes apparent only when they have to operate with groups or arrangements of elements. If these patients are asked, "Point to the pencil with the key drawn on it" or "Where is my sister's friend?" they do not understand what is being said. As one patient put it, "I know where there is a sister and a friend, but I don't know who belongs to whom." This is typical of patients suffering from semantic aphasia who are unable to grasp immediately the relations between various elements of a grammatically complex construction.

Long practice, mechanical learning, or practical training do not, as a rule, improve the ability of these patients to grasp the conceptual relations involved in such constructions. Grammatical constructions that are within the grasp of a five- or six-year-old child remain incomprehensible even to highly educated patients whose ability to synthesize words simultaneously is disturbed. Our basic method of therapy in such cases was to avoid the difficulties that are insuperable for the patient and to replace the direct perception of relations with successive reasoning using various external devices.

These methods were usually used when we taught the patient to understand inflected or prepositional constructions. For example, we gave patients who could understand the relation expressed in the phrase "the circle above the triangle" or "the triangle above the circle" the following drawing, which they could use to break down the complex relationship into simpler ones:

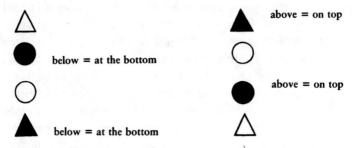

Beside each shaded figure is a caption that converts the relative preposition (*above, below*) into an absolute expression (*at the top, at the bottom*). This drawing enabled the patient to replace the incomprehensible relationship "the circle above the triangle" with ones that he could directly understand: "the circle is at the top, and the triangle is at the bottom." By breaking down the complex grammatical formula, the patient could master the relations it denotes even though he could not experience the "direct impression of relationship" which is normally essential to understand such phrases successfully.

We used analogous rehabilitative methods when patients failed to grasp such possessive relations as the "father's brother," or the "sister's friend." Although our particular therapeutic techniques for overcoming the patients' defective comprehension of such possessive relations critically depended on the structure of the Russian language, which changes word endings to mark grammatical relations, the basic method remained the same. The patients were taught to break such phrases down into a simplified form in order to carry out the appropriate analysis. Indirect analyses of complex grammatical structures are often the only way patients suffering from this kind of aphasia can understand these constructions. With time, this process becomes increasingly rapid and automatic. Only in rare cases, however, can it become so automatic that it resembles the "direct perception of relations" by which normal individuals understand such phrases. Although reconstruction of the functional system does not restore the damaged cortical function in its original form, it has resulted in the desired outcome in all cases that we analyzed.

Not only may individual functions be disturbed as a result of brain injury, but the more generalized functional system that underlies active thinking can also be disturbed as a result of injury to the frontal lobes, particularly in the vicinity of the premotor zone. Distinctive in this kind of injury is the disturbance of spontaneous thinking. Patients with frontal lobe lesions show no gross disturbances of the structure of individual mental operations. The logical structure of their abstract thinking remains intact. In fact, on first impression these patients may seem to have suffered no appreciable disability from their wound apart from a slight clumsiness or slowness. Their articulation of words and their auditory recognition are not affected. The patients are usually able to read and write and have no particular difficulty solving relatively simple intellectual problems. But more careful investigation shows that those suffering from this kind of frontal lesion have defects that are in some ways more serious than the disturbances of specialized operations. These defects are associated with a breakdown of productive activity and active thought. Although the patients have preserved their mental processes almost completely, they cannot actively use them.

The first complaint that we usually encountered with these patients involved the flow of their thoughts. Characteristic were such statements as, "My thoughts will not flow. My head is empty. When I have to write a letter, I don't even know how to begin, and it takes me all day to write." Our investigations showed that these complaints were in fact based on profound disturbances in the flow of thought.

Patients suffering from this kind of lesion usually reply readily to questions and show no signs of disturbance in their dialogue or in their responses to speech during an examination. But they have considerable difficulty if they are asked to give a detailed and lucid description of a picture, or if they are asked to write an essay on a particular topic. Under these conditions, the patients complain that they have nothing to say, and they find it difficult to go beyond passive description of what they see into the realm of interpretation. It seems impossible for these patients to create an inner concept and develop it by subsequent reasoning.

A number of simple tests bring these difficulties to light. For example, patients with frontal lesions have difficulty producing a smooth train of free associations (cat-dog-horse-cow-chicken). They cannot put together pairs of words whose meanings are logically connected, such as pairing red with its opposite or giving the opposite of low. They cannot produce a complete chain of reasoning, in which the individual links follow from each other, although they can easily draw a logical conclusion from any arguments presented to them. In short, with this kind of lesion, the patients become capable only of passive, reactive behavior. The active flow of their complex psychological processes is disturbed.

Experience showed that a reorganization of thinking in such cases is to a limited extent possible. To achieve it, we had to replace the internal synthesis of psychological processes by a regulation of those processes that depend initially on interaction with another person. Put differently, to overcome the patient's difficulties in active thinking, we used external stimuli to organize and activate his thought. For example, it was found to be characteristic of such disturbances that the patient can tell a story fluently only with the help of successive questions. Sometimes these questions consisted of little more than "What then?" or "What happened after that?" Such questions convert the patient's narrative speech into dialogue and replace his train of thought with successive reactions. These reactions provide links that make it possible for him to transmit his thoughts in a connected way. This finding indicated that patients suffering from this kind of frontal lesion retain the content of their thought and that their difficulties are in the dynamics of their thinking.

The course of therapy required us to use the patient's existing capacities and to discover some way for him to compensate for the missing links in his thought. Since our observations had shown that the patient's speech flows more actively when he is talking to someone else, we began by suggesting that he imagine that he was talking to a person who asked him questions. He would then be conducting his speech as an internal dialogue with an imaginary interlocuter. This device sometimes worked, but it did not always provide enough help. It was more effective to provide the patient with a series of auxiliary signs which could serve as external aids for organizing his narrative. When we instituted this practice, the patient's behavior became like that of a skilled mnemonist who can recall a long series of words with the help of a series of self-generated, internal, auxiliary stimuli, except that in the beginning the patient must rely on external stimuli provided for him. We began by asking the patient to read a passage and make suitable remarks while he read. We then showed him how to use these remarks as auxiliary pegs which he could use to help him organize the narrative. With experience the patient can become quite successful at reproducing tests using this method.

While this method can play an important role in the restoration of smooth narrative speech in patients who are suffering from some kinds of frontal lesion, it is limited in its applicability. It is suitable only for relatively simple narrative speech. What is more, it does not help to restore the active flow of the patients' thought, which normally operates by means of internal connections and cause-and-effect relations, nor does it help them to make transitions from one event to another or from one thought to another. Further aid to the patients' thinking is necessary for the real restoration of narrative speech to occur. In order to work, these aids must in some way create the "experience of transition" and gradually develop into stimuli which the patients can use to generate these dynamic transitions themselves. The method we arrived at for doing this was to give the patient phrases that were transitional formulas. For example, we gave the patient a card on which was written a series of words, such as "however," "whereas," "although," "after," and "since." We then asked him to find the necessary transition formulas from those on the card and use them to construct his narrative. We were guessing that at first the card would make the necessary orientation of thought accessible to the patient, but that with practice the patient would begin to produce these transitional formulas for himself.

Our hypothesis was justified, and the use of cards with transitional formulas has often been decisive in restoring considerable smoothness to the flow of narrative speech in such patients. For example, in one case we asked a patient who had great difficulty repeating familiar stories to tell us Tolstoy's story "The Mad Dog." The patient was given a card on which the transitional formulas were written to help him compensate for his difficulties. He carefully examined the card and then told the story fully and fluently. The story began as follows, with the formulas used by the patient appearing in italics: "*Once upon a time* a rich man bought a small puppy and *when* it grew up the rich man took it hunting with him. *Once* a mad dog came into the garden where the children were playing. The rich man saw it and began to shout, the children heard and ran to meet the mad dog. *Then* the man's own dog appeared, and they began to fight."

The effect of using the transitional formulas was to create the necessary links between the action being described at the present moment and the next meaningfully connected action. In terms of our general theory, the transitional formulas create necessary intentions; the patient both selects a meaningful next step and uses that step as a goal to reach the following step. The general idea of the story and the task of remembering it make up a general plan of behavior within which the individual phrases are subgoals, each requiring that the patient carry out current action in terms of the necessary next steps that the overall plan dictates. Within this framework the transition formulas take on the function of intentional links.

In this example the use of the formulas was external. During the following months the patient's powers of description and narrative became reorganized, and new transitional formulas appeared spontaneously. His narration became more continuous, and particularly important, his written accounts of passages that had been read to him ceased to show any signs of pathology. In addition, he was able to describe the contents of pictures spontaneously, which he had been unable to do previously.

This method of restoring active thinking is roughly analogous to the level of restoration of individual words and phrases in afferent aphasia. The suggested formulas for transitions are useful when the subject matter to be transmitted is sufficiently obvious to the patient whose only defect is in his dynamic patterns of thought. But the formulas are inadequate in cases where the patient does not understand the plan of the story and must reconstruct the meaning for himself.

It is as if the pieces of a jigsaw puzzle are piled up haphazardly before these patients, who can see no general pattern and who cannot arrange them in their proper sequence. "I can see one piece here, one piece there, and another there," said one of our patients, "but I cannot grasp the general plan." The spontaneous thought of these patients is disrupted not only because they have an absence of intention and cannot orient their thought, but also because they cannot mentally make the necessary plans to arrange the details of the narration in their proper order. We have helped patients compensate for this defect by reorganizing the processes of planning a composition so that it becomes externalized. Our technique for teaching these patients how to plan a composition is to have them write the fragments of narration they remember on separate pieces of paper without paying any attention to the order in which they are written. They then try to order these fragments by rearranging the pieces of paper, which are all laid out in front of them where they can be seen at once. In ths way the plan of a composition is broken down into two successive stages: deciding on the individual fragments to write and then arranging them in a coherent order.

We had striking results with several of our patients when using this method, which we called the "index card plan." The following example illustrates how the method worked. We read Tolstoy's story "How the Thief Gave Himself Away" to a patient who found it extremely difficult to retell the story. We then instructed him to write down on cards all the fragments of the story he could remember and to arrange them in order. Finally we asked him to write the story. He performed the first two steps as follows:

### Original Notes

1. How he began to sneeze and gave himself away.
2. Once a thief wished to rob a strange merchant.
3. When they were in the attic and found nobody.
4. The merchant told a workman that somebody had climbed up into the attic.
5. How the thief hid in the pile of tobacco.

### Final Arrangement

1. Once a thief wished to rob a strange merchant.
2. The merchant told a workman that somebody had climbed up into the attic.
3. How the thief hid in the pile of tobacco.
4. When they were in the attic and found nobody.
5. How he began to sneeze and gave himself away.

After he had composed this plan, the patient told the story lucidly and fluently. "Before all five sentences were turning over in my head, one after the other, and I did not know what to discard," the patient explained, "but now I think about only one sentence at a time and everything works out properly."

Later we asked this patient to write the story of how he was wounded. He wrote three lines and then insisted he could write no more. All of our attempts to prompt him to continue were unsuccessful. The patient refused to go on, saying he could not sort out the chaos that was in his head. Once again we suggested he use the index card plan method. In the course of the next hour he wrote down fourteen different sentences as he remembered them without bothering to put them in any order. Then he arranged them and wrote the following account of how he was wounded:

On 11 December 1942, I was in the front line. It had been cloudy since the morning, snow was falling and there was a slight breeze. I was at the command post accompanied by the senior political agent, comrade P. and a few soldiers. There was a little artillery fire. The soldiers began to ask me if we should soon open fire on the enemy. I told them the time had not yet come. An hour later the command to open fire was given. At this time the soldiers were in good heart and we had suffered no losses. I observed that the shells burst on the enemy's positions.

At 4 P.M. I was severely wounded in the head. I can remember comrade P. saying that the commander had been killed. I could not tell him I was alive, but I was thinking how easy it was to die . . . then I remember no more.

How they took me to hospital I do not know. I can remember them taking me from an airplane, at the airport at the town V. Then I realized that the Surgical Hospital was in this town, and an operation was performed on me. When I reached the hospital in V., the surgeon came on his round and told me that the operation would be done in the evening. That was 13 December 1942. Evening came, the orderlies took me to the operating theater and put me on the table; it was very difficult to lie down and I only asked how quickly the operation would be over. They told me: "Just be patient a little longer," but of course I had to go through with it all.

The use of this method never quite became automatic for the patient, and a long time elapsed after his discharge from the hospital before he could use it to write a report to his commanding officer.

These examples represent only fragments from the thousands of cases I have analyzed over the years. In each case the progress of diagnosis and the methods of treatment bear an obvious and close relation to the principles put forth by Vygotsky, who first suggested that the dissolution of higher psychological functions could serve as a path for their analysis. I think the examples show clearly both the logic of our general approach to the analysis of higher psychological functions and the important link between diagnostic theory and restorative practice. The methods of therapy that have proved useful are exactly those methods that would have been predicted by Vygotsky on the basis of the general theory of the sociohistorical origins of higher psychological functions. This work, carried out with the assistance of dozens of highly talented researchers, occupied my attention for more than twenty-five years. The work is still incomplete. A great deal remains to be done in order to perfect the methods that we developed. But a foundation for future progress has been laid.

9 . . .

# Mechanisms
# of the Brain

BY THE END of the war we had obtained a far better understanding of the "morphological organization" of higher psychological processes. Our progress had occurred along two fronts. First, we knew a great deal more about the structure of those inner activities, hidden from view, that we term "psychological processes." Second, we had greatly increased our understanding of the role played by separate areas of the brain in fulfilling these activities. The time was long past to consider psychological processes as the result of either strictly localized brain activities or the "mass action" of the brain in which all of its parts were "equipotential." It was time for us to begin the next step in our work: to explain the neurophysiological or, to use the Russian phrase, "neurodynamic" mechanisms underlying the activity of brain loci implicated in specific syndromes. If this step could not be taken, we would remain on the level of pure description. Such descriptions, though valuable, are not the endpoint of scientific enterprise.

Progress depended upon advances in both of the areas that had concerned me all of my life. On the one hand, I had to move from brain structures to a deeper understanding of the neurophysiological mechanisms that were operating in these structures. On the other hand, our psychological analysis of higher cortical functions was by no means complete, and we needed improved psychological analyses as well. To signify the combination of these two enterprises, the "neurological" and the "psychological," the term *neuropsychology* was coined. Developing this field of science has taken a long time and the help of many people. I have been most fortunate to receive strong support from a group of young co-workers (former students from the Psychology Faculty at Moscow University), friends, and trusted colleagues. The work that has occupied me in recent years has benefited immeasurably from the assistance of E. D. Homskaya, with whom I carried out many investigations and who has become an independent and gifted scholar, rich in psychological experience and precise in experimental technique; N. A. Filippycheva, who contributed her outstanding skills as a clinical neuropsychologist and neurophysiologist; A. I. Meshcheryakov, who helped me to begin this line of research before moving on to his classical investigations of the deaf-blind child; L. S. Tsvetkova, who participated closely in work on the recovery and rehabilitation of functions; N. A. Bernshtein, who before his death in the early 1960s provided invaluable theoretical knowledge about dynamic systems: E. N. Sokolov, one of the most experienced and gifted psychophysiologists in the world, who became closely involved in our studies of memory and orienting activity; and of course Olga Vinogradova, a brilliant experimenter and highly gifted thinker, who played a key role in a good deal of my work.

Among the younger generation E. G. Simernitskaya contributed her knowledge of interhemispheric functions, N. K. Kiyashchenko provided important insights into memory defects, and many other people provided indispensable assistance at every step of the way. To all of these people and many more whom I cannot name for lack of space I owe the deepest debt of gratitude. They made possible what was beyond the grasp of one man.

During recent years we have focused on two main problems, each of which illustrates a different path toward specification of the mechanisms underlying complex psychological functions. In dealing with these two lines of research, I shall emphasize their underlying logic. The first area of research was the neurophysiology of the frontal lobes.

During the 1940s and 1950s important progress was made in the study of brain organization. This research provided a basis for investigations into the neurophysiology of brain processes, which we had heretofore studied only at a more global level. H. Magoun, G. Morruzzi, N. Jasper, Donald Lindsley, and Wilder Penfield added enormously to our understanding by their studies of the brain stem, particularly the role of the ascending and descending reticular formation.

As Magoun and Morruzi showed in 1949, the reticular formation is a formation in the brain stem that is specially adapted, both in its structure and in its functional properties, to play a role in the regulation of the state of the cerebral cortex. Unlike the cortex, this formation does not consist of isolated neurons, capable of sending single impulses along their axons. Instead it is constructed like a nerve net with the bodies of nerve cells that are connected with each other by short axons distributed throughout it. Excitation spreads over the net of this nervous structure gradually, not in an all-or-nothing fashion. Consequently, the level of excitation in the system as a whole can change gradually, thus modulating the whole state of the nervous system.

Whereas formerly we could characterize approaches to the brain as "horizontal," that is, as concerned with processes organized at a given level of organization, this new wave of research turned our attention to "vertical" relations between the structures deep within the brain and nearer the surface. This reorientation clarified the ways in which the brain both generates and controls the level of its own activation.

Initially it was shown that the reticular formation is crucial to activating the brain. This activation was at first thought to be quite nonspecific. That is, any stimulation, such as a loud sound, the smell of sausage, or the sight of a butterfly, was assumed to have a generalized effect on the reticular formation, which in turn activitated other parts of the brain stem without regard to specific characteristics of the initiating stimuli. Another way of putting matters is that the reticular formation was assumed to control the quantitative level of activation in the brain, but was not responsible for the qualitative differences in activitation, which depended on characteristics of the specific stimuli. But specific characteristics of the stimuli to which the person, or animal, was exposed were soon demonstrated to exert an effect on the kinds of activitation that resulted; sausages and butterflies activated other parts of the brain in different ways. It became necessary to consider both a nonspecific and a specific activating function of the reticular formation.

A second important distinction that had to be made concerning brain activation was the direction of the excitatory influence. In the earliest work, investigators were impressed by the way that excitation proceeded from lower to higher brain formations, corresponding to the way in which the environment impinges on the organism. But it soon became apparent that it was also necessary to recognize that there were fibers which reversed the direction of neural activity. Upper levels of the brain's organization activated (or modulated the activity of) lower or more peripheral levels.

In due time neuroanatomists discovered that the structure of the reticular formation included both ascending and descending fibers, some of which were discharged only by specific forms of stimulation, while others were activated in a nondifferentiated way that seemed to affect the brain as a whole.

Because there are many different indices of neural activity, we experimented a good deal to determine which indices were best suited to our needs. Like many other investigators of intellectual functions and the brain, we make extensive use of the electroencephalogram, a device that records electrical activity of the brain from electrodes placed on the surface of the skull. The electrical activity or "brain waves" of the normal, awake adult who is not being exposed to any special stimulation, such as an adult sitting in a comfortable chair in a dark room, is dominated by small, rapid brain waves known as alpha waves. When a stimulus is introduced and the person is altered, alpha activity is suppressed, giving us a key indicator of activation.

When these electrophysiological techniques began to make their appearance in the 1950s, we decided that special attention needed to be paid to the role of the frontal lobes in the organization and support of adequate levels of brain activation. We hypothesized that frontal lobe symptoms that we had previously described might be linked to disturbances in the brain's ability to coordinate levels of activation among its subsystems. It was to this problem that Homskaya turned her attention in the mid-1950s, initiating a line of research that has continued for more than twenty years. We established a special neurophysiological section in our laboratory at the Burdenko Institute of Neurosurgery, where our neuropsychological and neurophysiological research could be carried out with the close coordination that they demanded.

A cornerstone of our work was Sokolov's research on the orienting reflex, or as Pavlov had called it many years earlier, the "what is it" reflex. The orienting reflex was particularly useful because it manifested both the specific and nonspecific characteristics that we knew to be central to the brain's activation mechanisms. The basic experimental model for our work came from a technique I had developed with Vinogradova in the early 1950s. Although in that case we had used galvanic skin response and peripheral blood flow as indicators of specific and nonspecific activation, the logic remained the same when desynchronization of alpha waves was used, as countless subsequent experiments have shown.

Subjects were first adapted to sitting quietly in a chair in a bare room where nothing special was happening. Then they were read a list of common words over a speaker system from a control room. The words were presented at intervals of a minute or so with just enough variability in time between words so that there was no point in the subject trying to anticipate when the next word would come.

The initial response to the first word was a clearly marked nonspecific activation, which manifested itself as an increase in skin resistance to electricity, a decrease in peripheral blood supply, and desynchronization of the alpha rhythm. As new words were presented, the magnitude of the activation, or orienting reflex, decreased. When the orienting reflex had almost disappeared, after presentation of ten to fifteen words, we followed presentation of one word, say "house," by a mild electric shock to the person's hand. Needless to say, this shock produced a new orienting reflex and a high level of activation. More important, it produced the higher activation not only in response to the shock but in response to later words in the sequence as well.

When we completed the experiment without further shocks, we discovered that the gradual presentation of spoken words would again fail to evoke any appreciable level of activation. But by presenting shocks selectively to certain words, we imbued these words with special significance, which then enabled us to trace the selective activation controlled by word meaning. For example, if we included in our series of common words the word "home" to go along with the word "house," we discovered that practiced subjects demonstrated no special activation to any of the words in the sequence except those two; both words evoked high levels of activation. We could demonstrate that word meaning was the basis of selection by including words that were like "house" in other ways. For example, we could include "louse" to see if acoustic similarity controlled activation. In normal adults it did not.

With this experimental model we could carry out further neurophysiological investigations of the way in which the frontal lobes affect activation of the brain as a whole. We could trace the nonspecific effect of all kinds of stimuli, and we could imbue certain stimuli with special significance in order to distinguish between specific and nonspecific activation. It was not always necessary to use conditioned reflex techniques, as we had in the 1950s; a great variety of methods, including simple instructions, were often just as useful.

The results of the work carried out by Homskaya and her colleagues were of the greatest significance for our understanding of frontal lobe functions. Working with either normal subjects or patients who had suffered damage to posterior portions of the brain, such as patients with a parietal lobe lesion, they reliably found the patterns of specific and nonspecific activation. Working with a technique based on preliminary instructions, such as "Listen for the word *house*" or "Listen to the words as I say them," Homskaya found that the instructions which required selective activation produced both a higher level of activation overall and appropriate changes when the target stimuli occurred. With instructions of the second type that required no special selective attention, activation was less durable as well as nonselective.

A completely different picture emerged in research on frontal lobe patients. These people as a rule exhibit diminished active behavior, and lack of spontaneity is a basic symptom of their pathology. In this new research their response to stimulation as measured by activation in the EEG pattern was significantly opposite to that obtained in normal subjects or patients with posterior lesions. In frontal patients, stimuli which had no special significance evoked marked EEG changes which were more or less like those observed when normal subjects were presented such stimuli. But no change occurred in the EEG pattern of frontal lobe patients when stimuli were imbued with special significance by means of verbal instruction. If we dealt with patients who had suffered really massive bilateral lesions, we even saw inhibition of the cortical processes in response to significant words, reflected as a slowing of EEG activity, where we might have expected it to increase. These results indicated that the frontal lobes are responsible for modulating the tonus, or, the level of neural activity, of the cerebral cortex. In normal individuals, the stabilizing effect of the frontal cortex in accordance with verbal instructions is reflected directly in the EEG patterns.

Once we had developed the basic technique for tracing the level of activation using EEG indicators of *physiological pro-*

*cesses,* we were able to repeat and extend a number of our basic *psychological* observations, tracing their physiological bases. The subsequent research, reported in monographs by Homskaya and in a number of my own publications, demonstrated that in the normal adult the frontal lobes exert control over behavior in part as a result of their control over the level of activation aroused by different kinds of verbal stimuli. For example, we repeated many of the basic experiments modeled on the combined motor method. Sometimes we asked the patient to "press the key when the red light comes on." At other times we introduced elementary choices into the task: "When you see the red light, press with your right hand; when you see the green light, press with your left hand." In such cases the frontal lobe patient might be able to respond correctly for a few trials, but cortical tonus quickly broke down, and as it did so, errors began to occur. Sometimes the patient began to perseverate, continuing to make his responses even when the light was no longer on. Sometimes in the choice experiments he began to respond only with one hand no matter what the stimulus, which indicated that selectivity was lost.

The ability of the patient to retain verbal instructions was not lost in these cases. He could repeat the instructions. But the instructions had lost their controlling function. Purely imitative verbal responses were also maintained. Such patients could say "red" whenever a red light appeared, but they could not control their motor responding in accordance with their verbal behavior.

We think it of real significance that these results mirror the results obtained in our earlier research with children. In the case of three to three-and-a-half year old children we were dealing with young people whose brains were still developing. It is at this period that mylenization of the neurons of the frontal lobes begins to reach completion; and it is at this age that young children begin to control their behavior in accord with verbal instructions. In both cases, there is evidence that the complex organization of human conscious action depends critically on the operation of neurophysiological mechanisms in the frontal lobes. In the case of children, the brain is developing at the same time that the child is acquiring higher forms of behavior, social in origin and verbally mediated in structure. In the adult who suffers a lesion of the frontal lobes, these higher forms become inaccessible as the result of insult to the basic neural structures of the brain.

Progress toward the explanation of higher psychological functions required progress along two fronts. The work extending "downward" into neurophysiology pointed in one direction. But we must also achieve a more detailed understanding of the psychological processes that are organized as a part of the interaction between the brain and man's social environment.

Illustrative of the effort required to explore this second dimension of neuropsychology are the forty years of research on the psychology and brain organization of language. So complex is this enterprise that I have coined a special phrase, "neurolinguistics," to indicate the problems it poses for scientific analysis, problems that are critically bound up in our understanding of human language. Although linguistic phenomena have played a role in much of my research, I have given little of the background which led me to use particular linguistic devices in my diagnostic work. Nor have I considered the psychology of, and brain organization of, language *per se*. However, the problem of language and the brain has been of great concern to me in recent years, and it illustrates the general approach to psychological analysis that is essential to neuropsychology.

My interest in linguistic phenomena grew naturally out of my early research using the combined motor method and Vygotsky's theory, which emphasized language as a key tool, unique to human beings, for mediating their interactions with the world. But a serious study of language as a highly organized system of human behavior began in earnest only after I had begun work on the problem of the neuropsychology of sensory and semantic aphasia.

Sensory aphasia is a condition in which patients can speak but are unable to understand spoken language. I knew that their defect could not be attributed to a loss of hearing or any general decrement in intelligence. I also found that patients suffering from semantic aphasia could understand isolated words but were at a loss when presented with relational terms, such as "brother's father" or "the circle under the triangle."

While these observations were interesting and of potential diagnostic value, I could not be sure of what the diagnoses meant. As a clinician, I was busy studying O. Pötzl's *Die Aphasielehre vom Standpunkt der Klinischen Psychiatrie* and Head's *Aphasia and Kindred Disorders of Speech,* along with the work of Gelb, Goldstein, and others. The work of these neurologists suggested that I had to understand the way information about spatial or quasi-spatial information is stored in the brain and how people come to construct a synopsis of a scene with many details. To learn more about these phenomena, I knew that I also had to master what the linguistics of that period, the late 1930s, could teach me.

One of the first important influences in my early linguistically oriented work was N. S. Trubetskoy's "Grunzuge der Phonologie," which was published in Prague in 1939. It was immediately recognized as a revolutionary account of the mechanisms of the acoustic organization of language. Trubetskoy argued that language processing depends critically not only on the physical features of sound, such as pitch, but also on the value of sounds as a means of distinguishing word meaning. He emphasized this phonemic aspect of speech instead of its phonological aspect because the organization of sounds into different phonemes is what distinguishes different languages, not the physical or phonological aspects of sound alone. If I was to understand aphasia, I knew that I would have to analyze the breakdown of the system of phonemes, not just the physical deteriorization of acoustic analysis. When I first began this line of work, the lesson I learned from Trubetskoy was not at all obvious; after all, I was observing patients who failed to distinguish between *b* and *p*, or *d* and *t*, who suffered what was then called "alienation of word meaning" (For example, a patient might repeat quizzically: "*Posture* . . . what does it mean? . . . *bosture* . . . *bolstul* . . . ?").

I knew that patients who had suffered temporal-parieto-occipital lesions suffered severe comprehension difficulties, but I did not know what it was about certain grammatical functions that implicated these areas of the brain. Here I was helped by V. V. Vinogradov, who drew my attention to the publication of a young Swedish linguist, C. Svedelius. In his *L'analyse de language,* published in Uppsala in 1897, Svedelius divided all forms of verbal communication into two basic classes: communication of events, the contents of which can be expressed in images, and communication of relations, such as "Socrates is a man" or "Kathy is prettier than Mary," in which special linguistic devices such as prepositions or variations in word order are necessary to express the ideas being communicated. I needed to undertake a special study of these constructions, an enterprise to which I devoted two years.

I began by studying model constructions of the type "brother's father" or "father's brother," constructions that included the attributive form of the genitive case. My patients could not understand these constructions, which in Russian take the form of *otets brata* and *brat otsa* respectively, but they could understand other forms of the genitive case, such as the genitive of parts, as in a "piece of bread," *kusok khleba.*

I began to understand that in the attributive genitive constructions there was a conflict between the two words that required the person to make a mental transformation in order to overcome the conflict and to understand the phrase. One had to abstract the immediate, concrete meaning of the word "brother's" and convert the semantic content of a noun into the semantic content of an adjective; mentally, the sequence of words had to be reversed. This was true because in Russian adjectives precede nouns, as in *vkusnyi khleb,* "good bread." But in a construction like *brat otsa,* "father's brother," the genitive form of the noun "father" performs the function of an adjective yet follows the noun it modifies. This kind of transformation can be made only if the relational meaning of the whole expression is grasped. But that transformation in the service of relational meaning was exactly what the patients in question found difficult to make.

When I looked into the area of historical linguistics, I found that relational constructions of this kind appeared late in the development of the Russian language. They did not appear at all in old Slavic chronicles. Instead, one finds simple appositions: not *deti boyar*, "children of the Boyars," but the simpler expression *boyare deti*, "the boyar children." The same lack of attributive genitive constructions appeared to be true of old German and old English texts as well. In German, for example, instead of *mit Leidschaft der Liebe*, there appeared the apposition *mit Leidschaft und Liebe*. This evidence suggested that the attributive genitive, which was especially disturbed in cases of semantic aphasia, was a construction of relatively recent historical origin and required special mental work. The attributive genitive is necessary for the communication of relations of a special kind that are not involved in either the genitive of parts or the communication of events.

The two years I spent in the study of linguistics early in my career stood me in good stead when I began to work seriously on the problem of semantic aphasia because I could understand more fully the different mental requirements that seemingly similar linguistic acts placed on people. I was thus in a beter position to carry out differential diagnosis of pathological symptoms which previously had been lumped together in the neurological literature. As my work continued to involve me in attempts to understand the brain basis of language-related behavior, I found it necessary to continue to study the psychology of language at the same time that I searched for its neurological bases. And just as advances in neurology and neurophysiology were instrumental to our study of brain mechanisms, advances in the study of linguistics were crucial to advancing our understanding of those phenomena of speech which brain pathology was interrupting; the two enterprises are inextribably bound together. Time and again I found myself returning to old data, armed with new insights from advances in linguistics.

One of the distinctions which began to appear in linguistics with the work of de Saussure in the 1920s and which I came to use heavily in the 1940s owing to the work of Roman Jakobson was the difference between the "paradigmatic" aspects of language, which refers to the placing of words and the things they denote into categories, enabling people to use language to make comparisons and generalizations, and the "syntagmatic" aspect of language, which enables people to join words together into coherent expressions. The paradigmatic function of speech allows the codes of language to be used to separate out significant cues in the environment, and it also makes it possible to take whole categories of cues into consideration at a single moment, which is what we do when we use categories. The paradigmatic function of speech is intimately related to the basic motives that direct activity. It links our intentions to our thoughts.

In trying to understand the cortical organization of language, we must recognize the existence of both the categorizing and the intention-fulfilling functions which intermingle in every utterance. Moreover, recognizing that they carry out different, if related, functions, we can expect their cortical localization to be different. Looking back into the history of neurology, we can see that as early as 1913 Pick was pointing to the syntagmatic function when he sought to determine how condensed thought patterns can be expanded into smooth, sequentially organized statements, and Jackson's reference to the "propositionizing" aspect of speech showed that he too recognized the importance of this function.

Working with this distinction, which was anticipated and used by Vygotsky in *Thought and Language* and in his preliminary articles on brain localization, we found the anticipated difference in the brain localization of syntagmatic and paradigmatic language functions. Lesions in the forward parts of the left hemisphere, which are known to be closely related to motor functions, selectively impair fluent, syntagmatically organized speech, but complex verbal codes based on paradigmatic organization remain more or less intact. Patients with such lesions easily name single objects, but their speech takes on the classic "telegraphic" style that many early investigators noted, owing to a breakdown of the predicative function which is basic to fluent speech.

From the point of view of this linguistic distinction, just the opposite pattern of disturbance occurs in patients with lesions in the rear of the head. These people can speak fluently, but the relations between individual words break down. This is the linguistic basis for observations in which grammatical relations such as "father's brother" are destroyed by lesions in the parieto-occipital area.

I could extend these examples, showing how a combination of linguistic, psychological, and neuropsychological analysis is required in order to understand the mechanisms underlying each particular form of speech pathology. It suffices, however, to point out that exactly the same principles for understanding individual words and simple phrases apply as well to longer, more complex phrases and to the comprehension of entire paragraphs and texts or narratives. A full discussion of these issues may be found in my *Basic Problems of Neurolinguistics*. Instead of multiplying examples, I shall give a single example which makes clear the ways in which the various disciplines that contribute to the understanding of an activity as complex as language must be combined to understand its brain organization. The example relates to the phenomenon known as "elicited imitation" in the literature on children's language, but in aphasiology it is referred to as "conduction aphasia."

In 1875 Wernicke described a special form of aphasia in which the patient retained his full understanding of speech addressed to him and to some extent could produce coherent speech spontaneously, but he was unable to repeat sounds, words, or sentences. This phenomenon was considered paradoxical because the patient was heard to make very complex remarks at the same time that he failed to repeat back the simplest phrases provided by the examiner. Wernicke hypothesized that this disturbance was caused by a break in the direct connections between the sensory and motor "speech centers," although each of these centers remained intact and each retained connections to the hypothetical "higher centers." In the years to follow, several additional cases of this kind were reported, and the concept of a special kind of conduction aphasia was passed down through generations of textbooks.

As is often the case, in the face of such a simple schema, contradictory data were overlooked. In their encounters with so-called conduction aphasia, workers noted that in some patients the difficulty in repeating words seemed to arise from a difficulty in naming objects; in other cases, individual objects could be named but complex material could not be repeated. Difficulties in narrative speech, which hypothetically ought to be under the control of only the higher centers, were also observed.

In my opinion the beginning of an understanding of this phenomenon came from neither a strictly linguistic nor a strictly neurological source, but rather from a psychological analysis of the activity demanded of someone repeating what someone else says. As early as the 1870s Jackson suggested that naming objects and repeating individual words are not the most elementary or natural forms of speech activity. In a series of investigations, Goldstein directed special attention to the importance of making a psychological analysis of speech repetition. His argument is that neither the naming of individual objects nor the repetition of words is the basis of most natural speech activity. Instead, the basic form of speech communication is the formulation of ideas as whole propositions which are intimately bound up with the motives and conditions of the activity in which the individual is engaged. When the neurologist begins to ask the patient to repeat phrases that are arbitrary and totally unrelated to anything he is supposed to do, the patient is really being asked to engage in an abstraction of speech from action at the same time that he is being asked to speak.

The major finding of Goldstein's analysis received support

from quite a different source. Long ago Piaget, as well as Vygotsky and his students discovered that after young children had learned to speak, they still experienced difficulty in carrying out presumably simple imitation tasks in which all they were required to do was to repeat some action or phrase after an adult. Quite recently, Daniel Slobin and his colleagues in America made a study of a child's spontaneous utterances around the home. From time to time they would ask the child to repeat something that he had said just a few minutes earlier. In addition to confirming observations made half a century earlier but appearing now in the context of the burgeoning field of developmental psycholinguistics, Slobin pointed out that the child's spontaneous speech was organized by the motives which guided his activity as a whole; deprived of the organizing motive, the child's speech lost its guiding principle. The child's failure represents the phenomenon that would have been called conduction aphasia if Slobin had been working with an adult who had a brain injury instead of a healthy two-and-a-half year old.

Because the general approach initiated by Vygotsky formed the basis for our research, we adopted the fundamental proposition that a change in the goal of a task inevitably leads to a significant change in the structure of the psychological processes which carry it out. A change in the structure of activity, in other words, implies a change in the brain organization of activity. Therefore the transition from spontaneous to elicited speech, whether in dialogue or in monologue, not only changes the task and the structure of the speech process but also changes the functional systems of the brain that support these activities. To believe that conduction aphasia constitutes a loss of abstract attitude—the erroneous direction toward which Goldstien's psychological theorizing carried him—or that it reflects a mere severing of connections between two brain centers is to misunderstand the structure of the task, the nature of the activity, and the significance of the brain injury.

Once the true complexity of language phenomena are understood, there is no further need to ignore the seemingly anomalous cases of conduction aphasia, since they are no more than indications that conduction aphasia is not a single syndrome but a set of disturbances which express themselves differently according to the demands placed on the patient and the particular areas of the brain that are affected. Just as we found that sensory, motor, and semantic aphasias were terms covering a multiplicity of related phenomena, so our later analysis has shown that several subcategories of disturbance are covered by the loose term "conduction aphasia."

These examples illustrate a process which has no endpoint. If one wants to understand the brain foundations for psychological activity, one must be prepared to study both the brain and the system of activity in as great detail as contemporary science allows. In many cases important clues can be gotten from specialists in related fields. This was true in our studies of neurolinguistics. It was true as well in our studies of the disturbance of memory and problem solving. But in each of these cases, we found that we must use the work of specialists as a starting point, modifying tasks and theories as we want, because the conditions of clinical work do not permit the well-controlled application of many experimental methods. And in dealing with patients, we must never forget that an individual human life is at stake, not a statistical abstraction which, on the average, supports a theory.

# 10

# Romantic Science

AT THE BEGINNING of this century the German scholar Max Verworn suggested that scientists can be divided into two distinct groups according to their basic orientation toward science: classical and romantic. These two basic orientations, he noted, reflect not only the scholar's general attitude toward science but his personal characteristics as well.

Classical scholars are those who look upon events in terms of their constituent parts. Step by step they single out important units and elements until they can formulate abstract, general laws. These laws are then seen as the governing agents of the phenomena in the field under study. One outcome of this approach is the reduction of living reality with all its richness of detail to abstract schemas. The properties of the living whole are lost, which provoked Goethe to pen, "Gray is every theory, but ever green is the tree of life."

Romantic scholars' traits, attitudes, and strategies are just the opposite. They do not follow the path of reductionism, which is the leading philosophy of the classical group. Romantics in science want neither to split living reality into its elementary components nor to represent the wealth of life's concrete events in abstract models that lose the properties of the phenomena themselves. It is of the utmost importance to romantics to preserve the wealth of living reality, and they aspire to a science that retains this richness.

Of course, romantic scholars and romantic science have their shortcomings. Romantic science typically lacks the logic and does not follow the careful, consecutive, step-by-step reasoning that is characteristic of classical science, nor does it easily reach firm formulations and universally applicable laws. Sometimes logical step-by-step analysis escapes romantic scholars, and on occasion, they let artistic preferences and intuitions take over. Frequently their descriptions not only precede explanation but replace it. I have long puzzled over which of the two approaches, in principle, leads to a better understanding of living reality.

This dilemma is a reformulation of the conflict between nomothetic and ideographic approaches to psychology that concerned me during the first years of my intellectual life. Within psychology the conflicting approaches underlay the crisis between explanatory, physiological psychology and a descriptive, phenomenological psychology of the higher psychological functions. One of the major factors that drew me to Vygotsky was his emphasis on the necessity to resolve this crisis. He saw its resolution as the most important goal of psychology in our time. But our work did not take place in a vacuum. Rather, it was carried out in a larger social and scientific context which shaped the attitude of all scientists, including myself.

Since the beginning of this century there has been enormous technical progress, which has changed the very structure of the scientific enterprise. It can be assumed that this progress began in the first half of the nineteenth century with the discovery that single cells constitute the elementary particles of all living organisms. This discovery paved the way for Virchow's cellular physiology and pathology. Reductionism, the effort to reduce complex phenomena to their elementary particles, became the guiding principle of scientific efforts. In psychology it seemed that by reducing psychological events to elementary physiological rules, we could attain the ultimate explanation of human behavior. Reductionism in the study of learning led to an emphasis on contiguity and reinforcement as the basic elements, the combination of which could explain even the most complex forms of behavior, including human conscious activity. In this atmosphere, the rich and complex picture of human behavior which had existed in the late nineteenth century disappeared from psychology textbooks.

Later, as a result of the enormous progress made in biophysics, another wave of reductionism was launched. During this period many scholars supposed that the explanation of behavioral processes, including such higher psychological processes as memory and attention, could be found at the molecular and even submolecular level. These attempts to reduce complex forms of conscious behavior to a microscopic level were especially dominant in the study of the brain as the basis of behavior. During this period the study of human conscious activity became submerged in a sea of molecular speculation.

Then came what was perhaps the most striking breakthrough of all. Electronic devices whose detection capabilities and speed greatly exceeded those of individuals were invented, and self-regulating electronic computers became one of the basic tools of science. Many scholars began to suppose that observation could be replaced by computer simulation and mathematical models. Psychological textbooks and monographs overflowed with such models and schemas. This deluge brought a still graver danger: the reality of human conscious activity was being replaced by mechanical models.

This tendency to reduce living facts to mathematical schemas and to leave investigation largely to instruments was especially great in medicine. The medicine of previous years had been based on the effort to single out important syndromes by describing significant symptoms. This activity was considered essential both for diagnosis and for treatment. With the advent of new instrumentation, these classical forms of medical procedure were pushed into the background. The physicians of our time, having a battery of auxiliary laboratory aids and tests, frequently overlook clinical reality. Observation of patients and evaluation of syndromes have begun to give way to dozens of laboratory analyses which are then combined by mathematical techniques as a means of diagnosis and as a plan of treatment. Physicians who are great observers and great thinkers have gradually disappeared. It is rare now to find a really good physician who is equally adept in observing, judging, and treating. I do not intend to underrate the role of instrumentation in medicine. But I am inclined to reject strongly an approach in which these auxiliary aids become the central method and in which their role as servant to clinical thought is reversed so that clinical reasoning follows instrumental data as a slave follows its master.

In the previous century, when auxiliary laboratory methods were rare, the art of clinical observation and description reached its height. One is unable to read the classical descriptions of the great physicians J. Lourdat, A. Trousseau, P. Marie, J. Charcot, Wernicke, S. Korsakoff, Head, and A. Meyer without seeing the beauty of the art of science. Now this art of observation and description is nearly lost.

Simple observation and description have their shortcomings too. They can lead to a description of immediately perceived events that seduces observers into pseudoexplanations based on their own phenomenological understanding. This kind of error jeopardizes the essential role of scientific analysis. But it is a danger only when phenomenological description is superficial and incomplete. Truly scientific observation avoids such dangers. Scientific observation is not merely pure description of separate facts. Its main goal is to view an event from as many perspectives as possible. The eye of science does not probe "a thing," an event isolated from other things or events. Its real object is to see and understand the way a thing or event relates to other things or events.

I have always admired Lenin's observation that a glass, as an object of science, can be understood only when it is viewed from many perspectives. With respect to the material of which it is made, it becomes an object of physics; with respect to its value, an object of economics; and with respect to its form, an object of aesthetics. The more we single out important relations during our description, the closer we come to the essence of the object, to an understanding of its qualities and the rules of its existence. And the more we preserve the whole wealth of its qualities, the closer we come to the inner laws that determine its existence. It was this perspective which led Karl Marx to describe the process of scientific description with the strange-sounding expression, "ascending to the concrete."

The observation and description of psychological facts should follow the same process. Clinical and psychological observations have nothing in common with the reductionism of the classicist. The clinical analysis of my early research is a case in point. Such an analysis seeks out the most important traits or primary basic factors that have immediate consequences and then seeks the secondary or "systemic" consequences of these basic underlying factors. Only after these basic factors and their consequences have been identified can the entire picture become clear. The object of observation is thus to ascertain a network of important relations. When done properly, observation accomplishes the classical aim of explaining facts, while not losing sight of the romantic aim of preserving the manifold richness of the subject.

I have tried to preserve the spirit of clinical analysis while using instrumental laboratory aids as a means to meaningful scientific advancement. In a good deal of this work my approach has been as much that of the classical scholar as the romantic one. But from time to time in my life I have had an opportunity to pursue my interests in a more purely romantic style.

My efforts to revive the traditions of romantic science resulted in two books, *The Mind of a Mnemonist* (1968) and *The Man with a Shattered World* (1972). In each of these works I tried to follow in the steps of Walter Pater in *Imaginary Portraits*, written in 1887, except that my books were *unimagined* portraits. In both books I described an individual and the laws of his mental life. But since it is almost impossible to write an analytical description of the personality of someone taken at random from a crowd, I chose to write about two men, each of whom had one feature that played a decisive role in determining his personality and which set him apart from all other people. In each case I tried to study the individual's basic trait as carefully as possible and from it to deduce his other personality traits. In other words, I tried to do a "factor analysis" of my subjects.

The first book in which I used this approach was *The Mind of a Mnemonist.* S. V. Sherashevsky, the famous mnemonist who was the hero of this book, had an outstanding memory which dominated his personality. However, his memory itself was not the subject of my book, but rather its influence on his personality.

Sherashevsky's memory was of a complex, eidetic-synesthetic type. He easily converted each impression, even acoustically perceived words, into optical images, which were closely associated with other sensations, including sounds, taste, and tactile sensations.

I remember one day when we were to go together to the laboratory of the Russian physiologist L. A. Orbeli. "Do you remember how to get there?" I asked Sherashevsky, forgetting that he permanently preserved all of his impressions. "Oh," he answered, "how could I possibly forget it? After all, here's this fence. It has such a salty taste and feels so rough; what's more it has such a sharp, piercing sound." He informed Vygotsky, "You have such a yellow and crumbly voice." He told me about an occasion when he was buying ice cream. The woman selling it asked in a deep voice, "Do you prefer chocolate?" Her voice seemed so terribly squawking to him that in his mind's eye black flecks immediately covered the ice cream, and he was unable to taste it. As he explained the process:

I recognize a word not only by the images it evokes but by a whole complex of feelings that the image arouses. It's hard to express . . . it's not a matter of vision or hearing, but some overall sense I get. Usually I experience a word's taste and weight, and I don't have to make an effort to remember it—the word seems to recall itself. But it's difficult to describe. What I sense is something oily slipping through my hand . . . or I'm aware of a slight tickling in my left hand caused by a mass of tiny, lightweight points. When that happens, I simply remember, without having to make the attempt. (Record, May 22, 1939)

These synesthetic components furnished him with additional information that guaranteed accurate recall. If he reproduced a word inaccurately, the additional synesthetic sensations he experienced would fail to coincide with the word, leaving him with the sense that something was wrong and forcing him to correct his error. But they were secondary to the visual quality of his recall. When he heard or read a word, it was at once converted into a visual image corresponding with the object that the word signified for him. As he described it: "When I hear the word *green,* a green flowerpot appears; with the word *red* I see a man in a red shirt coming toward me. As for *blue,* this means an image of someone waving a small blue flag from a window . . . Even numbers remind me of images. Take the number 1. This is a proud, well-built man; 2 is a high-spirited woman; 3 is a gloomy person" (Record, September 1936).

When Sherashevsky read through a long series of words, each word elicited a graphic image. Since the series was usually fairly long, he had to find some way of distributing these images in a mental sequence. Most often he would "distribute" them along some roadway or street he visualized in his mind. This technique explains why he could so readily reproduce a series from start to finish, or in reverse order, and why he could rapidly name the word that preceded or followed the one I had selected from the series. To do so, he would simply begin his walk, either from the beginning or from the end of the street, find the image of the object named, and "take a look" at whatever happened to be situated on either side of it.

These images and sensations were remarkably stable, and he could read off at will material from performances or conversations that had occurred decades before. It was impossible to establish a limit to the capacity or the duration of his memory, or to find any indications that his memory traces were extinguished over the course of time.

This stability became a special problen to him when he began his career as a professional mnemonist. He wrote: "I'm afraid I may begin to confuse the individual performances. So in my mind I erase the blackboard and cover it, as it were, with a film that's completely opaque and impenetrable. I take this off the board and listen to it crunch as I gather it into a ball . . . Even so, when the next performance starts and I walk over to that blackboard, the numbers I erased are liable to turn up again" (Letter, 1939). He tried writing things down so that he would no longer have to remember them, but this was not satisfactory either. He went further and started to throw away and even burn the slips of paper on which he had written items he wished to forget. But he still remembered. Then,

One evening—it was the 23rd of April—I was quite exhausted from having given three performances and was wondering how I'd ever get through the fourth. There before me I could see the charts of numbers appearing from the first three performances . . . I thought I'll just take a quick look and see if the first chart of numbers is still there. I was still afraid somehow that it woudn't be. I both did and didn't want it to appear . . . And then I thought: the chart of numbers isn't turning up now and it's clear why—it's because I don't want it to! Aha! That means if I don't want the chart to show up, it won't. And all it took was for me to realize this!

A description of Sherashevsky would have been inadequate if it had been limited to his memory. What was required was a careful analysis of how his fantastic memory influenced his thinking, his behavior, and his entire personality. During the decades I studied him, both the strengths and the limits of his intellectual capacities became clear. When he could imagine all the data of a problem, he could deal with it much better and faster than persons with normal memories. He could become more deeply involved in a narrative than most people, and he never missed a single detail and often spotted contradictions writers themselves had failed to notice. His solutions to riddles had a highly aesthetic quality.

But his use of immediate images, both visual and synesthetic, in solving problems presented certain difficulties that he was unable to overcome. For instance, when he read a passage from a text, each word produced an image. As soon as he began a phrase, images would appear; as he read further, still more images were evoked. If a passage was read to him quickly, one image would collide with another in his mind; images would begin to crowd in upon one another and become contorted. The problem for him then, was how to understand anything. If a text was read slowly, this too presented problems: "I was reading this phrase: N. was leaning up against a tree." I saw a slim young man dressed in a dark blue suit (N., you know, is so elegant). He was standing near a big linden tree with grass and woods all around . . . But then the sentence went on: and was peering into a shop window. Now how do you like that! It means the scene isn't set in the woods, or in the garden, but he's standing on the street. And I have to start the whole sentence over from the beginning" (Record, March 1937).

Thus, trying to understand a passage, to grasp the information it contained, became a tortuous process for Sherashevsky. The images kept rising to the surface of his mind, and he continually had to struggle against them in order to concentrate on what was essential. Inasmuch as his images were particularly vivid and stable and recurred thousands of times, they soon became the dominant element in Sherashevsky's awareness and came uncontrollably to the surface whenever he touched on something that was linked to them even in the most general way. His figurative thinking was a particular hindrance when he tried to read poetry. Each expression gave rise to an image, which conflicted with another image that had been evoked.

Abstract ideas meant another round of problems and torments for him: "*Infinity*—that means what has always been. But what came before this? What is to follow? No, it's impossible to see this . . . In order for me to grasp the meaning of a thing, I have to see it . . . Take the word *nothing*. I read it and thought it must be very profound. I thought it would be better to call nothing something . . . for I see this nothing and it is something. If I'm to understand any meaning that is fairly deep, I have to get an image of it right away." Sherashevsky was perplexed and overwhelmed when faced with abstract ideas, the way young people are when they first realize that abstract ideas cannot be understood in graphic terms. But most adolescents shift from thinking in concrete terms to dealing with abstractions, and the problem ceases for them. The role that graphic images once played in their thinking is replaced by certain accepted ideas about the meaning of words. Their thinking becomes verbal and logical, and graphic images are relegated to the periphery of their consciousness. But this is a transition that Sherashevsky never made. He was unable to grasp an idea unless he could actually see it, and so he tried to visualize the idea of "nothing" and to find an image with which to depict "infinity."

His behavior was also affected by his memory. He was able to control his involuntary processes, such as his heart rate and the temperature of his body, in the same way that a yogi does. A clear image of himself running fast increased his pulse rate. An image of a piece of ice on his hand decreased the temperature of his hand. And an image of his hand holding a glass of hot water increased his skin temperature. By this process he could increase or decrease the temperature of his hands by 5 degrees. But in cases where his inner image conflicted with a real situation, he was lost. "I had to go to court, and I prepared," he told me. "I had imagined the judge sitting here, and myself standing there . . . But when I arrived at court, everything was different. I was lost and could not deliver my speech."

Sherashevsky's entire personality was determined by his fantastic capacities. As a child, he was a dreamer whose fantasies were embodied in images that were all too vivid, constituting in themselves another world, one through which he transformed the experiences of everyday life. He tended to lose sight of the distinction between what formed a part of reality and what he himself could "see." For instance: "This was a habit I had for quite some time: perhaps even now I still do it. I'd look at a clock and for a long while continue to see the hands fixed just as they were, and not realize time had passed . . . That's why I'm often late" (Record, October 1934).

His dreams became a substitute for action in that they were based on his experiences of himself which had been converted into images. His ability to "see" himself in this way, to "cut himself off," to convert his experiences and activity into an image of another person who carried out his instructions, was of enormous help to him in regulating his own behavior, as when he controlled his autonomic processes. Yet sometimes cutting himself off in this way interfered with his having complete control of his behavior; the "he" seen by Sherashevsky slipped out of control and began to operate automatically.

Because Sherashevsky's entire personality was shaped by his incredible memory, I could study the structure of his mind in the same way that I studied syndromes. By contrast, my second book using the approach of romantic science began, not with an outstanding capacity, but with a catastrophe that had devastated a man's intellectual powers. A bombshell wounded a young man, destroying the parietal lobe of the left hemisphere of his brain. His whole world was shattered. He forgot his name, his address. All words disappeared. As he described it later: "Because of that wound I'd become an abnormal person . . . I was abnormal because I had a huge amount of amnesia and for a long time didn't even have any traces of memories . . . I'm in a fog all the time, like a heavy half-sleep. My memory's a blank. I can't think of a single word. All that flashes through my mind are images, hazy visions that suddenly appear and just as suddenly disappear, giving way to fresh images. But I simply can't understand or remember what these mean."

He was unable to read, or even to say whether the newspaper was in a foreign language. During our first interview at the rehabilitation hospital where he had been sent after his injury, I asked him to read something:

"What's this? . . . No, I don't know . . . don't understand . . . what *is* this?" he asked. He tried to examine the page more closely, holding it in front of his left eye, then moving it further to the side and scrutinizing each of the letters in amazement. "No, I can't," was all he could reply. I then asked him to write his first name and home town for me. This too led to a desperate struggle. Awkwardly he picked up the pencil, by the wrong end at first, then groped for the paper. But again, he could not form a single letter. He was beside himself, he simply could not write and realized he had suddenly become illiterate.

As a result of his wound, his body became strange to him. He often "lost" the right side of his body, which inevitably occurs when the parietal area of the left hemisphere is injured. He also thought that parts of his body had changed: "Sometimes when I'm sitting down I suddenly feel as though my head is the size of a table—every bit as big—while my hands, feet, and torso become very small. When I remember this, I myself think it's comical, but also very weird. These are the kinds of things, I call bodily peculiarities. When I close my eyes, I'm not even sure where my right leg is: for some reason I used to think it was somewhere above my shoulder, even above my head."

And his vision was damaged so that he could not perceive anything completely. He had to use his imagination to fill in the gaps in what he saw: "That is, I have to picture them in my mind and try to remember them as full and complete—after I have a chance to look them over, touch them, or get some image of them." This was because he had lost the right field of vision in both eyes. It meant that if he focused on a point with either eye, he could see only what was to the left of the point. Everything to the right was blocked out. In addition, there were blank spaces in his vision. But then one day, in the course of therapy, a discovery was made which proved to be a turning point:

At first I had just as much trouble with writing—that is, even after I thought I knew the letters, I couldn't remember how they were formed. Each time I wanted to think of a particular letter, I'd have to run through the alphabet until I found it. But one day a doctor I'd come to know well, since he was always very informal with me and the other patients, asked me to try to write automatically—without lifting my hand from the paper. I was bewildered and questioned him a few times before I could even begin, but finally picked up the pencil and after repeating the word *blood* a few times, I quickly wrote it. I hardly knew what I'd written since I still had trouble reading . . . It turned out I could only write certain words automatically—short ones.

After intensive training for about six months he learned to read and write. Writing came far more quickly because writing was an automatic skill for him with a series of built-in movements that had not been affected by his injury. However, he continued to read slowly, breaking words down into letters and syllables because the part of the cortex which controls visual functioning had been damaged. Nonetheless, he could write automatically, even though he had to rack his brain for words and ideas with which to express himself. As he described it:

When I look at a word like *golovokruzheniye* [dizziness], I just can't understand it. All the letters—even parts of the word—are as meaningless to me as they would be to a child who'd never seen a primer or an alphabet. But soon something begins to stir in my mind. I look at the first letter *g* and wait until I remember how to pronounce it. Then I go on to the letter *o* and pronounce the whole syllable. Then I try to join it to the next syllable. I take a quick look at the next letter, wait a little, then quickly look at the letter o. While I'm looking at that letter the two letters to the left of it escape my vision—that is, I see only the letter o and two of the letters on the left. But the first two or three letters in the word are no longer visible. To put it more exactly, at that point I see only a gray mist in which spots, threads, and little bodies seem to shift and flicker back and forth.

Despite this difficulty, he decided to write a journal, describing what had occurred to him and his struggles to overcome the damage to his brain. He worked on this journal day after day for twenty-five years, struggling with every word and sentence. Sometimes it took him an entire day to write half a page. He first called his journal "The Story of a Terrible Brain Injury" but later changed it to 'I'll Fight On." His diary is now more than three thousand pages long.

I observed this patient for more than thirty years. The book about him is in no way an "imaginary portrait." Mr. Zassetsky exists. To write a portrait of him, I used portions of his journal to describe what it felt like to have such a wound. But the book also contains digressions in which I explained the psychological structure of the difficulties he was experiencing and how they were caused by the type of lesion he had suffered. So this book is not only a portrait but also an attempt to come closer to understanding some psychological facts through the use of neuropsychology.

There have been many times when I felt that I would very much like to write a third book, or even a short series of such books. I could describe a man with a complete loss of memory and all that happened to his personality as a result of this loss. Or I could write about a patient with a frontal lobe lesion which caused a complete breakdown of his ability to formulate goals and plans and how this had affected him. Until now such attempts have more often been made by writers, such as Alexander Green, the Russian writer, who wrote "Hell Lost and Regained," a short story describing a patient whose frontal lobes had been wounded. But this is only an "imaginary portrait," as is the Jorge Borges short story "Funes the Memorious," in which some of my observations of Sherashevsky are repeated.

To perform more research for a book of this kind would be very difficult for me. One has to find individuals with exceptional qualities—an overdevelopment of some trait or a breakdown of some primary function—which have caused a complete change of personality. Then one has to spend decades following up that "unimagined story," singling out decisive factors and step by step constructing the whole syndrome. Unfortunately, I do not have such an opportunity.

The only remaining possibility has been to turn to myself and describe "The Life of a Soviet Psychologist in Retrospect," bearing in mind that the components of such a story are far different from those of preceding books. There is no subject with exceptional abilities—I have none. Nor is there a specific capacity or a specific disaster. But there is the atmosphere of a life, beginning at that unique time which was the start of the Revolution. There is a period of exploration, the meeting with a genius and falling under his influence, and the series of deeds that a scholar could accomplish during a rather long life.

People come and go, but the creative sources of great historical events and the important ideas and deeds remain. That is perhaps the only excuse I had for writing this book.

# Epilogue:
# A Portrait of Luria

So I shall never waste my life-span in a vain useless hope, seeking what cannot be, a flawless man among us all who feed on the fruits of the broad earth. But I praise and love every man who does nothing base from free will. Against necessity, even gods do not fight.

—Simonides

LURIA'S AUTOBIOGRAPHY, as well as my introduction to it, were written in accord with Alexander Romanovich's philosophy that people are transitory, that only their ideas and actions are of enduring interest. In an important sense he was right. But as applied to the story of his own scientific life, this depersonalized view of ideas belies the substance of his theory of psychology as well as his view of the importance of social circumstances in shaping individual human achievements.

When my wife Sheila and I first read the manuscript that served as the foundation of this autobiography, we were forcefully struck by the omission of all personal information. The march of ideas and experiments are presented in a vacuum. In a series of exchanges by letter and in the course of several discussions that I held with Alexander Romanovich in the year prior to his death in 1977, I attempted to extract some details of the social and personal context of his work. This effort met with slight success. He manifested as little interest in his personal history as his autobiography suggests. But my curiosity would not permit me to let matters rest.

*189* . . .

To find out about Alexander Romanovich's career, I had to ask others. I learned a great deal from conversations with Lana Pimenovna Luria, his wife of forty years, with former students, and with colleagues. During my last visit to Moscow before Alexander Romanovich's death I also asked him to arrange a gathering of the small band of psychologists who had labored in the 1920s with him and Lev Vygotsky to construct a new, Soviet psychology. It was my hope that their reminiscences would spark his memory. Miraculously, all were alive. Six arrived for tea. In the course of the discussion I heard old women recite poems they had composed fifty years earlier in honor of the group's struggles with their detractors. Alexander V. Zaporozhets, only slightly junior to Alexander Romanovich, smiled broadly as he recalled the energetic way that Alexander Romanovich had organized their work and how he had proudly presented them to Vygotsky at their oral exams. These people had not forgotten, nor did they want the world to forget, what they had done and how they had struggled. I promised those people, Alexander Romanovich among them, that I would not forget, nor would I allow their efforts to be forgotten. I decided then to write this essay.

Because I lack training as an historian of science and society, and because only a limited amount of documentary material is available about both the life of Alexander Romanovich and Soviet psychology at the time, I cannot pretend to present a comprehensive account of his life and times to supplement the portrait provided by his autobiography. Excellent discussions of Soviet science are already available, particularly Loren Graham's *Science and Philosophy in the Soviet Union*. But very little of the personal flavor of what life and work were like for a Soviet psychologist comes through these scholarly treatises. To construct a picture of the precise conditions, the excitement, the fears, and the hopes that energized Alexander Romanovich's work through more than half a century of relentless hard work, I have supplemented this information with not only the limited documentary evidence but also details I cannot document, picked up in casual conversation.

In writing this essay, I could not escape the perspective and limitations of my own education and my own views concerning the quest for a more powerful and humane scientific psychology. Trained in the tradition of American learning theories of the 1950s, I arrived in Moscow ill prepared to understand the work of a man whose scientific, political, and philosophical ideas constituted a coherent world view very different from any I had previously encountered. And although styles of American academic theory and research in psychology have changed considerably in the past twenty years, they still differ from Soviet research and theory in their limited range and pragmatic focus.

The gulf that separates Soviet scientists of Alexander Romanovich's generation from American psychologists of mine cannot be overcome by ignoring its existence. Rather, sympathetic study of our respective overall goals, the history of our ideas, and the structure of our theories must be carried out with the differences very much in mind. Once the dimensions and contour of our misunderstandings have been discerned, rational attempts at rapprochement can be considered. In the present embryonic state of such activity, however, the impossibility of a complete and objective account of the life and work of a Soviet psychologist by an American psychologist should be as apparent to the reader as it is to me.

Faced with these difficulties, I begin the account where it began for me, with my first visit to Moscow in 1962. In that fall Sheila and I, fresh from graduate school at Indiana University, arrived in Moscow where I was to engage in a year of postdoctoral research with Alexander Romanovich. He was at his dacha on the day of our arrival, but he thoughtfully sent a former student and colleague who spoke rather good English to help us find our way to the university. The following afternoon we went to the Lurias' for tea. Alexander Romanovich introduced us to Lana Pimenovna and ushered us into the sitting room, which doubled as his bedroom. In excellent English he asked if we spoke Russian. "A little," I admitted. It was the last time we spoke together in English, although my skill in Russian never matched his in English.

In the course of the next hour we wrote a "scientific plan" which laid out my work for the year. Since I had arrived in Moscow with only the vague hope of learning about "semantic conditioning", or the study of conditioned responses to word meaning, the idea of committing myself to a concrete plan on my first full day in Russia was appalling. It was also necessary. The plan might be modified, but it could not be ignored. It was my first lesson in doing things in the Soviet style. Only as I learned how written plans could be modified to fit on-going needs did I come to appreciate Alexander Romanovich's own unique style of work.

The scientific plan disposed of, Alexander Romanovich turned to Sheila. What, he inquired, were her plans? And what did we intend to do besides study? Sheila was uncertain of her future, although eventually she studied at Moscow University's journalism school and, thanks to Alexander Romanovich's intervention, wrote for an English language newspaper. But we were both certain that we wanted to learn as much as possible about Russian culture.

This declaration pleased Alexander Romanovich greatly. Complaining of a former foreign student who had done nothing but study, he forthwith wrote out a "cultural plan" that was every bit as detailed as the scientific plan. We soon learned that Alexander Romanovich was a devotee of Central Asian art, a connoisseur of the opera and theater, and one of the world's most omniverous consumers of detective novels. We left the Luria apartment filled with cake, tea, and a strong sense of having encountered a whirlwind.

This impression was only reinforced by further experience. On Monday I found my way to Alexander Romanovich's laboratory in the Institute of Neurosurgery. There was a guest speaker that day, the physiologist Nicholas Bernshtein. His topic, mathematical models in psychology, surprised me because I had been taught that Soviet psychologists rejected quantification. My surprise quickly turned to distress when Alexander Romanovich introduced me as a mathematical psychologist and asked me to speak on recent developments in the field in the United States. I doubt if my audience learned anything, but under such unremitting pressure my fluency in Russian improved rapidly.

In the following months Alexander Romanovich graciously arranged for me to do the kinds of conditioned reflex experiments I had come to learn about. Although I soon discovered that he had ceased using this technique a decade earlier, my experiments were made part of a general series of investigations that his colleague Evgenia Homskaya was conducting. I worked as conscientiously as I could, little realizing how uninteresting my labors were to my host.

From time to time Alexander Romanovich would take me on rounds as he visited patients awaiting surgery or recovering from a recent operation at the Institute of Neurosurgery. The enormous respect he evoked was transferred to me, a youthful foreigner in an ill-fitting white laboratory jacket. I understood nothing of the significance of his clinical examinations, although I found the tasks that he set for patients and their responses an interesting curiosity.

My overwhelming impression of Alexander Romanovich during that year was of a man in a hurry. His appetite for work exhausted me. Even his lunch breaks were more than I could keep up with. On occasions when we lunched together, he would walk rapidly from his laboratory to a small coffee-shop near the institute. Although he was sixty years old at the time and I was only twenty-four, I found it difficult to keep in step. At the coffee shop he would then order two rolls and two scorchingly hot cups of coffee, which we ate standing at the counter. At least I ate and drank. Alexander Romanovich seemed to inhale the scorching coffee while I blew timidly on the glass to cool it. Leaving me to deal with my tender palate, he loped back to the laboratory, where I could catch up with him when I was ready.

## . . . *Epilogue*

At irregular intervals during the year he talked a little about his past and about his mentor, Vygotsky. He gave me copies of Vygotsky's recently reprinted works, urging me to study them. On one occasion he took me into his study and sat me down at a large, glass-covered table, then went to a bulging cabinet and brought out some bulky folders tied with string. Opening one, he began to tell me about a trip he had made to Central Asia many years ago to conduct psychological experiments. The unusual, not to say bizarre, responses that he had obtained from peasants in these experiments amused me, but I attached little significance to them at the time.

Nor could I make much of Vygotsky. He had been Luria's teacher, and Luria made it clear that he considered him a genius. But both Vygotsky's prose and the style of his thought defeated my attempts to understand Luria's admiration for him. I had read Vygotsky's *Thought and Language* as a graduate student, but except for some observations on concept learning in children, which at the time I knew nothing about, I could see little in his work to generate enthusiasm. Still, I was polite. I read what I could and listened. Alexander Romanovich did not push the topic unduly. He knew that he could only plant seeds of understanding and hope they would germinate. He also knew that the more seeds he sowed, the more likely that one would grow. He waited a long time.

In the years that followed I maintained contact with Alexander Romanovich and visited him on several more occasions. He was anxious to arrange for publication in English of a two-volume compendium of Soviet psychological research, and I agreed to help. At about the same time that my co-editor, Irving Maltzman, and I completed work on this project, I became the editor of *Soviet Psychology,* a journal of translations. Over the years I thus had several opportunities to read the work of Alexander Romanovich and the many other Soviet psychologists who grew to maturity before or shortly after World War II. Consistent with the traditions of my graduate training, I continued to be interested in the Soviet research using Pavlovian conditioning techniques. On my initial visit to Moscow I learned of research on the conditioning of sensory thresholds, of internal organs (which suggested an important approach to understanding psychosomatic symptoms) and of early adaptive responses in newborn infants.

Other lines of research were also intriguing. I learned of Soviet studies with chimpanzees that threw new light on Wolfgang Kohler's classic studies of insight, of interesting attempts to link methods of programed instruction to theories of mental development, and of unusual demonstrations of the human capacity to learn sensory abilities such as perfect pitch. I even succeeded in applying a little of this information in my own work. For example, when happenstance led me to do research in West Africa, I remembered Alexander Romanovich's work in Central Asia and arranged to replicate some of his observations.

What impresses me in retrospect is how little I understood about the key concepts and concerns of those whose work I studied. Finding individual experiment interesting, I selected an idea here, a technique there. But the threads that bound the individual elements escaped me. I often found myself totally bored by work that absorbed Alexander Romanovich. For example, he urged on me the work of Alexander Zaporozhets on the development of voluntary movement in children or the studies of Lydia Bozhovich on motivation in young school children. Yet I could make nothing of such global, "soft" topics. Alexander Romanovich seemed to see their connection with his clinical work or his studies of language and thought in children using Pavlovian conditioning techniques. But I could not.

I experienced the same difficulty in trying to reconcile different stages of Alexander Romanovich's own career. What did the cross-cultural work have to do with his work in the Institute of Neurosurgery? Why was he no longer doing conditioning experiments? Why, in his book about S. V. Sherashevsky, the man with an unusual memory, did he spend so much time discussing his personality when his memory was at issue?

When I tried to discuss these issues with Alexander Romanovich, I got little help. He would answer with formulas. Phases of work done long ago were treated as youthful aberrations, almost as accidents of personal history. Mention of his work in Central Asia quickly drifted into anecdotes about the food, the difficulties of travel, or the errors of Gestalt psychologists. His very early work using the combined motor method was reduced to "some experiments which created the first lie detector." Talk of Sherashevsky and his memory generated additional anecdotes. At the same time, Alexander Romanovich's steady pressure on me to read Vygotsky and Vygotsky's students continued. When I discovered some bygone tidbit of information, Alexander Romanovich would be pleased. But rarely did a small discovery unlock more than a little new information from the man within whom was held an entire history.

Then two projects began significantly to alter my understanding of the links between the many activities that had occupied Alexander Romanovich and his colleagues for so long. The first project was the publication in 1978 of selected essays of Vygotsky, which had not appeared previously in English. Alexander Romanovich had urged this undertaking on me almost from the beginning of our relationship. But as I did not understand Vygotsky well, I could see no point in it. Then, as part of a large publishing enterprise in which both old and new Soviet psychological monographs were to be published, I agreed in the early 1970s to see to it that two of Vygotsky's long essays would appear in English. The enterprise turned out to be an extremely difficult one, occupying the energies of three colleagues and myself over a period of several years. But it was crucial in allowing me to glimpse the vast terrain covered by Alexander Romanovich's view of psychology and society. In struggling to understand Vygotsky well enough to resolve our editorial group's different interpretations of his ideas, I slowly began to discern the enormous scope of his thinking. His goal had been no less than the total restructuring of psychological research and theory. This undertaking would never have occurred to me or, I suspect, to very many other psychologists of my generation as anything but a crackpot scheme. Yet Vygotsky was no crackpot, and his scheme was extremely interesting.

The second project was Alexander Romanovich's autobiography. It began as an outline for a documentary film about his work. But when he fell ill at the beginning of the project, he decided to turn the scenario into a full-blown intellectual autobiography. Having started in English because the film makers were American, he continued in English, and a rough manuscript emerged. Sheila and I began to edit the manuscript at the same time as I was working on the Vygotsky manuscript. The confluence of the two tasks was instrumental in helping me understand Alexander Romanovich's career.

Alexander Romanovich often spoke of his work as merely continuation of Vygotsky's. Although there were important similarities between their two approaches, the autobiography made it immediately apparent that the topics of concern to Alexander Romanovich at the beginning of his career differed from those to which he turned after meeting Vygotsky. To understand how Alexander Romanovich's career and thought developed, I had to go back to the books and ideas that stirred him when he was still a university student in Kazan. Many of the names were unfamiliar to me: Windelband, Rickert, Dilthey. Others I had heard about, or even read, but always from a different perspective: psychologists such as William James, Franz Brentano, and Kurt Lewin; writers and social thinkers such as Alexander Herzen, Nikolai Cherneshevsky, and Leo Tolstoy. I read, or reread, the work of these people, trying to imagine myself into Alexander Romanovich's mind as he pondered the social and political problems of his day.

Then I turned to the writings of Alexander Romanovich himself, beginning with the little monograph on psychoanalysis that he had published himself in 1922 just before leaving Kazan. I searched American libraries for long-forgotten articles of the 1920s and 1930s. Alexander Romanovich was a tenacious collector of his own writings. After I had learned enough to question him about a particular article, a copy, or the copy of a copy, would materialize in his study. Those early works, most of them published in limited editions or in small circulation journals, are now difficult to obtain, even in the Soviet Union.

I also read all of his writings available in English, beginning with the brief abstract describing his work in the Proceedings of the Ninth International Congress of Psychology held in New Haven in 1929. When I correlated the content and style of his writings with the general political and social controversies of the day, the otherwise disjointed, zigzag course of Alexander Romanovich's career began to make sense. His interest in psychoanalysis no longer appeared a curious anomaly in an otherwise single-minded career. His strong attraction to Vygotsky, his cross-cultural work in Central Asia, the Pavlovian style of his writings in the 1940s and early 1950s, and his apparent shifts of topic at frequent intervals, all took on the quality of an intricate piece of music with a few central motifs and a variety of secondary themes.

It is not known when the Luria family moved to Kazan, a major commercial center on the Volga southeast of Moscow. But Luria is a very old family name, which was associated in the sixteenth and seventeenth centuries with Jewish scholarship.

In the last decades of the nineteenth century, the Jews of Russia led lives that were as stringently regulated by the state as the tsarist government could manage. Travel, education, and work were all restricted. The severity of the restrictions varied with where one lived and how much money one had to evade them. These constraints affected the Luria family's educational and professional opportunities. When Alexander Romanovich's father, Roman Albertovich, was a young man, only 5 percent of the students in the University of Kazan were permitted to be Jewish. Those who failed to qualify in this tiny quota and who had the financial resources went abroad to Germany to study. It was a matter of family pride that Roman Albertovich had qualified and had completed medical school in Kazan.

But academic distinction did not guarantee work upon graduation. Roman Albertovich, after being invited to join the faculties of medicine in Kazan and St. Petersburg, was denied employment in both cases because he was a Jew. For a time he practiced medicine privately in the countryside near Kazan. Then he returned to the city to open a private office. Practice was difficult, because hospitals and clinics were closed to him.

While internal opportunities were restricted, travel abroad was not, so Roman Albertovich spent several summers in Germany, where he continued to study medicine. Whether or not Alexander Romanovich ever traveled to Germany with his father is not known, but German was the second language of the household, and Alexander Romanovich mastered it at an early age. By his own account nineteenth-century German political, social, and scientific ideas were very important in shaping his intellectual life prior to the Revolution.

Equally important to his intellectual development were the Russian intellectuals who wrote about the serious problems in tsarist Russia and who proposed solutions of varying degrees of radicalism. As a youth, Alexander Romanovich considered himself a follower of Tolstoy, whose works on social injustice in Russia had wide appeal at the turn of the century. In many of his writings, especially *War* and *Peace,* Tolstoy struggled to reconcile two conflicting approaches to history and the role of individual human effort in producing social change. One approach, popular among such intellectuals as Herzen, Cherneshevsky, and Marx, was to assume that history can be studied as a science in which general laws can be abstracted from the flux of small events and accidents that make up daily life. However attractive this idea, Tolstoy repeatedly chose the opposite notion that historical events can be understood only in terms of the complex interplay of individual decisions and human effort. Abstract notions such as "power" or "historical necessity" by their very nature obscure the reality they purport to describe. Tolstoy's efforts to reconcile these conflicting approaches came to naught with the Revolution, which swept aside his exhortations to reform. But the basic contradictions remained, because they were not the creatures of his imagination alone. In a different form, they were exactly the problems Alexander Romanovich found in the conflict between Dilthey and Wundt, between the "nomothetic" and the "idiographic" views of psychology. These paradoxes, the province of no one social science discipline, were the common uncertainty of all.

Against this background, the liberating effect of the Revolution on the Luria family was profound. Instead of having to struggle for years in a gymnasium in the hope of securing a place in the university, without any certainty that places would even be open, Alexander Romanovich was able to race through his education, molding it to his own expansive intellectual ambitions. Meanwhile his father, so long excluded from Russian professional life, was provided an outlet for his talents. First he was offered a position at the University of Kazan, where he helped to create a new postgraduate medical school program. From there he went to Moscow, where he became a leading organizer of medical education throughout the USSR.

By all reports, Roman Albertovich was a man of strong opinions who took an active interest in his son's career. The younger Luria, in search of direct links between his utopian socialist ideals and his professional life, entered the social science department at the University of Kazan. His father never approved of his choice of careers, wanting him to go into medicine instead. Their disagreement was long a matter of tension between them. Perhaps it was to placate his father that Alexander Romanovich maintained a connection with medical schools and medical psychology throughout the twenty-year period between his entrance to the university and his full-time commitment to medicine following the death of Vygotsky in 1934. But whatever their disagreements about career, father and son shared an interest in German medical science, particularly psychosomatic medicine. One of Alexander Romanovich's last accomplishments was to oversee the reissue in 1977 of a small monograph on psychosomatic medicine that his father had written decades earlier.

In the chaos that immediately followed the Revolution Alexander Romanovich simultaneously held down a research position in one institution, did graduate work in another, attended medical school part-time, and ran tests of therapy on mentally ill patients. He also started a journal, organized a commune for wayward adolescents, directed a psychoanalytic discussion group, and published his own study of psychoanalysis. The contrast between these diverse activities and the limited possibilities for professional fulfillment that existed before the Revolution reveals the fundamental source of Alexander Romanovich's strong identification with the Revolution and the party which organized it. An activist down to his toes, he was set free by the Revolution. It gave him life. In return, he applied all of his energy to realizing the hopes and ideals that had been liberated in October 1917.

The situation that greeted Alexander Romanovich in Moscow was a challenge. Kornilov, who had succeeded in removing the prerevolutionary director of the Institute of Psychology in 1923, seemed to have a free hand in molding a Marxist, Soviet psychology. The similarity between Kornilov's and Luria's uses of the reaction time experiment gave them reason to think that they were at the beginning of a fruitful collaborative relationship.

Once in Moscow, Alexander Romanovich took up his research where he had left off in Kazan. The work proceeded on two fronts. First, he initiated a major series of experiments designed to perfect the combined motor method for diagnosing the way in which emotions organize, and disorganize, voluntary behavior. His audaciousness in this enterprise was astounding in light of the present-day atmosphere surrounding psychological experimentation. Nowhere is there an account of how the twenty-one year old Luria and his equally youthful companion Alexey Leontiev managed to get permission to pull students out of the line where they were awaiting interrogation by university authorities. Perhaps they managed the feat informally. Even more puzzling is how they convinced the criminal prosecutor to allow them to interrogate murder suspects.

An irony in this work was their naive good faith in the benign outcome of the research. When Horsely Gannt translated Alexander Romanovich's *The Nature of Human Conflicts,* he referred to the authorities' interrogation of Moscow University students as a "cleansing." Not until the 1930s did the procedure in question come to be known as a purge. The shadow of that word was very dim as Alexander Romanovich set out to do his work. Instead, before him loomed the notion of a unified science of man in which the distinction between laboratory and everyday life was rendered irrelevant.

To create such a science, he needed to develop its theoretical underpinnings in addition to developing experimental techniques. Alexander Romanovich saw in an experimental version of psychoanalysis the promise of an approach which would bridge the experimental-objective, but arid, research growing out of German structural psychology and the humanistic descriptive psychology of Dilthey. But what this formulation left out, and what conditions in Moscow now demanded, was a way of linking psychological and sociohistorical theory as embodied in the writings of Marx and Engels. Whatever the strengths or weaknesses of a psychological theory, its eventual acceptance depended heavily on questions of methodology. In Soviet parlance, "methodology" referred to the assumptions and logic of the overall approach to the subject. No psychological theory that failed to take Marxism as a starting point could succeed.

In the winter of 1924 in an article entitled "Psychoanalysis as a Theory of Monistic Psychology," Alexander Romanovich made his first contribution to the debate on how to create a properly Marxist psychology. Psychoanalysis and Marxism, he argued, share four important suppositions. First, they both hold that the world is a single system of material processes of which human life, and psychological processes in particular, are only one manifestation. Second, they both hold that the philosophical and scientific principles that apply to the material world apply to man as well. As Alexander Romanovich phrased it, both psychoanalysis and dialectical materialism require one "to study objectively . . . the true relations among perceivable events; and this means to study them not abstractly, but just as they are in reality." Both approaches also require that events be studied "in such a way that the knowledge we acquire will help us later to exert an active influence on them." And finally, both approaches require that events be studied dynamically in the process of changing: the interacting influences of man on his environment and the environment on man must always be kept in view" (Luria, 1925, pp. 8–10).

In the same article Alexander Romanovich defined the major shortcoming of psychoanalytic study as its failure to consider the influence of the social environment in shaping individual psychological processes. Although he promised to take up this topic again, the promise went unfulfilled for two major reasons. First, in 1924 he met Vygotsky, who had a far broader view of psychology as a social and natural science than Alexander Romanovich had yet imagined. Second, in the Soviet Union psychoanalytic ideas were increasingly considered anti-Marxist.

American scientists have long held the stereotype that articles by Soviet psychologists begin with an obligatory bow to Marx, Engels, and perhaps Pavlov, then go on to the real substance of the topic. The implication is that such philosophical framing is irrelevant to the scientist's work. There have been periods in the history of the Soviet Union when this was indeed the case. Alexander Romanovich was himself by no means immune to pressures to make his views conform to political and philosophical requirements, the distinction between political policy and philosophy being one that is not always easy to maintain in Soviet science. However, it would be a mistake to interpret the inclusion of Marxism in Soviet psychology in the 1920s as the reflection of political pressure. Quite the opposite spirit seems to have motivated those who engaged in the many-sided debate over the future direction of Soviet psychology. There was uncertainty, and there was sharp disagreement; but there was also enthusiasm and optimism.

In psychology, the initial discussions of Marxism in the 1920s were characterized by what I call a "conjunctive" approach. Each scholar—including Chelpanov, whose Wundtian orientation made him an unlikely candidate—explained how his brand of psychology was consistent with Marxist principles, and here I include Alexander Romanovich. Points of contact were noted between Marxism and the psychological theory, be it Kornilov's reactology, Bekhterev's reflexology, or Luria's psychoanalysis, and their interdependence was argued. But all the discussions had an ad hoc quality, for it was unclear whether the wedding of a particular psychological theory and Marxism would generate new kinds of research, let along form the basis for a wholly new approach to psychology. It was in precisely this respect that Vygotsky's approach to psychology and Marxism was distinctive. He held that a new kind of psychology could be *derived* from Marxist principles.

The volume *Psychology and Marxism,* edited by Kornilov in 1925, reveals the difference between Alexander Romanovich's and Vygotsky's approaches at the time. Luria's Marxism was based on the peripheral Marxist writings with obvious psychological implications, such as Marx's *Theses on Feuerbach* or Engel's *Anti-Dühring.* Vygotsky began with *Das Capital.* When Engels' *Dialectics of Nature* appeared in 1925, Vygotsky immediately incorporated it into his thinking. Whatever other shortcomings Vygotsky's thinking may have had, opportunistic parroting of Marxism was not one of them. As he remarked: "I don't want to discover the nature of mind by patching together a lot of quotations. I want to find how science has to be built, to approach the study of mind having learned the whole of Marx's *method*" (Vygotsky, 1978, p. 8).

Despite initial differences of emphasis, Alexander Romanovich was attracted to Vygotsky in part because he possessed a more comprehensive view of the relation between Marxism and psychology. Vygotsky's approach pointed the way to an all-inclusive study of man in nature and in society, which subsumed Alexander Romanovich's previous work. Although he had always been concerned with the larger social forces that organize individual psychological processes, Alexander Romanovich had only succeeded in developing techniques for the study of individual motivations and actions. In his modifications of psychoanalytic method through the use of the combined motor method he may have provided one means of bridging laboratory precision and clinical complexity. But society was conspicuously missing from his work. He acknowledged this shortcoming when he promised to explore the applications of psychoanalytic theory to problems of social determinism. Vygotsky's approach, which gave him such an analysis as a derivation from Marxism, was a gift not to be overlooked.

Alexander Romanovich, Vygotsky, and Leontiev began meeting regularly in the mid-1920s to work out the new Soviet psychology. Their program proceeded simultaneously on several fronts. At the level of theory they reviewed major developments over the preceding fifty years of psychology, sociology, and biological theory. Vygotsky and Luria read German, French, and English. Leontiev read only French, which became his specialty among the group. What they read they also wrote about. Both Luria and Vygotsky were prolific writers. They published many articles summarizing important lines of foreign work in the late 1920s and early 1930s. They also promoted the translation of books, for which they wrote prefaces interpreting foreign ideas.

In addition to analyzing western European and American authors, they studied the major pre- and postrevolutionary Russian social and biological thinkers. Both the linguist A.A. Potebnya and the biologist V.A. Vagner influenced Vygotsky and, through him, Alexander Romanovich who referred to Potebnya's work in his last book on language and the brain. In the 1920s no Soviet psychologist could ignore Pavlov, though he was by no means accorded the role of supreme arbiter of Soviet psychology that he would acquire in the 1950s. Rather the "troika"—as Vygotsky, Luria, and Leontiev regarded themselves—accorded Pavlov a restricted role in psychological theory and had the temerity to question the generality of his physiological theory as it applied to integrated behavior. This critical attitude came through clearly in *The Nature of Human Conflicts,* where Alexander Romanovich rejected the "telephone switchboard" analogy of the brain, which he identified with Pavlov, opting instead for a "systems" approach which he identified with the Karl Lashley. At the same time, Pavlov's contribution to a physiological theory of mind was acknowledged, and his experimental studies of conflict and neurosis were important to Alexander Romanovich's thinking.

Initially the troika, located as they were in the Institute of Psychology, borrowed ideas from Kornilov's reactology. But that narrow framework could not contain them. As their ideas branched out, so did they. In 1927–1928, while continuing to hold positions in Kornilov's institute, the troika became associated with the psychology laboratory at the Institute of Communist Education, and Vygotsky began to put together the Institute of Defectology, where the development of anomalous children was studied.

In addition to surveying and criticizing existing schools of psychology, the troika began to train students in their own style of thinking and research. Forced to the conclusion that their new theory required new methods, they used a small but enthusiastic group of students to try out their ideas. They were joined by the "pyatorka," or group of five, including L.I. Bozhovich, R.E. Levina, N.G. Morozova, L.S. Slavina, and Alexander Zaporozhets. These students, several of whom would become prominent in Soviet psychology following World War II, conducted their work directly under Luria's guidance. As they later related to me, Luria, Vygotsky, and Leontiev would meet to discuss a set of issues and speculate on how to create experimental models of them. Alexander Romanovich would interpret the discussion for the students, who in turn conducted pilot studies. In the main this work was aimed at constructing concrete models of the idea that adult thought is mediated by culturally elaborated "instruments of thought." Vygotsky's experiments on the idea that language is the major adult means of mediating thought produced the best-known results of the period, first reported fully in his introduction to Piaget's *Language and Thought of the Child*. An entire year was also spent studying children's growing ability to represent thought in schematic pictures. Luria himself conducted studies of protowriting activities, showing how very young children come to understand the mediated nature of remembering by using marks on paper long before they learn the formal written code for spoken language.

Although centered in psychology, Alexander Romanovich's curiosity about human nature was virtually boundless. He and Vygotsky, for example, met regularly with Sergei Eisenstein to discuss ways in which the abstract ideas that formed the core of historical materialism could be embodied in visual images projected upon the movie screen. By happenstance Zaporozhets, who had been an actor in the Ukraine before going to Moscow and had been recommended to Sergei Eisenstein, eventually ended up a psychologist. At the end of the 1920s he played the role of psychology's "ear" in the world of film, attending Eisenstein's discussions, which he reported to Vygotsky and Luria. Eisenstein enlisted his psychologist friends' help in solving not only the difficult problem of translation between verbal and visual concepts but also the empirical problem of assessing success. With their aid he constructed questionaires for audiences composed variously of students, workers, and peasants, to determine if they had understood his images as he intended. It is a measure of the breadth of his interests that, for Alexander Romanovich, the relation between modes of representing ideas and modes of thought was no less important in the cinema than in the laboratory.

During the last half of the 1920s Alexander Romanovich continued to study adults by elaborating on the applicability of the combined motor method as a technique for probing the workings of complex behavior. But more and more of his energies went into tracing the rise of organized behavior in the history of the individual and human history. Simultaneously he began to explore the dissolution of behavior under conditions of trauma and disease. Through it all, he increasingly had to defend his work against charges that he borrowed uncritically from non-Soviet sources.

Little of Luria's thought during this period is available in English. Read in the proper way, *The Nature of Human Conflicts*, spanning the period 1924–1930, is a unique source of information; but read in isolation from his 1925 article on psychoanalysis or the early articles influenced by Vygotsky, this book seems opaque because of its many theoretical positions. Three articles, one each by Vygotsky, Leontiev, and Luria, which were submitted to the *American Journal of Genetic Psychology* in 1928, contain formulations of their theorizing at that early date, along with descriptions of experimental procedures.

Particularly important in the light of later controversies was the fact that they saw a significant relation between the cognitive development of the child, which they referred to as the cultural development of the child, and the evolution of human culture. The same notion can be found in *The Nature of Human Conflicts* where Luria approvingly cites the custom of drumming as an accompaniment to farm work in primitive groups to show how people at an earlier stage of culture rely on an external mediator to maintain their attention in a manner analogous to the way adults in "civilized" societies maintain the attention of young children. This analogue between cultural evolution and individual development was very much a part of early twentieth-century developmental psychology. It was explicit in the writings of Lucien Levy-Bruhl, who influenced Piaget and the German developmental psychologist Heinz Werner, both of whom were known to Luria in the mid-1920s. It was also compatible with the general idea, which the troika had been pursuing, that development is characterized by the evolution of ever more complex forms of mediated behavior. Further explorations of the developmental analogy were made in *Studies in the History of Behavior* by Vygotsky and Luria, published in 1930. The dangers of a strong interpretation of the developmental analogy were made very clear by one reviewer: "These authors consider a primitive still not a human being . . . Cannibals, Indians, etc., are not primitives from our point of view, but people whose culture is not a reflection of biological capacities (as Vygotsky and Luria assert) but the result of specific means of production" (Frankel, 1930). Frankel went on to the mistaken claim that the sociohistorical theory implied that once a child had passed the chimpanzee-like stage, he or she progressed to the stage of primitive man, whose illiteracy and "weak" memory were the reflection of biologically determined capacities.

Other lines of research into which Luria was led in the last half of the 1920s were natural extensions of ideas being developed as part of the sociohistorical approach to the study of psychological processes. Developmental studies, whether of individual children or of entire cultural groups, were only one aspect of the general conception. Just as important were studies of the dissolution of psychological processes, since disease and trauma undo what evolution and cultural experience have helped to construct. Here Alexander Romanovich's family tradition atuned him especially to the theoretical possibilities of problems that might otherwise have been considered purely medical.

One of his earliest statements on the possibility of a fruitful interplay between psychology and medicine appeared in 1929 in the article "Psychology and the Clinic." In it he reviewed contemporary psychology, including not only Pavlov's work on experimental neuroses and his own work on the combined motor method, but also such western European work as Jung, Freud, and Adler's on psychogenic disorders, Binet's on differential psychology, and Piaget's on the development of thought. One of his central messages was the possibility of using clinical methods to conduct scientific research on human behavior. Thus, while doubtful about the therapeutic claims of the psychotherapists or about the basis for alternative personality theories, he saw in their attacks on the classical laboratory methods a common, healthy movement toward a psychology that would be both scientific and relevant to medical practice: "Little by little the abstract and statistical psychology of Wundt has been reborn in a fundamental way; it has approached the concrete tasks of life and willingly or not it has begun to overcome the mechanistic nature of previous natural sciences. With the new content have come new principles and a new method" (Luria, 1929, p. 51).

The troika's attack on problems of the dissolution of behavior proceeded on several fronts. Leontiev carried out studies with mentally retarded subjects, first using the combined motor method and later the mediated memory task, which was one of the first standard experimental techniques devised by the socio-historical school. Vygotsky had a long-standing interest in the retarded from his early days as a schoolteacher. Working with his collaborator L.S. Sakharov, he developed a concept formation task which he used in studies of both mentally retarded and schizophrenic subjects.

At some point in these investigations, Alexander Romanovich obtained a copy of Henry Head's classic description of thought disorders associated with aphasia. Not only the general phenomena but his very terminology seemed to match perfectly Vygotsky's notion that thought is crucially mediated by language, so that if language is lost, thought should regress to a "prelanguage, unmediated" state. According to Head, in aphasics the direct perception of the likeness of two figures is "complicated by failure to record their similarity by means of a name," whereas in normal persons "the power of recording likeness and difference by means of a symbol enormously extends the power of conceptual thinking and underlies all scientific classification" (Head, 1926, p. 525). The great potential which brain disorders held for their approach to the study of the mind induced both Luria and Vygotsky to enter medical school, adding clinical studies to their already full schedules.

The period 1925–1930 was one of incredible enthusiasm and excitement. All of the participants in the nascent psychological movement felt themselves part of a vanguard. Far from experiencing resistance, the most prevalent response they reported was indifference. Perhaps the major exception was the response to psychoanalysis. During this period, articles critical of Freudian theory appeared in both theoretical journals and *Pravda*.

This criticism came from Luria's friends and colleagues, including Sapir, as well as from his antagonists. As a result, in 1927 Alexander Romanovich resigned from his position as Secretary of the Soviet Psychoanalytic Society.

Despite this pressure, Alexander Romanovich, who had plenty of reason to join in the renunciation of Freudian theory as a result of his own theoretical work, failed to engage in denunciations. Instead, he confined his references to psychoanalytic research to purely methodological and empirical points. For example, his development of the combined motor method, which dominates *The Nature of Human Conflicts,* was conceived as a kind of neo-Freudian experimental reconciliation of experimental-explanatory and clinical-descriptive approaches to the study of mind and emotion. Although Freud and Jung are barely mentioned in the monograph, this fact is not an egregious slight but rather, considering the pressure to expunge them altogether, a stubborn insistence that the historical record not be completely obliterated.

The same characteristic of Alexander Romanovich's writing was in evidence a decade later when he contributed an article on psychoanalysis to Volume 47 of the *Great Soviet Encyclopedia.* In a more or less straightforward description of the major concepts and history of psychoanalysis, he asserts that the psychoanalytic method for studying unconscious drives is a central contribution. His major criticism of psychoanalysis as a general system is that it errs in giving too much weight to biological drives in the determination of behavior, underplaying the significance of historically evolved cultural factors. These ideas, which were apparent in his thinking as early as 1925, were fully consistent with the viewpoint he had developed in conjunction with Vygotsky.

Around 1930, public attention veered suddenly to the field of psychology, including the hitherto unnoticed Vygotskian school. As a result, constraints were placed on much of the work in progress. In discussions held by educational and scientific research organizations throughout the country, all existing schools of psychology and their participant members came under scrutiny. Psychological research was assessed in terms of its contribution to scientific-Marxist goals.

The attitude of Alexander Romanovich and his colleagues toward this controversy is unclear. In the beginning they may have viewed it as little more than a continuation of a debate over the course of Soviet science that had lasted throughout all of their careers. Certainly they did not back away from the positions they had adopted, although there is evidence that they were not insensitive to what they viewed as serious criticism. In response to the situation, Vygotsky continued to refine his understanding of developmental abnormalities and methods to deal with them, at the same time that his basic treatment of mediated behavior, especially his view of the relation between signs and meaning, underwent important change. For his part Alexander Romanovich continued in his role as data gatherer, embarking on two projects designed to test, for almost the first time, the implications of the cultural-historical theory. These were the expeditions to Central Asia and the massive study of the roles of culture and heredity in shaping mental development in twins.

Perhaps the clearest institutional response to the varied pressures was the group's effort to found their own department of psychology in 1930. Failing to find an institution in Moscow that would accept the entire group and allow them to set up a curriculum and research program, they accepted an invitation from the Psychoneurological Institute at Kharkov University to form a new department of psychology under its auspices. Luria, Leontiev, Vygotsky, Zaporozhets, and Bozhovich all moved to Kharkhov. But the group did not stay together for long. Soon Alexander Romanovich was back in Moscow, where he carried out a variety of developmental studies. Vygotsky traveled regularly between Kharkhov, Moscow, and Leningrad until his death from tuberculosis in 1934. Only Leontiev, Zaporozhets, and Bozhovich remained, forming a distinctive school of psychology. In time distinguished new figures such as P.I. Zinchenko and P. Y. Galperin were added to its ranks. But the dream of a unified department was never realized.

In the spring of 1931 Alexander Romanovich and a number of staff members from the Institute of Psychology in Moscow traveled to Samarkand where they held a two-month seminar with members of the Uzbek Research Institute to design an expedition into remote areas of Uzbekistan. The purpose of the expedition, as explained in an article in the American journal *Science* upon completion of the first trip in the summer of 1931, was "to investigate the variations in thought and other psychological processes of people living in a very primitive economic and social environment, and to record those changes which develop as a result of the introduction of higher and more complex forms of economic life and the raising of the general cultural level." A great variety of topics were investigated, including several forms of cognitive activity, the perception of printed material, personality formation, and self-analysis. A similar expedition was planned for the following summer, "to continue the same work. It will have an international character, as it is planned to invite foreign psychologists to participate" (Luria, 1931, pp. 383–384). When the second expedition set out, the Gestalt psychologist Kurt Koffka was a member. Although Koffka became seriously ill shortly after arriving in Central Asia and had to return home, Alexander Romanovich and his colleagues completed the second summer of experimentation. This work, begun with such high hopes and high ideals, led to consequences that were far more dangerous and complex than anyone at the time anticipated.

Alexander Romanovich's enthusiasm for the research was enormous. He and Vygotsky were particularly anxious to show that Gestalt perceptual principles were the result not of enduring characteristics of the brain but of ways of perceiving intimately bound up with culturally transmitted meanings of objects. One of their first experiments demonstrated the virtual absence of classical visual illusions, which caused Alexander Romanovich to wire excitedly to his friend and teacher Vygotsky: "The Uzbekis have no illusions!" The relish with which he anticipated reporting these findings to his German colleagues is easy to imagine.

*. . . Epilogue*

Unfortunately, Alexander Romanovich's work proved problematic. The central issue of debate in 1932–1933, as foreshadowed in Frankel's reactions to *Studies in the History of Behavior,* concerned his concept of culture and the nature of the link between culture and individual development. In Alexander Romanovich's description of his expeditions and in all of his other writings at this time, his use of the term *culture* derived from a tradition of European, especially German, thought in the nineteenth century. Culture in the tradition of the German Romantics was associated with the progressive accumulation of the best characteristics of mankind in science, art, and technology, all those accomplishments that reflected mankind's increasing control over nature and his freedom from domination by reflex, instinct, and blind custom. This sense of culture, which is still extant, orders human societies on an evolutionary scale. Those societies with writing systems and advanced technologies are considered more cultured or more advanced than societies without such tools. Since the cultural-historical school held that the development of the higher psychological processes proceeded according to the culturally organized means of intellectual activity, among which writing was considered primary, it followed that there would be qualitative differences between "cultured" and "uncultured" adults with respect to their higher psychological functions.

Depending upon just how cultural development was conceived and how cultural mechanisms were thought to become individual mechanisms of thought, this style of theorizing could be used to justify a number of conclusions about the mental and cultural status of Central Asian peasants in the period around 1930. Alexander Romanovich's work had a dual emphasis. Sometimes he stressed the fact that different cultural traditions led to qualitative differences in the kinds of higher psychological functions in people. But overall, his writings emphasized the "improved" status of people following the advent of literacy and modern technology.

For a combination of reasons, including negative value judgments that could be read into his work and loose identification of his research methods with mindless IQ-testing, Alexander Romanovich's studies met with strong, not to say vitriolic, disapproval when he began to report his results. Whatever the scientific justification for criticism of the cultural-historical theory, the mixing of scientific and political criticism in 1934 had far-reaching implications. For example, I could not find any report of the results of the Central Asian expeditions prior to the late 1960s, save in an abstract in the *Journal of Genetic Psychology*.

Understanding little of this background but knowing of the existence of Alexander Romanovich's Central Asian data, I began to discuss it with him in the summer of 1966. At that time I had conducted some cross-cultural cognitive experiments in Liberia and was interested in seeing if the phenomena he reported could be replicated there. For an hour a day over the course of two months we worked our way through his meticulous notes. Seeing the volume of data he had collected and realizing that they would disappear forever if he did not organize and report them, I urged him to publish a monograph about that long-ago research. He was very reluctant to discuss the matter, feeling that the time was not ripe. But in 1968 he published a brief article about the research in a volume on history and psychology. Encouraged by the reactions it evoked, he dug into his files and produced a slim monograph on the subject which he felt lived up to current standards of scientific research. In the changed conditions of the early 1970s, this work was accepted as a positive contribution to Soviet science.

At almost the same time in the 1930s when he was engaged in controversy over his Central Asian work, Alexander Romanovich was participating in another ambitious undertaking which was to place yet another cloud over his career. In 1925, a medical-biological institute was founded in Moscow, whose task was to apply modern biological science, particularly genetics, to problems of medicine. The institute was directed by S.G. Levit, an academician of international standing, who was an early supporter of the Bolshevik party. It included as part of its research plan a study of the development of identical and fraternal twins. The controversy over genetic theory which was later to inundate Soviet biology had not yet taken shape, but the highly political nature of the institute's research, aimed at demonstrating the mechanisms that could be used for creating the Soviet citizen of the future, did not need a Lysenko to make it visible.

The point of view that Alexander Romanovich brought to this work was directly shaped by his cultural-historical theory. He expected a simple dominance of neither genetic nor socializing factors in his studies of twins; rather, he expected "nature and nurture" to interact in a pattern that would lead to the eventual dominance of "nurture" in the form of culturally organized, higher psychological functions. Few reports of this work have survived. Alexander Romanovich coauthored two or three articles for the proceedings of the institute in 1935–1936, and he published a partial account in the now defunct American journal *Character and Personality,* which was edited by the psychometrician Charles Spearman. But except for a brief early report in a Georgian journal and an equally brief report in *Problems of Psychology* in 1962, the developmental comparisons carried out on a massive scale have been lost, along with any report of the effects of different kinds of early educational experience on later development. Only a little monograph co-authored with F.A. Yudovich, which did not appear until 1956, offers some insight into the broad pedagogical aims and accomplishments of the work. Clearly, the data on twins was very controversial in 1935 and 1936. The controversy never had a chance to clear, since work at the institute was brought to a close in 1936.

By the middle of that year, Soviet psychology was a virtual minefield of explosive issues and broken theories. Every existing movement in the field had been examined and found wanting, including Vygotsky's. Of course, Soviet psychology, like any other science, had its share of mediocre figures. Moreover, enormous sacrifices were being asked of the Soviet people, and science was expected to make its contribution. In the early postrevolutionary days in particular a great deal of faith had been placed in the power of psychology to transform schools and clinics in line with the aspirations of the Soviet leaders.

Although the present political climate in the United States provides a reassuring contrast with events in the Soviet Union in the mid-1930s, the attitude of important American government figures toward science in general and psychology in particular is not so different as to defy comparison. Consider, for example, the attacks on basic research in the social sciences by members of the Senate who question whether tax dollars should be spent on identifying the behavioral basis of material bonding or the social forces that organize dialect variation. In many such cases the researchers in question have proven scientific merit and deep social commitment. But they, like Soviet psychologists of the 1930s, are vulnerable to criticism because they cannot fulfill society's highest expectations of their work. The pressures shaping budgets and priorities of American psychological research today reflect a noticable kinship with the pressures faced by Alexander Romanovich and his colleagues many years ago.

Just as all the different movements within Soviet psychology were scrutinized by 1936, so too was the work of each psychologist, including those on the staff at the institute. In this highly charged atmosphere, one voice spoke up against the blanket condemnation of Soviet psychology: "It must be said that Professor Luria, as one of the representatives of the cultural-historical theory, also did not consider it necessary to admit his mistaken theoretical position in front of this meeting" (G.F., 1936, p. 94). Yet at the time there was no real forum for Alexander Romanovich's point of view. Obvious lines of attack on the problems that had preoccupied him were closed, and nothing could be gained by continuing to protest the course of events.

It was in such circumstances that Alexander Romanovich decided to return to medical school as a full-time student. Perhaps because he had taken medical courses on and off for almost twenty years, he quickly completed his medical training and went to work in a neurological clinic. Blocked in the attempt to develop his ideas in developmental psychology or cross-cultural research, he picked up that strand of his theory which hypothesized specific changes accompanying the loss of language and began what was to be more than thirty years of research on the cerebral basis of those higher psychological processes that he had been studying in children. This was not to be the last shift in activity resulting from changes in social conditions, but it was the most timely. When World War II broke out, there could be no question of the relevance of Alexander Romanovich's neuropsychological research.

Just how important Alexander Romanovich's conversion into a neuropsychologist was for his future career is virtually impossible to judge. There is no doubt that from the beginning he viewed this activity as yet another extension of the cultural-historical theory into a new empirical domain. Even while studying in medical school and then working as a physician, he continued to be active in psychology to the limited degree that such activity was possible, as in the article on psychoanalysis that he contributed to the *Great Soviet Encyclopedia*. By this time in the late 1930s, self-criticism was absolutely essential, yet in this article Alexander Romanovich managed to say everything he believed to be true and to be self-critical at the same time. Each paragraph about important contributors to Soviet psychology contains a brief, factual account of their ideas, carefully differentiated from the criticism. When he turns to the important concepts of psychology, his own views shine through clearly.

The war provided him with an enormous store of data concerning the brain and psychological processes, which he reported on in a series of papers and monographs. When Moscow was no longer threatened, he returned from the Ural Mountains, expecting to continue this line of work at the Institute of Neurosurgery. For a while he continued his work uninterrupted. But once again, history intervened.

In 1948 when the Cold War was in force, Soviet science was again racked by a series of upheavals, the best known of which was the controversy over genetics. Less well-known in the United States was the debate throughout many branches of Soviet science, including physics and linguistics, which mixed issues of national and international politics with scientific philosophy and day-to-day scientific practices. In the midst of this controversy, in early 1950, Alexander Romanovich was dismissed from the Institute of Neurosurgery.

Although matters seemed grim, they were not hopeless. As a full member of the Academy of Pedagogical Sciences, Alexander Romanovich was entitled to a job in one if its institutions. Almost immediately he picked himself up and began where he had left off, providing the empirical basis for Vygotsky's theory. Blocked from work with children, the nonliterate, or the brain-damaged, he turned to an area close to Vygotsky's heart, the mentally retarded. Nor was he alone in this enterprise. Several of his students from the 1920s, including Levina and Morozova, were working at the Institute of Defectology, which was to become his scientific home for almost a decade.

In many respects, the decade from 1948 to 1958 must have been one of the most difficult periods in Alexander Romanovich's life. He was not only working in his third or fourth area of scientific specialization but was experiencing difficult social and scientific restraints as well. It was a time when science was emphasized as one of the basic factors shaping Soviet society, and when Pavlov's work was held up as a model to be adhered to strictly. The situation was peculiarly trying for Alexander Romanovich because he agreed with a good deal in the Pavlovian scientific program, especially the necessity for building psychological theories on a sound physiology of brain activity. But agreement on such matters of basic principle was not sufficient. A measure of the seriousness and narrow-mindedness of this "Pavlovian revolution from the top" can be gleaned from comparing Alexander Romanovich's self-criticism at meetings in the early 1950s with his analogous statements on similar occasions in the 1930s. No longer could he offer careful expositions of his basic views set apart from critical evaluation. Now he had to state that his work on aphasia and the restoration of brain function was deeply flawed because of his failure to apply Pavlovian teaching, without specifying which branch of Pavlovian physiology could or did apply. He also had to praise the work of men like A.G. Ivanov-Smolensky whose interpretation of the combined motor method he could not abide (and which he freely criticized later). His only freedom was to be self-critical where it counted least. Thus, he could say with a clear conscience, for it represented his highest aspirations, that "only with the help of detailed physiological analysis of even the most complex psychological facts can we construct a materialist theory of man's psychological processes; and this applies to both medical and general psychology" (Luria, 1950, p. 633).

In this highly charged atmosphere, Alexander Romanovich could continue his research within the Institute of Defectology, but he could not openly pursue Vygotsky's line. His solution to these constraints was an ingenious one. He returned to the combined motor method which has the general structure of a conditioning experiment and carried out research on the transition from elementary psychological functions, which according to his theory could be handled within a Pavlovian framework, to higher psychological functions, which existing Pavlovian theory could not encompass. Moreover, he concentrated on the role of language in producing the transition from elementary to higher psychological processes. This choice of foci was fortunate, because toward the end of his life Pavlov had begun to speculate on ways in which the principles of conditioning could be extended to account for human language. A very old man at the time, Pavlov made it clear that this was one area in which his theory needed to be elaborated; it was not *terra cognita*. Hence, anyone wishing to tackle it could do so with minimum need to ensure conformity to physiological theory laid down in the 1920s on the basis of Pavlov's research with dogs.

Reading Alexander Romanovich's publications during this period is unnerving to me now. Always an excellent student of languages, he used the Pavlovian argot like a true expert. In some cases I am relatively certain that he believed it a fruitful way to describe and explain the phenomena, as in his experiments with mentally retarded children. But in other cases, as in his study of the twins who developed their own language, he certainly believed Pavlovian theory to be inappropriate. In such cases, it is necessary to translate what he is saying into his own theoretical language. Sadly, in the 1950s many young Soviet psychologists could not make the translation, nor could I.

By the time my wife and I reached Moscow in 1962, these events were largely behind Alexander Romanovich. It was not that the search for a Marxist psychology had ceased to be of concern or that fierce arguments over the proper theoretical and methodological approaches to the study of mind had been settled. Rather, the terms of the discussion were now a matter of normal debate, with no one dictating a single acceptable route.

In 1955, after a twenty-year hiatus, psychology had been allowed its own journal, *Problems of Psychology,* with Kornilov as its editor. Both Alexander Romanovich and Leontiev sat on the editorial board. Then in 1956 the first edition of Vygotsky's collected works was published, with a long preface by the two remaining members of his troika, for the first time making his ideas available to a generation of students who scarcely knew his name.

In the late 1950s Alexander Romanovich once again began to travel abroad. The large glass cabinet in Lana Pimenovna's sitting room filled with mementos from Japan, England, western Europe, and the United States, to complement her collection of Soviet and eastern European memorabilia. Wherever Alexander Romanovich went, he lectured, often in the language of his hosts. He appeared before the world's psychological community in many different guises. At first he appeared as a developmental psychologist in the Pavlovian tradition, a specialist on mental retardation whose conditioning experiments on the properties of the "second signal system" were in tune with the theorizing then in progress in many different laboratories around the world. Later, when he returned to the Institute of Neurosurgery, another Luria appeared on the world scene, this time an aphasiologist with distinctive techniques for restoring damaged brain functions and a typology of aphasia that appeared somewhat askew of current ideas on the topic available outside the USSR.

In both his lecturing abroad and his publishing activities at home, Alexander Romanovich was working to reconstruct and make available the contents of Soviet psychology, which represented his own life's work, but which the vagaries of time had made inaccessible. The enormity of the task sometimes produced strange anomalies in the order and timing of his publications. His work on twins and his Central Asian research were published only in part, twenty and thirty years respectively after they had been carried out. No sooner had they appeared in Russian than English translations became available. *Traumatic Aphasia,* published in the USSR in 1947, contained material that was a part of Alexander Romanovich's doctoral dissertation, supplemented by the enormous quantity of material gathered during the war. That major work did not find its way into English until 1965, thanks to the prodigious effort of Douglas Bowden, a physician who had studied with Alexander Romanovich in the early 1960s. Because the Pavlovian phase of his work which postdated this research was summarized in lectures delivered in English in London in the mid-1950s, it was the first to become generally available to an English-reading audience. Nowhere did Alexander Romanovich hint at the complex ideological and institutional constraints that had produced his various research careers and which had shaped the conditions under which they were being made available to a wide audience.

For me, the misunderstandings produced by this series of events was fortunate. The message provided by the work being published in the 1950s was one that could attract my interest, if not my deep understanding. It brought me to Moscow.

During my year at Moscow University a constant stream of visitors came by the laboratory to visit with Alexander Romanovich. Except when severely pressed for time or when ill, Alexander Romanovich would not turn them away. Several times a week he lectured at one of the many institutions with which he was associated: Moscow University, the Institute of Neurosurgery, and the Institute of Psychology. He also headed a discussion group for foreign students to which he took visitors, and he was active in party affairs.

Early in the morning and late into the night he would read and write, scratching out a voluminous, multilingual correspondence with an old-fashioned fountain pen. Before leaving for work, he would be on the phone. Many directors of departments and institutes around Moscow joked to me of being awakened weekday mornings by Alexander Romanovich, reminding them of a job undone or an enticing project to be carried out.

In addition to his other chores, Alexander Romanovich followed his lifelong habit of reading the latest in foreign psychological research and seeing to it that the most important articles and monographs found their way into Russian, as likely as not with his own introduction. He was a consulting editor for foreign as well as Russian journals, and when conditions permitted, he wrote original articles in English, French, Spanish, and German for publication abroad. Mindful of his students and colleagues, he tirelessly promoted their work, arranging many translations from Russian into English and other European languages.

I realize now that by the time I reached Moscow, Alexander Romanovich was devoting as much of his energy to preservation of the past as to contemporary and future work. No wonder he was in such a hurry. There was a great deal to be done if that past were to survive the ravages of the historical epochs through which he had traveled.

My greatest sadness is that I understood so little of the content of Alexander Romanovich's work for so long. Only in the last year of his life was I prepared to ask him the kinds of questions that I should have been able to ask in 1962. He appreciated my questions—about Vygotsky, the rationale for the combined motor method, the events surrounding his work in defectology. But full answers, real discussion, were rarely forth-

coming. It was then more than forty years since his first meeting
with Vygotsky, and he could no longer tell me why the man had
so excited him. "He was a genius," I was told again and again.
Alexander Romanovich's early inclination toward psychoanalytic concepts was passed off as a boyhood caprice. His use of the
combined motor method was reduced to a means by which he
had stumbled on the prototype of the lie detector. All true, but
so misleading.

As I reached the end of my own research on Alexander Romanovich's life, I began to understand, and to regret, the way in
which living ideas from his past had been reduced to formulas.
In the course of a single lifetime he had found it necessary to
think in several different scientific languages, each of which
coded the same reality in different, seemingly disconnected
ways. His standard formulas were not intended as obfuscations;
they were rather the benchmarks of the different epochs through
which his career had passed. He never succeeded completely in
creating a unified language for the entire corpus of his work.
The meaning of the whole could be learned only with years of
apprenticeship and was difficult if not impossible to discern
until each of the parts had been understood, forcing the issue of
their integration to the fore.

My fifteen years as an apprentice were insufficient to render
me a master. But they made me a witness to the full complexity
and range of issues that concerned Alexander Romanovich in a
way that was not generally available to his other students. This
experience opened before me the picture of an integrated
understanding of his life's work.

A highly personal testimony to the power and endurance of
the ideas that first attracted Alexander Romanovich to psychology was given me on the day I sat down to write this account. In
a modern psychology building on a campus of the University of
California seven colleagues and I had gathered to discuss a recent paper by a leading practitioner of the branch of computer
science known as the study of "artificial intelligence." We represented an unusually broad cross-section of the social sciences—

anthropology, psychology, communications, sociology, and linguistics. All of us are considered competent practitioners of our sciences' most modern technologies, including mathematics, computer modeling, and experimental design. But our topic that day was not one of method or fact, narrowly conceived. Rather, we had gathered to discuss a far-reaching attack on artificial intelligence research by one of its leading practitioners. His point: our models of mind are nomothetic idealizations that fail to capture the real nature of human experience. He exhorted us to find new methods that would bridge the chasm between our technologically sophisticated, but arid, scientific present and the still unobtainable, but necessary, future of a psychology that encompasses the full range of human experience.

It is indeed ideas that endure. But it is human beings who give them life.

BIBLIOGRAPHY

INDEX

# Bibliography

WORKS BY LURIA

Although A. R. Luria published extensively over a 50-year period, a complete bibliography of his published works does not exist. Many of his publications in Russian are unobtainable in the United States and are difficult to locate even in the USSR. His many publications in languages other than Russian have yet to be compiled. Included here in chronological order are only his major works in English, supplemented by important contributions in Russian sufficient to give a representative sample of his work.

Psychological Expedition to Central Asia. *Science* 74, no. 1920 (1931): 383–384.
*Psychoanalysis in Light of the Principal Tendencies in Contemporary Psychology.* Kazan, 1922. (In Russian.)
*Contemporary Psychology and Its Basic Directions.* Moscow, 1927. (In Russian.)
*Language and Intellect in Child Development.* Ed. A. R. Luria. Kazan: A. V. Lunacharskii poligrafshkola, 1927.
The Problem of the Cultural Behavior of the Child. *Journal of Genetic Psychology* 35 (1928): 493–506.
Psychology and the Clinic. *Zhurnal psikhologii, pedologii i psi-khotekhnii* 2 (1929): 33–58.
*Speech and Intellect among Rural, Urban, and Homeless Children.* Moscow-Leningrad: Government Publishing House, 1930. (In Russian.)
*Studies in the History of Behavior.* With L. S. Vygotsky. Moscow, 1930. (In Russian.)
*The Nature of Human Conflicts.* 1932. Reprint New York: Liveright, 1976.

229 . . .

The Development of Mental Functions in Twins. *Character and Personality* 5 (1936–1937): 35–47.

Psychoanalysis. *The Great Soviet Encyclopedia,* 1940, vol. XLVII, cols. 507–510.

Psychology. With A. N. Leontiev. *The Great Soviet Encyclopedia,* 1940, vol. XLVII, cols. 511–548.

Summary of Remarks. *Trudie Akademiya Meditsinskikh Nauk: Seriya Fiziologicheskaya,* 1952, 203–207.

Summary of Remarks. *Nauchnaya Sessia Akademii Meditsinskikh Nauk,* 1950, 629–634.

*Speech and Development of the Mental Processes of the Child.* With F. A. Yudovich. London: Staples Press, 1959.

*The Role of Speech in the Regulation of Normal and Abnormal Behavior.* New York: Irvington, 1961.

*The Mentally Retarded Child.* New York: Pergamon Press, 1963.

*Restoration of Function after Brain Injury.* New York: Pergamon Press, 1963.

*Higher Cortical Functions in Man.* New York: Basic Books, 1966.

*Human Brain and Psychological Processes.* New York: Harper and Row, 1966.

Speech Development and the Formation of Mental Processes. *A Handbook of Contemporary Soviet Psychology,* ed. Michael Cole and Irving Maltzman. New York: Basic Books, 1969.

*Traumatic Aphasia: Its Syndromes, Psychology and Treatment.* The Hague: Mouton, 1970.

*Cognitive Development.* Cambridge: Harvard University Press, 1976.

*Basic Problems of Neurolinguistics.* The Hague: Mouton, 1976.

*The Neuropsychology of Memory.* Washington: Winston, 1976.

*The Selected Writings of A. R. Luria.* Ed. Michael Cole. White Plains: Merle Sharpe, 1978. Esp. the chapters on "A Child's Speech Responses and the Social Environment," "The Development of Constructive Activity in the Preschool Child," "The Development of Writing in the Child," "Experimental Psychology and Child Development," "Paths of Development of Thought in the Child," and "Psychoanalysis as a System of Monistic Psychology."

OTHER REFERENCES

Boring, Edwin G. *A History of Experimental Psychology.* 2nd ed. Englewood Cliffs: Prentice-Hall, 1950, p. ix.

Brett, George S. Associationism and "Act" Psychology: A Historical Perspective. In *Psychologies of 1930,* ed. Carl A. Murchison. 1930. Reprint New York: Arno Press, 1973.

Frankel, A. Against Electicism in Psychology and Pedology. *Povesteniya Natsionalnostei,* 1930, no. 7–8.

G. F. On the Condition and Tasks of Psychological Science in the USSR. *Pod znamiem Marksizma* 9 (1936): 87–99.

Graham, Loren R. *Science and Philosophy in the Soviet Union.* New York: Alfred A. Knopf, 1972.

Head, Henry. *Aphasia and Kindred Disorders of Speech.* Cambridge: Cambridge University Press, 1926.

Leontiev, A. N. The Development of Voluntary Attention in the Child. *Journal of Genetic Psychology* 40 (1932): 52–83.

Lenin, V. I. *Teachings of Karl Marx.* London: Lawrence and Wishart, 1934, p. 14. Quoted in John McLeish, *Soviet Psychology: History, Theory, Content* (London: Methuen, 1975), p. 88.

Rahmani, Levy. *Soviet Psychology: Philosophical, Theoretical and Experimental Issues.* New York: International Universities Press, 1973.

Razmyslov, P. On Vygotsky and Luria's Cultural-Historical Theory of Psychology. *Kniga i proletarskaya revolutsia* 4 (1934): 78–86.

Paths of Contemporary Psychology. *Estesvoznanie i Marksism* 23 (1930): 63.

Results of the Discussion of Reactological Psychology. *Sovetskaya psikhotekhnika* 4–6 (1931): 387–391.

Vygotsky, L. S. The Problem of the Cultural Development of the Child. *Journal of Genetic Psychology* 36 (1929): 415–434.

Vygotsky, L. S. *Mind in Society.* Ed. Michael Cole, Vera John-Steiner, Sylvia Scribner, and Ellen Souberman. Cambridge: Harvard University Press, 1978.

# Index

# . . . Index

# Luria in Social Context

*May you not live in interesting times*
—Chinese saying

While Chapter 1 of the autobiography provides the fullest account of Luria's personal orientation to the events that swirled around him as a youth, readers may find it difficult to credit his claims about the rapidity with which he completed his gymnasium[1] and college education. But the circumstances and opportunities he describes were, in fact, commonplace owing to the virtual vacuum of power that immediately followed the revolution(s) of 1917.

Russia had been at war with Germany as an ally of England and France but was so unprepared for war that it had far more men in the armed forces than armaments for them to use and consequently the Russian armies suffered horrendous losses. Manufacturing and agricultural production were inadequate even without the burden of war, and were totally inadequate to serve a huge nation at war on several fronts simultaneously.

This disastrous situation led to strikes in the capital, St. Petersburg, which became more and more severe. Finally, on March 15, 1917, the Tsar abdicated his throne. But there was no agreed upon successor. The Russian parliament was divided among members with a range of political views. A provisional

---

[1]Gymnasium is a widely used term in Europe that corresponds to secondary education in the United States and other countries.

government was set up by the most powerful parties, but an internal power struggle ensued in which the most radical group, the most radical socialist Party, the Bolsheviks, headed by Vladimir Lenin, won out. The Bolsheviks led a successful coup against the Provisional Government on October 25, later named the Great October Revolution in Soviet historiography.

Over the next several months, many of the traditional arrangements upon which the society had been based were totally transformed. Workers councils (soviets) were authorized to supervise factory production and an 8-hour day was instituted. The power of the Russian Orthodox Church was reduced by seizing its extensive land holdings and denying it authority over marriage. Banks were nationalized. In March of 1918, the new government concluded a peace treaty with the Germans at great loss in the territory over which Russia had ruled. Poland, Finland, large areas of Byelorussia and Ukraine as well as the Baltic States of Lithuania, Latvia, and Estonia were removed from Russian control—a total of 1,300,000 square miles and 62 million people. The losses along Russia's western borders were so great that the capital was moved from St. Petersburg to Moscow.

Russia's withdrawal from the war and its domination by a radical socialist—soon to be communist—government, was viewed as a betrayal by the Allies ranged against Germany. By the time Luria began attending Kazan University, from which Vladimir Lenin had graduated less than two decades earlier, a civil war was raging in many parts of the country, plunging an already staggering economy and political system into further chaos.

In the late summer of 1918 a large number of Czechoslovakian troops, who had fought with the Russians against the Germans, sought to return to fight in the West. The Soviet government refused. In response, the Czech troops seized a large segment of the trans-Siberian railway and occupied several cities in central Russia, including Kazan.

Leon Trotsky had only recently been made commander of the fledgling Red Army. He quickly organized troops to take Kazan, and on September 12, 1918, the city once again fell into Soviet hands. Documents from Trotsky's archive indicate the chaotic situation that existed in and around the city. For example:

WARNING TO THE WORKING POPULATION OF KAZAN

You must get out of the city for the time being. After the seizure of Kazan by the Czech-White-Guard bands, the city has become a nest of counter-revolution. This nest has to be destroyed .... It is necessary to remove your children from the town as soon as you can. We advise the working population of Kazan to seek refuge on Soviet territory. We offer fraternal hospitality to all working and needy people. Within a few days the working population of Kazan will be able to return to a city cleansed of vermin, along with the Soviet troops

A second document refers to an event, which occurred quite close to the Lurias' house:

ABOUT THE BURGLARS WHO SEIZED IN KAZAN PART OF THE GOLD RESERVE OF THE RUSSIAN SOVIET REPUBLIC

In Kazan the White Guards and Czechoslovaks seized part of the gold which is the public property of the Russian Soviet Republic .... In order to extract their profits from the Russian workers and peasants, the foreign beasts of prey, acting through the Czechoslovak mercenaries and White Guards, seized part of the gold which belongs to the Russian people.

(From: LEON TROTSKY'S MILITARY WRITINGS, Volume 1, THE CIVIL WAR IN RSFSF IN 1918. THE FIGHT FOR KAZAN)

There is no doubt that these events affected the Luria family, but just how severely is uncertain. Although Alexander Romanovich had kept a detailed diary since April 15, 1915 and carefully saved it to the end of his life, the dark blue notebook named "The Great Revolution" lacks many pages. They could have been torn out by his parents, or perhaps it was a kind of auto-censorship carried out in subsequent years. But the surviving entries of August 1918 give us some picture of what was going on around him at that time:

> The morning of the 6th was quiet. We even visited the market, but most shops were closed. But after 5 o'clock a terrible firing began. Before 8–9 it turned into bombardment of our place. There was a skirmish and shelling adjacent to the bank. We hid ourselves in the pantry and only from time to time looked out of it. The cannonade was unimaginable. Some of us slept in the pantry, the others in the corridor.

> On the 7th we heard shooting around 3 pm. There were rumors that Czekoslovaks were approaching. At 9 pm panic began, because the firing became very heavy. Everybody hid in their homes. At 11 pm in the evening shouts were heard from the bank. The gold kept there was taken away (and, evidently, the bank was ransacked).

> On the 8th I awoke very early. There were absolutely no people in the street. But later people began to gather. They said that our town had been already taken by the Czechs. Suddenly two horsemen appeared, who, without reaching our place, looked around and rode back. Very soon we saw a detachment, the soldiers were in Serbian (or Czechoslovakian) uniforms, with big arm-bands. This was the first time that I saw White Guards. The soldiers lined up near the bank. Soon a weapon was carried out of the bank, then the Bolshevik guard who had been there was taken away somewhere. This is how the bank with the gold reserve from the whole of Russia was "taken."

> In the morning my father was arrested because he was mistakenly thought to be a Bolshevik. Very soon he got free. Everywhere in the town executions are held: they are searching and killing the Bolsheviks. In this connection the most horrible anti-Semitic mood is developing. There was already a provocation in the Synagogue: somebody reported that the Bolsheviks and the Jews keep bombs there. The search showed it was a lie. Nevertheless everyone is in fear of a pogrom. All of us are in low spirits.

It's a nightmarish time!!

Clearly the chaos and bloodshed impacted the Luria family, although we have only this scant record of their experience of the events. At the very least, the fact that fighting went on not only in their neighborhood but all over the city, and that the city was the site of struggle between pro- and anti-Soviet regimes, gives a somewhat clearer notion of the conditions that allowed Luria to finish high school so quickly, and that destabilized conditions at the University of Kazan.

In fact, despite the dangers, these events had a variety of positive impacts on the Luria family. As Cole wrote in his initial epilogue, the Tsarist policies that tightly restricted Jewish access to higher education and denied Jews access to professional life in the large metropolitan centers were removed.

Here is an extract from Semen Dobkin's memoirs about his childhood friend, Lev Vygotsky, Alexander Romanovich's mentor, which indicates how restrictive Tsarist policies were:

In the summer of 1913 Lev was finishing the gymnasium and was already taking the so-called "deputy exams," i.e., exams attended by a "deputy," a representative of the educational authority of the province who had the decisive say in giving marks. More often than not, the official appointed was a teacher from the public gymnasium, most of whom looked down on the teachers and pupils of the private gymnasium and were often extremely anti-semitic. Lev, however, did brilliantly at these exams and was almost certain to get an honors certificate. But midway through examinations a directive from the Minister of Education, Kasso, appeared. In Tsarist Russia there was a quota for the admission of Jews to institutions of higher education. This quota was three per cent at Moscow and Petersburg universities. In practice it meant that gold medalists were assured of admission, silver medalists had a fifty-fifty chance, while anyone who finished school without honours had no chance at all. While preserving the quota, the Kasso directive introduced a new rule whereby Jewish applicants were to be enrolled by casting lots. The idea was very simple: a university education should be received not by the most gifted but by average young people who were unlikely to be high achievers in the future.

Vygotsky showed me the newspaper with the report about the new directive, which meant a great misfortune for him personally and for his whole family since it dashed his career plans and hopes of getting a university degree.

"There," said Lev, "Now I have no chance."

The news seemed so monstrous to me that I replied quite sincerely:

"If they don't admit you to the University it will be a terrible injustice. I am sure they'll let you in. Wanna bet?"

Vygotsky, who was a great bettor, smiled and stretched out his hand. We wagered for a good book.

He did not make a single mistake on his final exams and received a gold medal. At the insistence of his parents, he applied to the medical department that was considered most suitable because it guaranteed a modest but secure future.

True, Vygotsky was more interested in the humanities, but what were his options? The history and philology departments were ruled out because they trained mainly secondary-school teachers, and Jews were not allowed to be government employees in Tsarist Russia. And the law department, too, generally turned out court officials, although it also opened opportunities to become an attorney.

And the incredible happened: late in August, the Vygodskys (the standard spelling of the family name, MC, KL) received a cable from their friends in Moscow telling them that Lev had been enrolled at the University by winning the lottery. On the same day he presented me with a volume of Bunin's poetry inscribed "To Senya in memory of a lost bet." I don't think anyone was ever so happy about loosing a bet." (Levitin, 1982, pp. 28–29)

A university diploma for a Jew meant the right of living in big Russian cities. It was so vitally important that even schoolchildren tried to do what they could to help Jews to leave the humiliating Pale. Here is a fragment from another memoir, this time of the prominent Russian writer Konstantin Paustovsky, that refers to his gymnasium experience in Kiev a year or two before WW1:

> Before the exams a get-together was organized in the city park. All the pupils of our class were invited, except Jews. The Jews should not know about this meeting. It was decided, that the best Russian and Polish pupils should get at least one "good" instead of "excellent" mark, so as not to get a gold medal. We agreed to leave all the gold medals to our Jewish class-mates, since without these medals they were not admitted to the university. All of us vowed to keep this decision in secret. (Paustovsky, 1955, p. 242)

If it were not for the revolution, Alexander Romanovich would have had limited chances to enter the university and practically no chance to move to Moscow. But as we know, he not only completed university in Kazan, but both he and his family took up residence and pursued their work in Moscow. The reason for this change of fate was very pragmatic: change of the national manpower policy. In Tsarist Russia people belonging to the nobility or clergy got all the preferences. Naturally, after the revolution the new state would discriminate against these two categories. By an irony of history the Bolsheviks proclaimed it their policy to destroy the state machine of the past, but the social-cultural roots of the Russian mentality made them copy the Tsarist bureaucratic system of preferences and discriminations according to national origin and religious affiliation. Being a Jew became a kind of a passport to any position because it automatically meant that a person could never have belonged to nobility or clergy, and a manpower officer need not spend time and effort checking up on his background and family connections. The Jews, whose dream always was to leave the Pale of forced, segregated, settlement, rushed to the big cities, mainly to Moscow, and were offered many opportunities in social life. This policy led to disproportionately greater numbers of Jews among the representatives of the new state, in particular in the secret police (variously referred to as the VCHK-NKVD-KGB) that later, in the seventies, gave birth to a trend of self-accusation among the Jewish intelligentsia. For example, the well known historian Mikhail Kheifets, who was imprisoned in 1974 for writing a preface to Josef Brodsky's collection of verses, even while he was imprisoned, wrote a book *I Am a Jew*, telling about his guilty feelings for the sins of Jews in organizing and governing the numerous Soviet punitive organs.

Gradually the threat of civil war receded. The last major threats from Russian counter-revolutionaries ended in late 1920, although it was not until October of 1922, when Alexander Romanovich was beginning his career in Moscow, that the last foreign troops were pushed out of the Far East. The country was in terrible economic trouble. It has been estimated that in 1921, 20% of the Russian population was suffering from famine and cholera. (Craig, 1971). This situation forced Lenin's government to compromise some of its socialist principles and allow a partial return to capitalism by permitting the revival of private industry and allowing peasants to produce and trade food for profit. This policy appeared to be successful. By 1927, farmers were more prosperous and factory production had risen to the level it had attained in 1913.

The early 1920s were a period of experimentation in all aspects of Russian society. Increased moderation in agricultural and industrial policies was accompanied by unprecedented freedoms in the nation's intellectual life. Isaiah Berlin, who spent a brief assignment as a cultural attaché at the British embassy in Moscow immediately following the Second World War summarized the early years of the Soviet Union in these terms:

> There was a genuine renaissance, different in kind from the artistic scene in other countries, in Russia during the 20s. Much

cross fertilization between novelists, poets, artists, critics, historians, and scientists took place, and this created a culture of unusual vitality and achievement, an extraordinary upward curve in European civilization. (Berlin, 1949, p. 158)

Berlin's views concerning cross-fertilization of intellectual life during the 1920's were based upon his knowledge of Soviet life and letters studied from abroad. But they were confirmed in a manner of special interest to understanding Luria at an official embassy dinner where Berlin sat next to Sergei Eisenshtein. The film director told him "the early post-revolutionary period was far and away the best in his own life as a creative artist, and in the lives of many others. It was a time, he said wistfully, when wild and marvelous things could be done with impunity" (1949, p. 164).

Berlin did not know, it appears, that the collaboration between Eisenshtein and Luria provided an excellent example of the cross-fertilization he was writing about. This collaboration extended beyond what Cole was able to write about in his initial epilogue; Eisenshtein's formulation of the principle of montage, in particular, his invocation of the idea that what emerges in the juxtaposition of images is a "generalized image" resonates strongly with Luria's and Vygotsky's notions of word meaning, for which they also invoked the notion of a "generalized image." From Eisenshtein's own essays, we know that he was present at least once during a research session with Luria's patient and the protagonist of his book *The Mind of a Mnemonist*, Shereshevsky, the person about whom it could be said that the lack of ability to effortlessly create generalized images served as the basis for his unusual memory and personality (Eisenshtein, 1942, pp. 148–149).[2]

In turn, Luria's activities during the early 1920's richly illustrate the idea that it was a time when wild and wonderful things

---

[2]Further evidence of their friendship was to be found in the Luria household where Eisenshtein's brain resided in a bottle in Luria's office, and original sketches for scenes in several of his films were kept.

could be done with impunity, a phrase which nicely captures Alexander Romanovich obtaining paper from a soap factory to print a journal or hauling students out of line to test his ideas about the nature of hidden psychological processes, or inviting Vygotsky, then an obscure educational psychologist whose dissertation was devoted to an analysis of *Hamlet*, to join a research group at the prestigious Institute of Psychology in Moscow.

It was, as Cole wrote in his initial epilogue, a time when a variety of attempts were made to develop the principles of Marxism in many intellectual fields. Alexander Romanovich's comments on his own efforts to combine Marx and Freud were part of this much larger field of similar explorations. Cole was correct in noting criticism directed at his efforts in this field, but subsequent scholarship has shown that it was more extensive and serious than he knew. Both Voloshinov (1986) and Vygotsky, neither of whom could be considered instruments of the Party, weighed in with their criticisms in print (see van der Veer & Valsiner, 1991, ch 5).

Perhaps most important, it was during this time that Vygotsky, Luria, and Leontiev undertook the wholesale reformulation of psychology along Marxist lines. As a result, cultural-historical psychology as a self-conscious solution to the "crisis in psychology" was born. Perhaps because of their current popularity in world psychology, it is sometimes thought that cultural-historical psychology was either *the* leading school of psychology in the USSR during and after the 1920s or at least *a* leading school, outshone, perhaps, only by Pavlov. In fact, Pavlov did not consider himself, and was not considered to be, a psychologist by his Russian colleagues. Moreover, several approaches in psychology, notably Kornilov's reactology, were more influential than the cultural-historical approach (Joravsky, 1989; van der Veer & Valsiner, 1991).

It is unclear to us how the impression of cultural-historical psychology's preeminence arose among non-Russian psychologists. Perhaps it resulted from Luria's membership on the board of the *Journal of Genetic Psychology* that published a set of three articles about the school between 1928 and 1930. Or it may have been because of the popularity of *The Nature of Human Conflicts*, the last section of which provides an introduction to cultural-historical psychology as if these ideas had provided the structure for the entire book, which they most certainly did not.[3]

In any event, the truth of the matter was that all manner of psychological theories laying claim to Marxist origins were stronger institutionally than cultural-historical psychology, which was widely criticized within the USSR (an excellent compendium of critical articles has been published by Renee van der Veer, 2000). A simple, but clear, example of such criticism can be found in Alexei Leontiev's doctoral thesis. Although the thesis was published as a book in 1929, it was published with a foreword from the publishers denouncing the ideas it contained as inappropriate use of Marxism in psychology!

Isaiah Berlin's comments on this period are again especially appropriate to characterizing how the social context impacted Alexander Romanovich's intellectual life.

> After a relatively relaxed period during the years of the New Economic Policy, Marxist orthodoxy grew strong enough to challenge and in the late 20s, crush all this unorganized revolutionary [intellectual] activity ... but since it was not always possible to predict which side would win, this alone, for a time, gave a certain grim excitement to literary life. (1949, p. 158–159)

The same remark appears to have been true of Luria and his colleagues. Their response to the editorial foreword was to hold a Party for Leontiev during which they mocked the criticism in music and poetry.

We now know that although the 1920s began as a period of relative openness and experimentation in all spheres of Russian

---

[3]This book, which constituted Luria's first doctoral thesis, was not published in Russia during his lifetime. It was only in 2002, 70 years after its publication in English, that the book appeared in Russian.

life, the foundations of the efficient totalitarian state to come were being gradually created by Lenin and his colleagues. On the surface, it might appear (and did so appear to many non-Russians) that the Bolsheviks had constructed a hierarchical system of government based on local democracy: that is, people from local Soviets were elected to represent their constituents. When the country adopted the constitution that marked the formal beginning of the USSR in 1924, a member of each local Soviet sent a representative to a regional Soviet, and so on up the line to the Supreme Soviet that elected those who governed on a day-to-day basis. But the appearance was built upon a carefully crafted illusion. As Leonard Schapiro, a well-known historian of the Soviet Communist Party, perceptively wrote many years ago, Lenin's form of government had

> the unique quality that it brought into being what were ostensibly independent political institutions—soviets, courts, trade unions and the like—but ensured from the first that every one of these institutions should function only under the control of a single Party and by strict discipline. (1959, p. viii)

Lenin suffered the first of a series of strokes in May 1922, and between this time and his death in January 1924, the leadership of the Politburo (the top-most organization in the governmental hierarchy) was shared, and disputed, among three men, one of whom was Joseph Stalin. By 1927, Stalin had manipulated the situation so that only he remained at the top of the pyramid of power. And he began to wield that power both to transform the economic foundations of the country and to eliminate any remaining opponents. The first of these transformations made itself felt to the population in the form of the first Five-Year plan, which called for collectivization of agriculture and direct state control over industry, but the implications of these events extended into the intellectual life of the country as well.

Collectivization met with stubborn resistance from millions of peasant farmers and this resistance brought ruthless imposition of state authority, carried out by the army. Villagers who resisted were deported to Siberia or simply shot. But resistance there was. Many peasants burned their crops and destroyed their livestock to keep them from passing into the hands of the government. By 1933, a large proportion of the houses in the Soviet Union had been destroyed and many millions of people had been killed (Craig, 1971). But collectivization was successfully imposed, and with it, increased state power, concentrated in Stalin's hands.

A similar fate befell the industrial sector, where those who resisted state control were accused of being saboteurs or foreign agents. Subsequent trials and executions of both Russian citizens and foreign experts who had been brought in to speed industrialization frightened people into line.

In intellectual life, as already noted, the Party began to exert more and more of an influence as well. But in this sphere, the Party was not as strong and the debates were not (yet) decided by force.

These events had direct effects on Luria's career, both positive and negative. On the positive side, it was the fact that collectivization was carried out in the Soviet republics of Central Asia (which he like many other Russian intellectuals viewed as a policy promoting modernization of the peasantry) that provided the conditions for his cross-cultural research in Uzbekistan.[4] On the other hand, increasing Party influence also made it more and more difficult openly to show one's sympathy to ideas from outside of Russia. Revealing in this regard was Luria's very sparse use of citations to Freud and Jung in *The Nature of Human Conflicts*, and increasing attacks on Vygotsky, Luria, and Leontiev for the close attention they paid to non-Russian psychology.[5]

---

[4]As James Wertsch has emphasized, from Luria's perspective, these studies were more properly thought of as cross-historical, since the advent of collectivization which brought modern bureaucratic institutions and literate practices into the everyday lives of peasant herdsmen were considered a new and higher historical stage as well as a cultural change (Wertsch, 1985).

[5]Not only did these men refer to Western psychologists in their published work, they actively promoted translations and wrote prefaces to the leading research being carried out in Europe and the United States at the time.

It was almost certainly in response to the increasing criticism that their work was evoking, and the increasingly strident political tone of that criticism, a tone that even then had ominous overtones, that motivated the move of the group to Kharkov and out of the political limelight. But, as Cole noted in the initial epilogue to the autobiography, despite the élan with which the move to Kharkov began, this period also marked the beginning of fractionation within the group. Vygotsky commuted between Moscow, Leningrad, and Kharkov while Luria spent a good deal of his time in Moscow. Moreover, Alexander Romanovich did not remain out of the spotlight. The work in Central Asia carried out in 1931–32 was harshly criticized in visible print media (Razmyslov, 2000). The work at the Institute of Medical Genetics, which began in 1934, was, if anything, even more dangerous.

One of the episodes illustrating these dangers that was deleted from the initial epilogue had been related to Cole by Luria's wife, Lana Pemienova. It occurred in 1935–36. Alexander Romanovich had been away from the Institute for some time. He returned to encounter a large, heated meeting in progress. The subject of the meeting was its director, S. G. Levit, who was being denounced for his supposed anti-Soviet views and his collaboration with foreigners. The evidence? He had hosted the well-known American geneticist, H. J. Mueller and corresponded with American colleagues. Initially, Alexander Romanovich sought to speak out in Levit's defense but a friend who had been observing the meeting dragged him away, aware that Levit had been marked for extermination. Levit was subsequently killed and the Institute closed.

The increase in Party-controlled state regulation of all spheres of life that accompanied the first Five Year Plan and collectivization, despite the opposition they met, were not without successes. After an initial period of chaos in agriculture and industry, production did increase, putting the Soviet Union on the path to becoming a major industrial power, although progress in agriculture was not as marked as in industry.

Having further consolidated his power, Stalin now turned the instruments of terror that had been used to control agriculture and industry against the Bolshevik elite itself. The key event that started the great purges of the 1930s began with the murder of Sergei Kirov, who was Party head in Leningrad in December, 1934. Although there is no definitive proof, it is widely believed that Stalin himself ordered the murder of Kirov. Whether he was directly responsible or not, Stalin used the murder to begin to liquidate a large proportion of the people who had formed the backbone of the Communist Party since the Revolution, including its top leadership. His method, as described by Nikita Khrushchev in 1956, was to sign a decree, endorsed by the Politburo, that deprived anyone accused of "preparing to engage in terrorist acts" of any legal rights. Even when individuals survived torture designed to extract confessions and provided convincing proof of their innocence, they were killed.

It is impossible at this distance in time and culture to imagine the extent of the terror waged against the country's political and intellectual elite. According to various accounts, as many as 800,000 Party members were killed, including 6 of the 13 members of the Politburo, all but a few of the 138 members of the Central Committee, almost all of the premiers of the various people's republics and high ranking members of the army, and about half of the army's officer corps.

One can only imagine the effect these events had on people like Luria and his colleagues. Friend turned against friend, children against their parents, husband against wife. No family among those in Luria's circle of acquaintances, including members of his own family, escaped unscathed.

Vygotsky apparently saw the direction in which matters were headed before the purges began. In another segment excised from the initial epilogue, Lana Pemienova told Cole that not long before he died, Vygotsky visited Roman Albertovich, Luria's father, to urge him to find a way to get his son out of the public eye as rapidly as possible. It was as a direct result of this conversation, she said, that Luria entered medical school on a full time basis. There was, of course, ample intellectual reason for entering medicine, but in this case, the major purpose was to become a non-person in order to survive. Vladimir Zinchenko once told Karl Levitin a story he had heard from his father, Peter Zinchenko, the prominent Soviet psychologist. Alexander Romanovich, being at that time responsible for distributing free permits ('putyovky') to sanatoria and hospitals, was lucky to get the best one for Vygotsky, but when he happily brought it to his friend and teacher, Vygotsky silently tore it to pieces: he could foresee the future events in Soviet politics and did not want to survive to become the cause, though obliquely, for his colleagues' tortures. As we would now say, he possessed a very high level of reflexivity.

The terror lasted into 1938. The decree against psychological testing came in the middle of this devastation, with Luria as one of its targets. Despite the fact that he did not succeed in making himself entirely into a non-person, the move into medical school achieved its aim. But at what costs to him and others who survived the terror we will never know. Isaiah Berlin's comments reflect our own impression of the scars left upon the psyches of the survivors:

> The activities of informers and false witnesses exceeded all previously known bounds; self-prostration, false and wildly implausible confessions bending before, or active cooperation with authority, usually failed to save those marked for destruction. For the rest it left painful and humiliating memories from which some of the survivors of the Terror were never to completely recover. (1949, pp. 159–160)

Those scars were clearly evident in the surviving members of Vygotsky's circle of close colleagues. While they were able to forge coalitions that brought them a few years of institutional power in Moscow following Stalin's death and the revival of psychology, residual suspicions and resentments from that earlier time were evident in what should have been purely intellectual arguments about matters of psychology, and they have not entirely disappeared to this day.

Luria and several other prominent cultural-historical psychologists survived the war, during which they were able to use their theoretical acumen to conduct outstanding research on basic and applied issues associated with restoration of people who had been wounded. Luria, of course, focused on restoration of brain function, but Leontiev and Zaporozhets, for example, carried out equally interesting work on the restoration of people who lost limbs and motor function (Leontiev & Zaporozhets, 1960).

The agony of Stalinism, unfortunately, did not end with victory in the war. As indicated in the earlier epilogue, Luria was dismissed from his position in the Institute of Neurosurgery in 1950. Not included in the epilogue, because VAAP would not allow it to be included, was the fact that his dismissal came at a time when the Party was seeking to increase its control over intellectual life. When this policy was first introduced in 1946, a disproportionate number of the people singled out for criticism were Jews who were criticized in the newspapers using the code term "rootless cosmopolitans."

Luria was devastated by this turn of events. According to Lana Pemienova, it was the only time she had seen him feeling, and acting totally defeated. She had never before seen this optimistic man cry. But she did then.

While matters improved as Luria put back together his work life at the Institute of Defectology, anti-Semitism in government/Party circles continued to increase. It reached its apogee in 1952 at approximately the same time that Luria and his colleagues were under attack for being insufficiently Pavlovian. The key event in this new assault was the announcement that a plot had been discovered among high ranking physicians with responsibility for care of the Kremlin elite, and, of course, of Stalin himself. Seven of the nine men indicted were Jewish. The announcement of this new conspiracy was widely interpreted as a replay of the initiation of the Great Purges of the 1930's and at this point, Luria anticipated that it was just a matter of time until he was arrested.

His reaction to this combination of assaults was recounted to us by his former student, Vladimir Lubovsky , now an old man (this account may be found on the accompanying DVD). At Luria's request, Lubovsky would come to Luria's apartment every morning and accompany him to work. At the end of the day, he would accompany him home. In addition to his briefcase, Luria carried with him a small suitcase with a change of underwear and toiletries in it. If he was arrested while on his way to or from work, Lubovsky was to inform his family so that they would not fear he had been hit by a car and waste their time running around to hospitals to find him.

He was not arrested. Stalin died on March 5, 1953. A month later the accused doctors were released (except one of them, who died in prison) and over the course of the next several years, the terror of his quarter century of rule over the Soviet Union abated.

After a 29 year-long interval, Alexander Romanovich got permission to travel abroad, first to Norway, then to the International Psychological congress in Brussels, then London and the United States. In 1958 Luria was allowed to return to his position at the Burdenko Institute of Neurosurgery and an approximation to normal life that he had not known for a quarter of a century. His laboratory of neuropsychology now consisted of only four people, all of them his former students (Filippycheva, Khomskaya, Pravdina, and Tsvetkova) and they were given only one room without any furniture, so they used the window-sills as desks. But it did not matter much to them—they could do their scientific work.

By 1962 when Cole arrived as a post-doctoral student, the laboratory at the Burdenko institute had grown somewhat but was still small and poorly equipped, requiring extraordinary effort and ingenuity to create needed equipment. Luria was lecturing regularly at Moscow University in the psychology department and at the Institute of Psychology where he began his career.

The international political situation was still tense (recall that 1962 was the year of the Cuban missile crisis) and the Communist Party continued to exert its authoritarian control over the population. However, it was also a time of lively debate inside the USSR, the year when Alexander Solzhenitsyn's novella, *One Day in the Life of Ivan Denisovich*, began to lift the veil of silence that had surrounded the instruments of terror upon which the Soviet state had long been based.

In 1966, in no small measure owing to Luria's unceasing efforts and international contacts, the International Congress of Psychology was held in Moscow and not long afterwards, psychology graduated from a department within the faculty of philosophy to become a full fledged discipline in its own right, with representation in the Soviet National Academy of Sciences. For a while it was even possible to make phone calls between the USSR and the United States. Various academic and cultural exchanges expanded. While life remained constricted and difficult, it no longer teetered on the edge of annihilation.

# Luria in Personal Context: Reconciling Contradictions

*Life flashes by in a succession of boring days.*
*It's a long time since I've written any tales.*
*I look around me and feel awful.*
*Life without tales is a stupid joke.*
—A. R. Luria, 14 July, 1923

It should be clear to the reader that writing his autobiography was an extremely complex task for Alexander Romanovich. He could not write truthfully about the linkages between his personal experience and his scientific work without severe reprisals from the State. As a matter of life long habit, he effaced himself among his peers, attributing his achievements to his good luck in working with people of greater talent. It is our belief that he firmly detested the cult of personality to which his country was inclined, and firmly believed that the facts of his personal life were of fleeting interest in comparison with the scientific ideas to which they contributed.

But it is one thing to argue that personality should not be used as an explanation of scientific progress and another to so thoroughly efface oneself that the efficacy of individual agency is totally eliminated. While respecting his preference for self-effacement, in this final section we add to the limited material that Michael Cole was able to obtain in the late 1970's when Russia

*255 . . .*

was still part of the Soviet Union and its citizens had to report all of their conversations with him to the secret police or face reprisals themselves.

We present this additional set of considerations in terms of a set of contrasts which appear to capture important aspects of Alexander Romanovich's personal context.

Luria was born, lived, and died in a country where people were accustomed to express their most important thoughts in Aesopian language, often in the form of brief, funny, stories, packed with concealed meaning—the ubiquitous Russian anecdotes. Such anecdotes were usually told at the kitchen table, far from the omnihearing telephone. In trying to characterize the personal life of Alexander Romanovich, we begin in this tradition.

Alexander Romanovich loved the bitter irony in a joke popular during those times: "What is happiness? It is to live in the Soviet Union. And what is misfortune? It is to have such happiness." He perfectly understood that his own life was full of such paradoxes.

## CLEVERNESS, HONESTY, AND COMMUNISM

In the Soviet era there was a saying: One might choose only two out of three things: to be clever, honest, or to be a member of the Party. That is, if you are clever and honest, you can't be a Communist; if you are a Communist, you are either honest but stupid, or clever but dishonest. Alexander Romanovich managed to combine all three of these qualities.

As he notes in the initial chapter of his autobiography, Alexander Romanovich was not a political person. Despite the high level of his social participation and his activism as a young man, he did not join the Communist Party until the German invasion of Russia, a time when many people joined the Party as an act of national solidarity.

Elkhonon Goldberg in his book, *The Executive Brain*, dedicated to his teacher, remarks several times about the paradoxical situation that Luria found himself in:

Coming from the westernmost edge of the Soviet empire, from the Baltic city of Riga, I grew up in a "European" environment. Unlike the families of my Moscow friends, my parents' generation did not grow up under the Soviets. I had some sense of "European" culture and "European" identity. Among my professors at the University of Moscow, Luria was one of the very few recognizably "European," and this was one of the things that drew me to him ....

As a multilingual, multitalented man of the world, Alexander Romanovich was completely at home with Western civilization. But he was also a Soviet man used to making compromises in order to survive. I suspected that in the deepest recesses of his being there was a visceral fear of brutal, physical repression. It seemed that this latent fear—the glue of the Soviet regime—was forever with him. This duality of inner intellectual freedom ..., and everyday accommodation was common among the Soviet intelligentsia. (p. 9)

Olga Vinogradova, a student of Alexander Romanovich's during the 1950's who went on to become a leading neuroscientist, described how Luria's adaptation to political pressure from the authorities manifested itself in his lectures:

The 1950s arrived and with them the "Pavlovian" session, as a result of which we psychologists learned that there was no such thing as a science of psychology, that there was not a soul, and that there were only conditioned reflexes. But this view found no echo in the lectures Alexander Romanovich gave us. He knew Pavlov's theory quite well and merely changed the vocabulary in his lectures: The beauty of a direct psychological language was replaced, but nonetheless the knowledge he gave us remained at the level of real science.

Nataliya Traugott, a contemporary of Luria, wrote about this same period:

They came to this kangaroo court and repented. They repented that they inadequately understood Pavlov and had devoted too much attention to the brain. Then, when they finished repenting, the Presidium would declare whether they had repented enough or not. If they thought it was not enough, they forced them to do it again. Shmar'yan, for example, appeared three times, because each time after he said, "Well, yes, I am guilty of this or that, but nonetheless one must still take cerebral factors into account" they replied, "You have not repented enough; you have not understood your own mistakes." He appeared before them again, and he literally collapsed before your eyes, like a balloon when you let the air out of it.

Alexander Romanovich also repented. But his case was decided quickly. They said that he had caused damage to the development of the theory of aphasia, and that this had to be put on record, and Alexander Romanovich did not particularly dispute this."

## FAMOUS ABROAD, A NOBODY AT HOME

One of the mysteries surrounding Luria concerns the contradiction between his status abroad and his position at home. He was a Soviet citizen who was allowed to travel abroad, where he was widely honored, but, at home, he was not treated as a distinguished person at all. When Luria visited the USA in 1957, American newspapers compared his lecture tour to the launching of the first satellite by the Soviet Union that same year. Subsequently, Luria became one of the best known Soviet Russian scientists outside Russia. But in his own country he never occupied an official position higher than head of a laboratory or departmental chair. His colleagues in the West could not imagine that Luria had never been elected to the Academy of Sciences of the USSR, nor was he ever appointed a director of any Soviet institute or hospital.

During the Soviet period, a person who had won fame abroad was either used as an example of the great achievements of Soviet society, and was given all the high academic ranks and official positions that the state had to bestow, or was proclaimed a dissident, a traitor, or even a spy and denied the possibility of traveling abroad or having contact with foreigners at home. But this did not happen to Luria. He became well known abroad where he received many awards and was elected to prestigious academies, while at home, he remained nothing more than the head of a laboratory. His international reputation was overlooked and he was permitted to visit foreign colleagues and to be their hosts in the Soviet Union.

A related puzzle is how Luria managed to escape being arrested or shot. In the 1930's his cross-cultural work in Central Asia was publicly denounced as an insult to the builders of socialism. At almost the same time, his work on the contributions of genetics and cultural experience to development at the Institute of Medical Genetics came under attack. Its program was accused of promoting genetic determinism. The Institute closed, and its director killed. He then entered the Institute of Experimental Medicine and became a student at the First Medical Institute. After completing the course with distinction, he did not return to psychology, but asked N. N. Burdneko, a famous Russian surgeon, to take him on as an assistant at his neurological institute. Many people believe that this move saved him from the Terror.

At the end of the 1940's, he was dismissed from the Institute of Neurosurgery and his laboratory was closed during the anti-Semitic "struggle against cosmopolitanism" (a code term applied to Jews). In the early fifties, during the infamous "Pavlovian" session of the Academy of Agricultural Sciences, it was proclaimed that Luria caused great damage to the development of the theory of aphasia; somewhat later in the middle of fifties, during the "Kremlin doctors affair," he lost all his jobs and expected to be arrested from one day to the next. His concern was so great that he asked to be accompanied from home to work and back and kept a small suitcase with him containing his necessities so that if he was taken off the street, his family would know what had happened (as described by Lubovsky on the accompanying DVD). Yet, in spite of all these difficulties, unlike his sister Lidiya, Luria was never imprisoned, nor was he shot as Lidiya's husband was.

These strange—by Soviet standards—circumstances gave birth to speculations that Luria had some special relation with the Soviet authorities. Some have even gone so far as to suggest that his research in Central Asia was conducted at the direct request of Josef Stalin as a means of assessing the minds and moods of peasants in the Soviet Central Asia republics. Others have intimated that his research on the combined motor method was sponsored by Alexander Vyshinsky, the Prosecutor General, who ordered Luria to produce the lie detector. Such speculations show a limited understanding of Soviet reality. For example, a lie detector was the last thing Vyshinsky needed. It was his well-known custom to prepare not only the written accusations against his victims but also their written "voluntary confessions" long before they were even arrested.

Examples of such speculative criticism can be found in an otherwise scholarly book by Renee van der Veer and Jaan Valsiner (1991). For example, on the basis of such speculations they criticize him for writing an apologetic letter to the Communist Party to excuse his work in Central Asia. They have never seen the letter. We have. It reads:

> To the Culture and Propaganda Section of the Central Committee of the Bolshevik Party,
>
> To the People's Commissar on Education
>
> The Moscow Control Commission of Workers and Peasants Inspection, which investigated the Institute of Psychology, demanded from me the material on work done under my leadership in the psychological expedition to Central Asia. Despite the fact that this material has not yet been properly analyzed and is in crude form, the commission felt it could hand down a decision on our work not having in its hands the conclusions without which neither the purpose of the study nor the raw material could be properly understood. Making a biased selection of individual facts and interpreting them incorrectly,

the commission made a number of extremely grave charges, presenting our work as a specimen of colonizing research based on a racist theory.

It is very difficult to interpret this letter as cowardly obedience to authority—especially when one realizes that it was written during the great purges of the 1930's when Bolshevik Party Commissions wielded the power of life and death over everyone. Luria seemed to be as unrepentant as was possible, while, at the same time, trying to avoid being killed.

It is true that Luria was compelled to find a balance between freedom and necessity. Without question his personal convictions and loyalties entered into his decisions. Luria made no secret of his support for the revolution in its early phases. It is far easier to make judgments from afar with decades of hindsight. But like Isaiah Berlin (p. 245) we doubt that the moral state of affairs in the USSR in the 1930s was as clear at the time.

## CREATIVE AND COMPULSIVE

Steven Toulmin, an American philosopher and then professor at the University of Chicago, wrote a year after Alexander Romanovich's death:

> The most distinguished of Vygotsky's comrades-in-arms was Alexander Romanovich Luria, whose extraordinarily range of interests and abilities ... made him possibly the finest all-round psychologist of the century ... Luria was Beethoven to Vygotsky, and Vygotsky can be seen as the Mozart of psychology as Sadi Carnot was of physics ....

Everyone who knew him remembers how artistic Luria was. His love for architecture, especially the Northern Russian churches, his deep knowledge of painting, his passion for making photos of tiny natural objects, his wonderful ability to mimic the speech patterns of people from different countries, the verses and fairy tales he wrote, his diaries and personal letters to his wife and his daughter, full of genuinely poetical pages, to say nothing of his two literary chef-d'oeuvres, *The Man with the Shattered World* and *The Mind of the Mnemonist* all speak to his artistic talent. These "unimagined portraits" created a new literary genre, a tradition ably followed by Oliver Sacks.

"He had a tremendous sense of drama; when we walked along the Red Square in Moscow, I felt as if Luria was showing me a movie," recollected Jerome Bruner during the Luria memorial conference in Moscow in 1997. "A great actor died with him," wrote Maria Knebel, a well-known Russian theatre producer and critic.

Although he was clearly artistic, Luria was also disciplined, punctual, and orderly to the point of being compulsive. He was notable for his punctuality. He never postponed or delayed anything. Vladimir Zinchenko recounts one manifestation of this characteristic which many experienced (see the interview on the accompanying DVD):

> At the Academic Council session where I presented a preliminary report on my thesis, he agreed to be my official opponent. Some days later he told me: "I have completed my comments on your thesis. When can I finally see it?" I suspect he wrote the comments right after the Council session.

One month before his death on his 75th birthday, Alexander Romanovich showed Karl Levitin how he had prepared himself for death. Folders with unpublished works were placed on lower shelves of the bookcase. He joked that only the easiest part of work remained: to take the folders to the publishing house.

He answered letters the day he received them; the same practice was used with the numerous articles he had agreed to prepare for various scientific journals. Professor Peter Galperin, whose pupils and colleagues used to rely on his wisdom in complicated situations, once said "What advice can I give to Alexander Romanovich? He writes faster than I read."

Luria's daughter Elena writes how insistent Alexander Romanovich was that everything in his study be in its proper place, how he always loved to have his pencils well sharpened,

and how he considered it a tragic loss when his favorite Parker
fountain pen broke.

## ACTIVIST-SCIENTIST

As a general rule, a scientist can be an activist, organizing con-
ferences, jobs, salaries, grants, visits, contacts with mass media
and industrial and agricultural companies, foundations and
other universities, or be a really good scientist. Luria was both.

At a memorial meeting in Amsterdam in 2002, Vladimir
Zinchenko reminded attendees about Luria the activist.

It should not be forgotten that for many years Alexander
Romanovich was president, or rather Father, of the International
Association of Foreign Psychology Students at Moscow State
University.

He was genuinely considerate of young scholars in general,
not only of his disciples. He helped many to get a job in their special field (which was not easy then). He also helped them to get
their books and articles published (which is always hard).

During the 1962–63 academic year Michael Cole was an at-
tendee at these informal seminars which were generally held
monthly in the dormitory at the main building of Moscow University, where most of them lived. Luria lived downtown, next to
the older part of Moscow University where the Psychology Department was located. The trip from the dormitory to Luria's
apartment was not an easy one, requiring either a long walk to
the metro (often in sub-zero weather), or a 45 minute ride on one
of the most notoriously crowded buses in all of Moscow. With
access to an automobile, Luria took it upon himself to go to the
students, rather than make them come to him. This seminar was
not a teaching activity Luria was paid to do, according to
Zinchenko. Rather, it was one he felt it his duty to do.

Cole was also present to witness Luria lead the organization
of the International Congress of Psychology in the summer of
1966. Luria's already voluminous correspondence mushroomed
under the pressure of finding housing, translating abstracts of

talks, organizing the delivery of food, and all the other minutia that go into organizing a large international congress in a country poorly equipped for such an undertaking.

All of this organizing did not seem to effect the pace of Luria's scientific work. He still went most days to his laboratory at the Burdenko Institute, and each afternoon that summer he and Cole spent an hour going over the data he had collected in Central Asia, 30 years earlier.

## MENTOR-DISCIPLE

Luria made a powerful impression on people both in his role as mentor and his role as disciple. In his book about the role of Vygotsky's students as champions of research on the blind-deaf, Levitin (1979, pp. 53–56) reported on Luria's role as a mentor.

Alexander Meshcheryakov, a student of Luria's who became famous for his work with the blind-deaf, commented during an interview that

> Alexander Romanovich was a very good man. I sensed this always, but as you grow older, you grow wiser. I really understood this only after we had already been friends for many years.
>
> We worked together at the Burdenko Institute of Neurosurgery, and studied the location of psychological functions in the brain. But as it happened, both of us had to leave this institute.[6] We moved to the Institute of Defectology—for only a temporary period, we thought. This was 1952. There was no job for me except as a technician. But I, of course, did not care what I was called. I took the job and began to work. We were interested in feeblemindedness—mental retardation. I, of course, wrote the obligatory annual reports and did what was necessary according to our contract; but the actual problem of mental retardation did not attract me.

---

[6]Note how Mershshchyakov phrases this transition. A more literal translation would be, " it befell us to leave the Institute" as if there were no agency involved in the event. This comment was made by one Russian to another within the framework of Soviet law. One can discern the full drama underlying the events at issue only if one understands enough of the historical context to interpret interpolation of the phrase, "This was 1952."

Mescheryakov continued,

> Ivan Sokolyanskii, who conducted work on the instruction of
> the blind-deaf worked at the same institute. At that time he was
> already old, the spark of life in him was already fading ... He had
> only one teacher and one blind-deaf little girl as a student ... I, of
> course, saw what a sorry state the practical work of Sokolyanskii
> was in; but his idea that by studying the development of the
> blind-deaf it would be possible to study the human mind in its
> purest form, of constructing everything with one's own hands,
> seized me. I began to work with Sokolyanskii out of a feeling of
> social obligation. Actually, I was his only scientific assistant. I
> devoted all my thoughts and almost all my time to work with the
> blind and deaf children, although I was counted as part of the
> laboratory for the feebleminded, to which they finally trans-
> ferred me officially from the ranks of technician.
>
> I don't know if my interest in the blind-deaf was embarrassing
> for Alexander Romanovich, but he did not once reproach me,
> never interfered with my work with Sokolyanskii, and indeed
> helped us as much as he could. Without his help we truly would
> not have survived.

As he reminisced about Luria, Mescheryakov told Karl about
a note that Alexander Romanovich had jotted down at his doctoral defense. Luria was in a great hurry, and was unable to wait
to the end, so he sent the note separately. In order not to lose the
note, Mescheryakov stuck it away in a folder with the other papers, and then later put the folder away. Karl reports that at first
Mescheryakov could not find the note, but finally said with sat-
isfaction, "Ah, here it is finally." It read: "I heartily congratulate
you for the triumph, but of course you absolutely deserved it.
You have found yourself, and your work will suffice you for
your entire life. But this is only the main investment in a great
achievement."

The note was in a most precise handwriting, that of a person
used to carefully ordering his thoughts. The words "triumph"
and "absolutely deserved" and "found yourself" are carefully

underlined. Below is a signature that is difficult to decipher, but Karl knew it said Alexander Romanovich Luria, Professor—the person under whose guidance Meshcheryakov had become a scientist, defended his candidate's dissertation, and whom he later left behind, so to speak, if one could squeeze life into the prescribed classic framework of relationships between teacher and pupil.

Jerome Bruner also commented on Luria as a mentor and father figure:

> I think the first time I met Luria was in 1956, at McGill University in Montreal. But is difficult to be sure of this: In the course of years we became so close to each other, that I can't imagine myself not knowing him—everyone always knows his father, uncle, elder brother. Luria was a perfect "adopting father." I understood after many years that though he had a talented and active daughter, he always suffered because of the absence of a son. That is why he was attentive to his "adopted sons"—such as Oliver Zangwill, Hans Lukas Teuber, and me. By the way, all three of us had some common features—all had developed literary and artistic tastes, all were more European-oriented than our contemporaries, and all three of us were well assimilated Jews.

Elkhonon Goldberg (2001) wrote as follows about this aspect of Luria's personality:

> My relations with Alexander Romanovich and his wife Lana Pimenovna, herself a noted scientist-oncologist, were virtually familiar. Warm and generous people, they had a habit of drawing their associates into their family life, inviting them to their Moscow apartment and country dacha, and taking them along to art exhibits. The youngest among Luria's immediate associates, I was often the object of their semi-parental supervision, ranging from finding me a good dentist to reminders to shine my shoes. (p. 11)

In an interview with Levitin, Olga Vinogradova, his pupil and collaborator, remembers:

They pointed out to Alexander Romanovich that there were too many Jews in his laboratory. He personally sought to find other jobs for Zhenya (Evgeniya) Khomskaya and Nelly Zislina, but could do nothing for them. Undoubtedly to save Alexander Romanovich, Evgeniya submitted her resignation. He found her a job in a specialized home for retarded children in Sokol'niki, and he himself went there for research and consultations. He thought that Evgeniya had behaved nobly, and throughout his life would say that he was indebted to her.

But Alexander Romanovich was also an outstanding disciple, whatever difficulties accompanied the dangerous and conflictual periods of his life.

Stephen Toulmin, in the article quoted earlier, which launched Vygotsky into the mainstream of American developmental psychology, wrote that

The wide-ranging intellectual possibilities pursued by Luria ... from literature across the board to neurophysiology by way of linguistics and educational innovation, had all been initially suggested in discussions with Vygotsky and his associates during the years around 1930. Luria's own comment in his autobiography ... reads: "Vygotsky was a genius. After more than half a century in science I am unable to name another person who even approaches his incredible analytical ability and foresight. All of my work has been no more than the working out of psychological theory which he constructed."

Ah, but what a "working out"! ... (1978, p. 57)

Finally, Gita Vygotskaya, Vygotsky's daughter, reported how Vygotsky's books were confiscated from the Institute of Defectology following the July 4, 1936 resolution of the Central Committee of the Party condemning pedology (the name given to work that Vygotsky was conducting at the time). In her words,

Lev Semenovich's works were banned—they could not be mentioned or referred to for 20 long years.

True, there were people who did not always obey this proscription. Lev Semenovich's portrait hung for many years in Luria's home and in Zaporozhets's home, and in their laboratories. And even before Lev Semenovich's name was rehabilitated, Luria and Zaporozhets would refer to his works and talk about them to their students.

Soon after the war, in 1947 (or perhaps 1948), a meeting took place at which Luria was one of the speakers. His words are engraved in my memory: "There is nothing in Lev Semenovich's works that could not be published. They can be published today, right now, changing only one word: In place of the word "pedology," one must put "child psychology."

Luria began to undertake a determined effort to publish Lev Semenovich's works. A great optimist, he spoke to me and Mama: "We are soon going to publish 'Thinking and speech,' and then we are going to publish everything in succession." In fact, in late 1956, thanks to Luria, the first of Lev Semenovich's books was published, *Selected Psychological Works*; it contained "Thinking and speech." In 1960, again thanks solely to Alexander Romanovich, the second book, "The development of higher mental functions," consisting of unpublished manuscripts, came out.

Then again came a long pause.

In 1966, in connection with the 70th anniversary of Vygotsky's birth, the Presidium of the Academy of Pedagogical Sciences decided to publish his works. But a long 16 years went between adoption of this resolution and publication of the first volume! I can say quite confidently that, if it had not been for the incredible efforts of Luria, the collection of Vygotsky's works might not have been published at all—or would still be awaiting publication .... Some complication or another was always arising, and Alexander Romanovich had barely surmounted one when another arose. First, it was a paper shortage; then it was necessary to get the agreement of someone about something; and then the person who was to make a certain decision had gone off on a trip somewhere, etc. This lasted for several years. The person to

whom we are mainly obliged [could not] see the first volume of
the six-volume set (Luria died in August 1977).

## THE SOCIAL AND THE PERSONAL:
## IN SEARCH OF SYNTHESIS

We have now reached the end of our exploration of the social and
personal contexts of Alexander Luria's life. Additional material
can be found on the DVD accompanying this text. As a means of
exploring how these two, interwoven, aspects of life might have
been combined in the person of Alexander Romanovich, we
conclude with a long excerpt from a book by one of his last students, Elkhonin Goldberg, currently a neuropsychologist prac-
ticing in New York and one by his daughter.

Elkhonin Goldberg:

> My mentor Alexander Romanovich Luria, and I were immersed
> in a conversation that we had had dozens of times before. We
> were strolling away from Luria's Moscow apartment, up Frunze
> Street and on toward Old Arbat .... The year was 1972. The
> country had lived through Stalin's murderous years, through the
> war, through more of Stalin's murderous years, and through
> Khrushchev's aborted thaw. People were no longer executed for
> dissent; they were merely jailed. The overriding public mood
> was no longer bone-chilling terror, but damp, resigned, stagnant
> hopelessness and indifference, a society stupor of sorts. My
> mentor was 70 and I was 25 .... As on many occasions before,
> Alexander Romanovich was saying that it was time for me to
> join the Party—the Party, the Communist Party of the Soviet Un-
> ion. (2001, pp. 7–8)

Goldberg, now an American scientist residing in New York,
continues his story in the same manner—with a bitter irony,
poorly concealed affection towards his teacher, and a hint of
nostalgia about the occasion. Luria, being a Party member, offered to nominate his young colleague and to arrange the second
nomination from his long time colleague, Alexei Leontiev, who

was then Dean of Psychology Faculty at the Moscow University. Goldberg fully understood that Luria's idea was based on the existing "rules of the game": Party membership served as an obligatory steppingstone to any serious aspirations for career advancement in the Soviet Union. Goldberg not only knew that his teacher's "love" for the Party was equivalent to his own, but also that nominating him for Party membership was a very generous gesture both for Luria and Leontiev. There were many reasons to consider his candidacy problematic. Goldberg came from Latvia, which was regarded as an untrustworthy province and was of "bourgeois" background. His father had spent five years in the Gulag as an "enemy of the people." Most importantly, Goldberg was a Jew. By vouching for him, Luria and Leontiev ran the risk of irritating the university Party organization for pushing "another Jew" into the rarefied strata of the Soviet academic elite. But there were no other ways to make it possible for him stay on at the University as a junior faculty member. These were the realities of Soviet existence.

But this is not the end of the story, so ordinary for the times in which Luria lived.

> On a dozen occasions over the past few years, whenever Luria brought it up, I would sidestep the subject, turning it into joke, saying that I was too young, too immature, not yet ready. I did not want an open clash and Luria did not force one. But this time he was speaking with finality. And this time I said that I was not going to join the Party because I did not want to .... (p. 8) ... Luria halted in the middle of the street. With a tinge of resignation but also a matter-of-fact finality, he said: "Then, Kolya (my old Russian nickname), there is nothing I can do for you." And that was that. This could have been devastating under a different set of circumstances, but that day I felt relief. Unbeknownst to Alexander Romanovich or almost anyone else, I had already made up my mind to leave the Soviet Union. By making Party membership a precondition for his continued patronage, he freed me from any obligation I felt toward him, which may have interfered with my decision .... (Goldberg, 2001, p. 11)

Goldberg summarizes his attitude toward Luria's involvement in the Party by writing, "I did not condemn Luria's Party membership, but I did not respect it either, and it was a source of nagging ambivalence in my attitude toward him. I sort of pitied him for that, and odd feeling for a student to have toward his mentor" (p. 10).

This truly Shakespearian combination of fidelity and betrayal, rendered in Goldberg's book in a matter-of-fact manner tells the reader a lot about what it could feel like for a young man to part ways with a teacher whom he really loved under difficult circumstances. Many years later, Goldberg re-experienced this unnatural situation in writing his book and tried to understand it more fully. Being a psychologist, he can't help using his scientific background to seek an explanation for his mentor's behavior and state of mind:

> Whatever his true beliefs were, publicly he had always been a loyal Soviet citizen. Was it only a patina, which he was careful not to drop? I suspected that it was something in between, that a constant conscious dissonance between what you said and what you felt was too painful to endure. The closest Luria had ever come to revealing his deeply buried discontent was through an occasional oblique muttering "Vremena slozhnye, durakov mnogo" ("These are complex times, many fools abound"). What was first adopted as protective mimicry in time became a form of "autohypnosis." (Goldberg, 2001, p. 16)

Ironically, the term "autohypnosis" was proposed in 1990 by none other than Luria's daughter, Lena, over dinner with Goldberg in New York, while they were talking about her parents, both long deceased, and about other people of her parents' generation. Lena, reports Goldberg, was fascinated by political autohypnosis as a psychological defense against tyranny. An echo, though deformed, of this conversation can be found in Elena Luria's book: "In 1956 I finished my school and decided to enter the faculty of fine arts of the Moscow University. But father said: 'There is nothing for you to do there! What kind of science is that? Art critics do not write what they think, but what is needed' " (1994, p.157).

This comment suggests to us that Alexander Romanovich inherited from his mentor Vygotsky a very high order of reflexivity: He was able to see himself and the situation he was in from outside. Perhaps the position he had chosen was dictated not by autohypnosis, but something else—perhaps a kind of wisdom, the rare human quality he so clearly demonstrated in his scientific work and so carefully concealed in day-to-day life. If so, it was wisdom which not only made him a great scientist but also allowed him to survive—to become one.

As for Goldberg's different choice about entering the Party, it may be worth remembering when Luria joined its ranks. It happened in 1943, when Alexander Romanovich was over 40 and his decision by no means could promote his career. Like millions of other Soviet citizens who swelled the Party's ranks in that critical juncture in world history, he knew too well the Nazi command "Jews and Communists—one step forward!" and he wanted to preserve the right if need be, to take more than two steps.

Of course, many people of Goldberg's generation did not understand these mundane facts of life in the USSR at war and its aftermath. Paraphrasing Luria, Karl would say in his mother-tongue "Vremena vsegda slozhnye, i durakov vsegda mnogo," which Mike will translate into his native English as "Times are always complex, and fools always abound!"

True, Luria was compelled to find his personal balance between freedom and necessity, according to the times in which he lived as he understood them. We hope that the materials in this book, especially the newly added materials, clearly indicate his value as a scientist whose work has, if anything, increased in significance over the years, and his value as a human being, taking energy from the opportunities that his historical era presented him as a youth and surviving the horrors that they meted out before his death.

So what remains two and a half decades after the death of a man whose earthly careers spanned three quarters of a century and who was recognized as the creator of a new science even during his lifetime? A long list of scientific degrees, titles, and prizes granted to him? Books, articles, pupils, and disciples? A few lines in encyclopedias? A granite plaque in a prestigious cemetery? Or twenty five years after his passing, does not the fond memory of Alexander Romanovich endure among his friends and relatives, so that it is still alive in their collective consciousness, as if he is still leading them through life and through science with his talent, his erudition, his knowledge, his rarely encountered combination of intelligence and goodness, and an unrepeatable combination of other uncommon personality characteristics?

—Michael Cole and Karl Levitin
San Diego-Amsterdam-Florence-Moscow

# Supplementary Bibliography

Berlin, I. (1949). "Meetings with Russian writers in 1945 and 1956." *Personal impressions*. New York: Viking Press

Craig, G. A. (1971). *Europe since 1815*. New York: Holt, Rinehart, and Winston.

Edelman, G. M. (1992). *Bright air, brilliant fire :On the matter of the mind*. New York: Basic Books.

Eisenstein, S. M. (1942). *The film sense* (Trans. and Ed., Jay Leyda). New York: Harcourt, Brace and company.

Geertz, C. (1973). *The interpretation of cultures*. London: Fontana.

Goldberg, E. (2001). *The executive brain :Frontal lobes and the civilized mind*. New York: Oxford University Press.

Homskaya, E. D. (2001). *Alexander Romanovich Luria: A scientific biography*. New York: Kluwer.

Joravsky, D. (1989). *Russian psychology, a critical history*. Oxford, UK: Blackwell.

Leontiev, A. N., & Zaporozhets, A. V. (1960). *Rehabilitation of hand function* (Trans. from the Russian by Basil Haigh, Ed. by W. Ritchie). Oxford: Pergamon Press.

Levitin, C. (1982). *One is not born a personality*. Moscow: Progress Publishers.

Levitin, K. (1998). A dissolving pattern. *Journal of Russian & East European Psychology, 36*(5/6).

Luria, E. A. (1994). *Moi otets A. R. Luria (My Father A. R. Luria)*. Moscow: Gnosis.

Paustovsky, K. G. (1955). *Povest' o zhisni (The Story of a Life)*. Moscow, Sovetsky Pisatel' Publishers.

Quartz, S. R., & Sejnowski, T. J. (2002). *Liars, lovers, and heroes: What the new brain science reveals about how we become who we are.* New York: William Morrow.

Razmyslov, P. (2000). On Vygotsky's and Luria's "cultural-historical theory of psychology." *Journal of Russian and East European Psychology. Special Issue: Criticizing Vygotsky, 38*(6), 45–58.

Ridley, M. (2003). *Nature via Nurture.* New York: Harper Collins.

Schapiro, L. (1959). *The Communist Party of the Soviet Union.* New York: Random House.

Toulmin, S. (1978). The Mozart of psychology. *New York Review of Books, 25*(4), 51–57.

Trotsky materials may be found at this URL: http://www.marxists.org/archive/trotsky/works/1918-mil/ch33.htm#bkazan

Vološinov, V. N. (1986). *Marxism and the philosophy of language.* Cambridge, MA: Harvard University Press.

Vygodskaya, G. L., & Lifanova, T. M. (1999). Lev Semenovich Vygotsky (Part IV). *Journal of Russian & East European Psychology,* September–October.

van der Veer, R. (2000). Criticizing Vygotsky. Special issue of the *Journal of Russian & East European Psychology, 38,* 3–94.

van der Veer, R., & Valsiner, J. (1991). *Understanding Vygotsky: A quest for synthesis.* Oxford, UK: Blackwell.

Wertsch, J. (1985). *Vygotsky and the social formation of mind.* Cambridge, MA: Harvard University Press.